PREDATOR™

TITAN BOOKS
LONDON

script
MARK VERHEIDEN

pencils
CHRIS WARNER & RON RANDALL

inks
CHRIS WARNER, RANDY EMBERLIN & SAM De La ROSA

colours
CHRIS CHALENOR

letters
JIM MASSARA & DAVID JACKSON

cover
DENIS BEAUVAIS

PREDATOR Vol 1
ISBN 1 85286 377 3
Published by Titan Books Ltd
19 Valentine Place
London SE1 8QH
by arrangement with
Dark Horse Comics Inc, USA

First British edition : April 1991
Copyright © 1990 Twentieth Century Fox Film Corporation
2 4 6 8 10 9 7 5 3

Printed in Singapore by Stamford Press Pte Ltd

CHAPTER 1

2

3

4

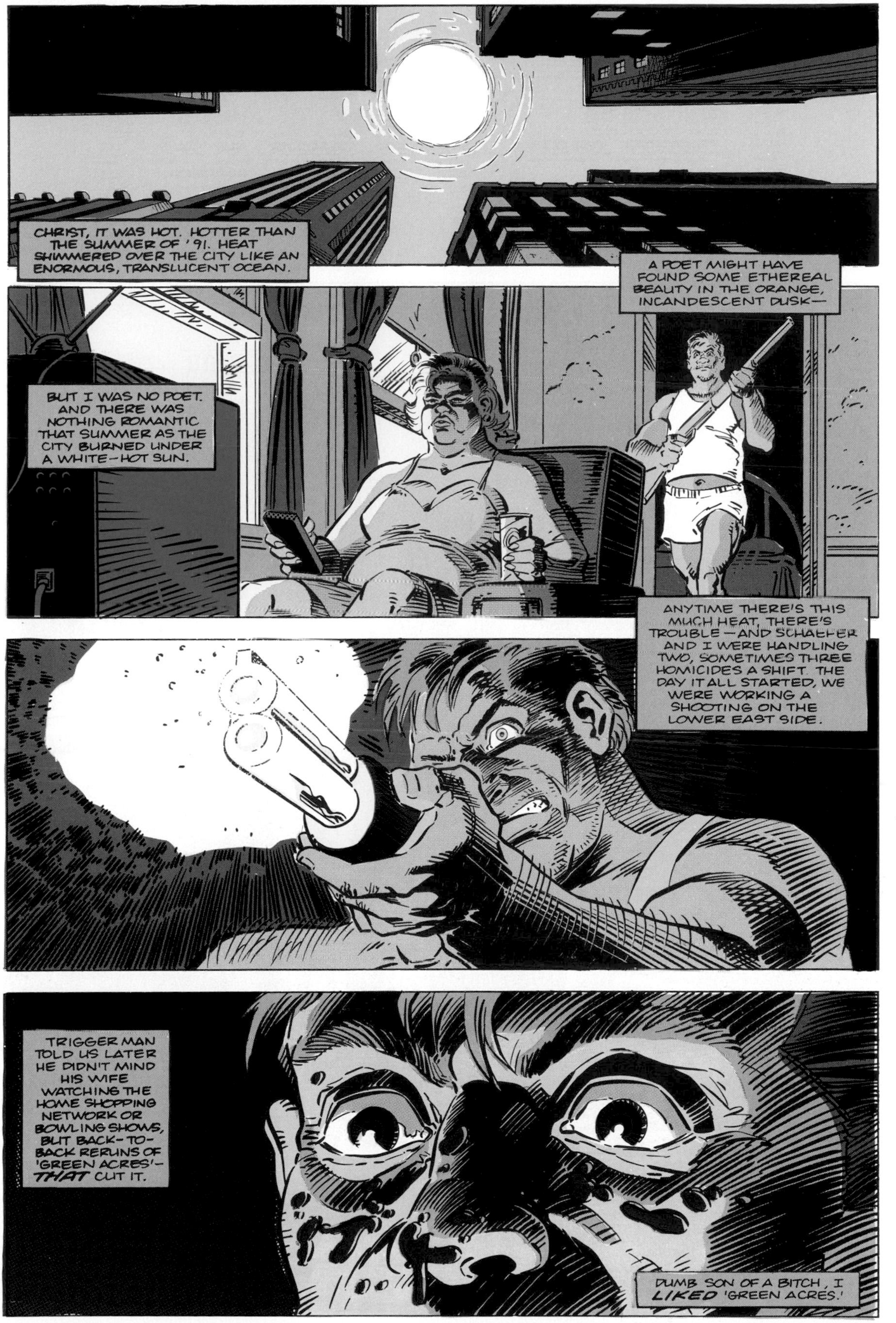
CHRIST, IT WAS HOT. HOTTER THAN THE SUMMER OF '91. HEAT SHIMMERED OVER THE CITY LIKE AN ENORMOUS, TRANSLUCENT OCEAN.
A POET MIGHT HAVE FOUND SOME ETHEREAL BEAUTY IN THE ORANGE, INCANDESCENT DUSK—
BUT I WAS NO POET. AND THERE WAS NOTHING ROMANTIC THAT SUMMER AS THE CITY BURNED UNDER A WHITE-HOT SUN.
ANYTIME THERE'S THIS MUCH HEAT, THERE'S TROUBLE—AND SCHAEFER AND I WERE HANDLING TWO, SOMETIMES THREE HOMICIDES A SHIFT. THE DAY IT ALL STARTED, WE WERE WORKING A SHOOTING ON THE LOWER EAST SIDE.
TRIGGER MAN TOLD US LATER HE DIDN'T MIND HIS WIFE WATCHING THE HOME SHOPPING NETWORK OR BOWLING SHOWS, BUT BACK-TO-BACK RERUNS OF 'GREEN ACRES'- THAT CUT IT.
DUMB SON OF A BITCH, I LIKED 'GREEN ACRES.'

THE HEAT

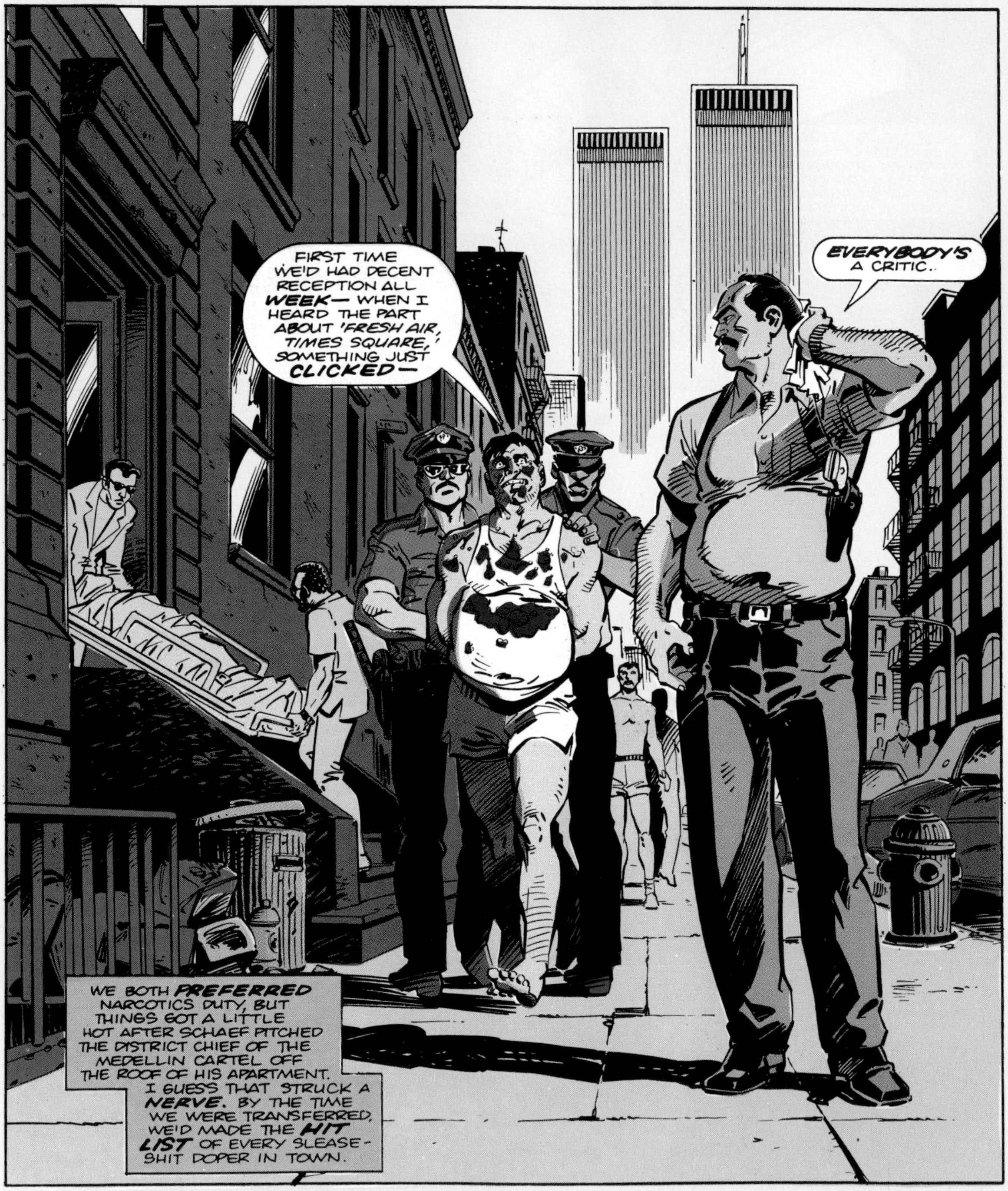
FIRST TIME WE'D HAD DECENT RECEPTION ALL WEEK— WHEN I HEARD THE PART ABOUT 'FRESH AIR, TIMES SQUARE,' SOMETHING JUST CLICKED—
EVERYBODY'S A CRITIC..
WE BOTH PREFERRED NARCOTICS DUTY, BUT THINGS GOT A LITTLE HOT AFTER SCHAEF PITCHED THE DISTRICT CHIEF OF THE MEDELLIN CARTEL OFF THE ROOF OF HIS APARTMENT. I GUESS THAT STRUCK A NERVE. BY THE TIME WE WERE TRANSFERRED, WE'D MADE THE HIT LIST OF EVERY SLEASE-SHIT DOPER IN TOWN.

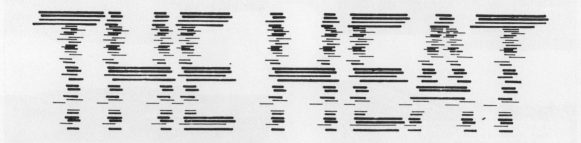

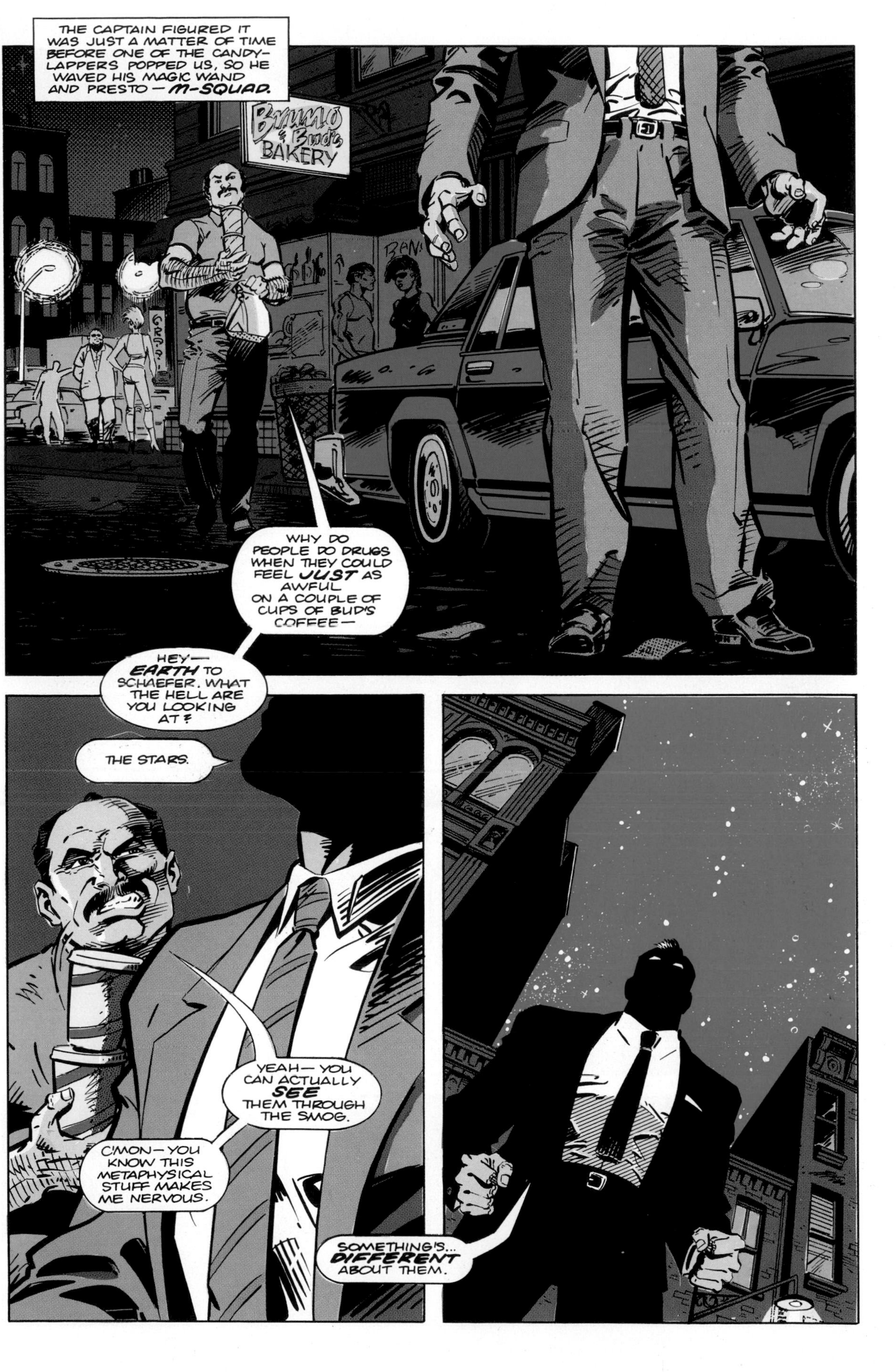
THE CAPTAIN FIGURED IT WAS JUST A MATTER OF TIME BEFORE ONE OF THE CANDY-LAPPERS POPPED US, SO HE WAVED HIS MAGIC WAND AND PRESTO — M-SQUAD.
Bruno & Bud's BAKERY
WHY DO PEOPLE DO DRUGS WHEN THEY COULD FEEL JUST AS AWFUL ON A COUPLE OF CUPS OF BUD'S COFFEE—
HEY— EARTH TO SCHAEFER. WHAT THE HELL ARE YOU LOOKING AT?
THE STARS.
YEAH— YOU CAN ACTUALLY SEE THEM THROUGH THE SMOG.
C'MON— YOU KNOW THIS METAPHYSICAL STUFF MAKES ME NERVOUS.
SOMETHING'S... DIFFERENT ABOUT THEM.

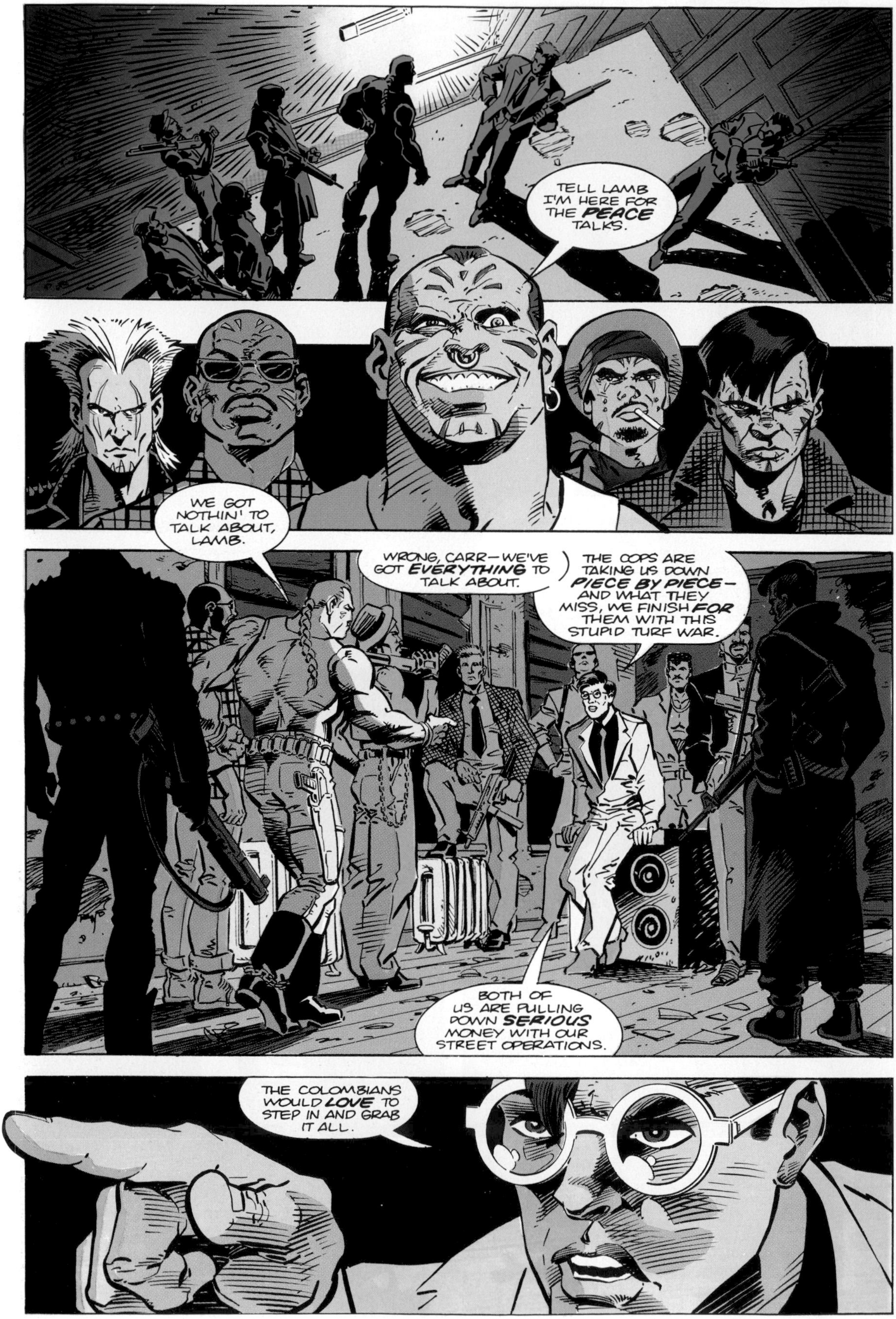

TELL LAMB I'M HERE FOR THE PEACE TALKS.
WE GOT NOTHIN' TO TALK ABOUT, LAMB.
WRONG, CARR—WE'VE GOT EVERYTHING TO TALK ABOUT.
THE COPS ARE TAKING US DOWN PIECE BY PIECE—AND WHAT THEY MISS, WE FINISH FOR THEM WITH THIS STUPID TURF WAR.
BOTH OF US ARE PULLING DOWN SERIOUS MONEY WITH OUR STREET OPERATIONS.
THE COLOMBIANS WOULD LOVE TO STEP IN AND GRAB IT ALL.

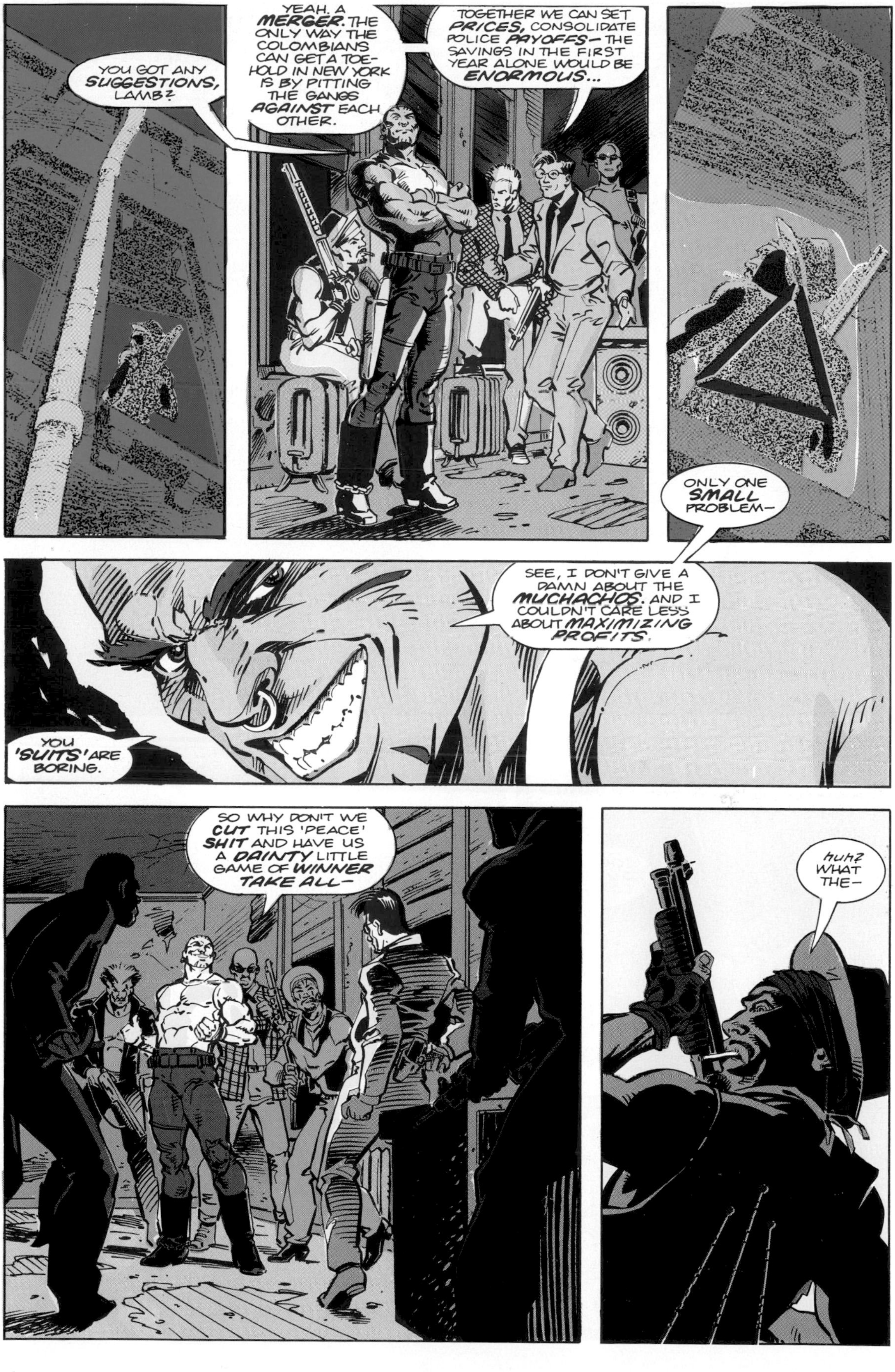
YOU GOT ANY SUGGESTIONS, LAMB?
YEAH. A MERGER. THE ONLY WAY THE COLOMBIANS CAN GET A TOE-HOLD IN NEW YORK IS BY PITTING THE GANGS AGAINST EACH OTHER.
TOGETHER WE CAN SET PRICES, CONSOLIDATE POLICE PAYOFFS— THE SAVINGS IN THE FIRST YEAR ALONE WOULD BE ENORMOUS...
ONLY ONE SMALL PROBLEM—
SEE, I DON'T GIVE A DAMN ABOUT THE MUCHACHOS. AND I COULDN'T CARE LESS ABOUT MAXIMIZING PROFITS.
YOU 'SUITS' ARE BORING.
SO WHY DON'T WE CUT THIS 'PEACE' SHIT AND HAVE US A DAINTY LITTLE GAME OF WINNER TAKE ALL—
huh? WHAT THE—

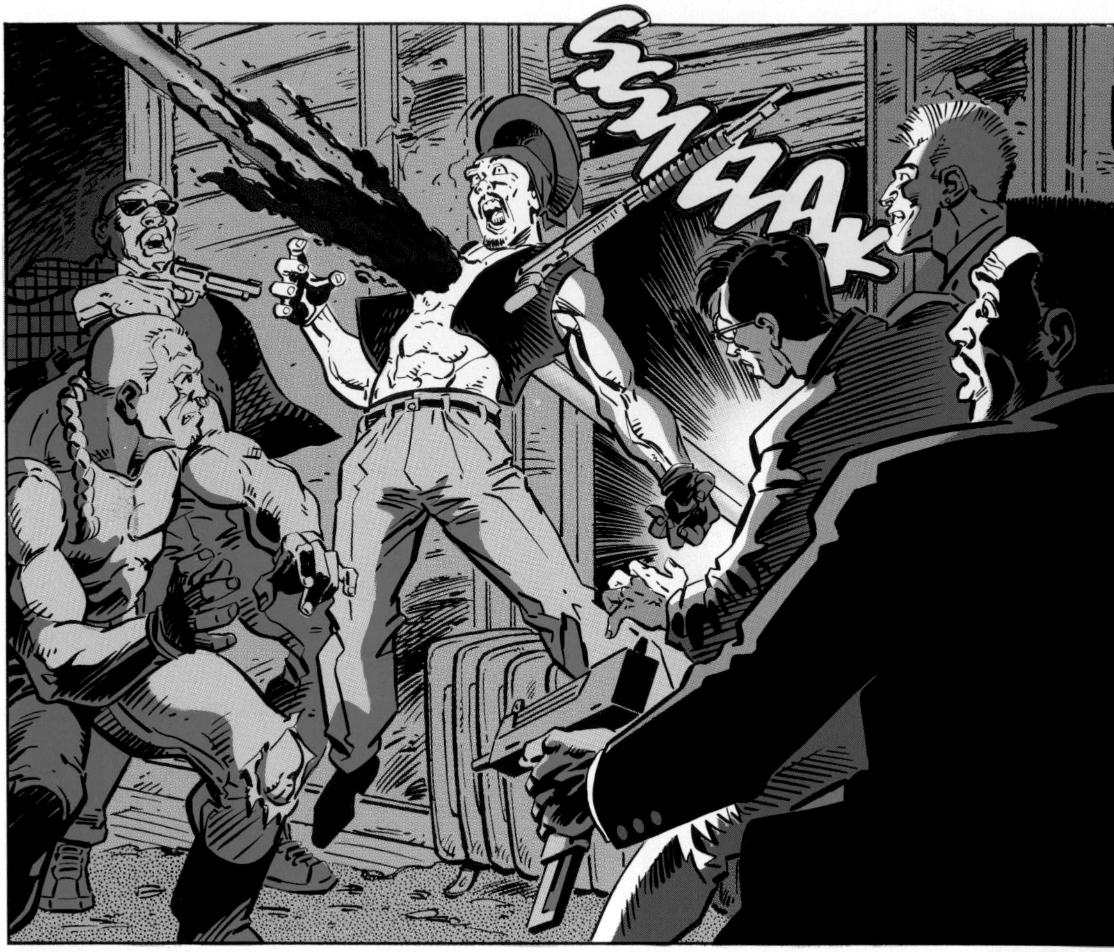
SSNNZAK

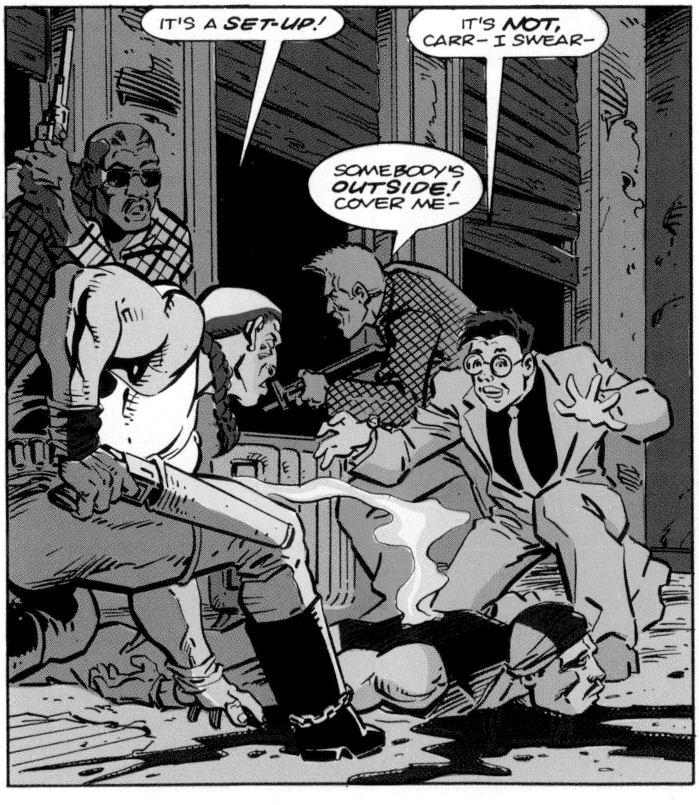
IT'S A SET-UP!
IT'S NOT, CARR– I SWEAR–
SOMEBODY'S OUTSIDE! COVER ME–

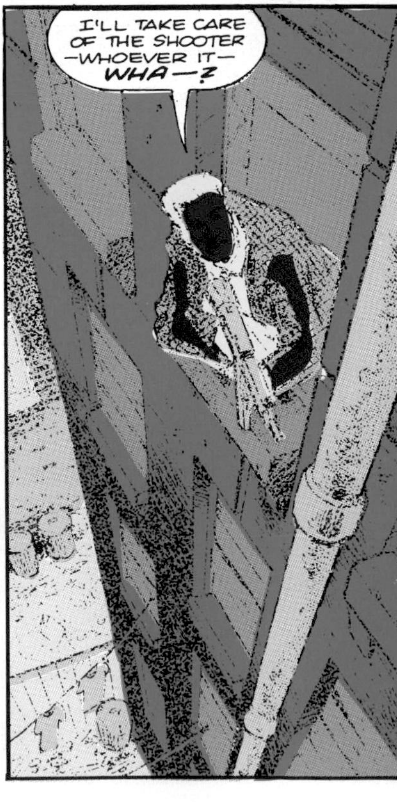
I'LL TAKE CARE OF THE SHOOTER –WHOEVER IT– WHA–?

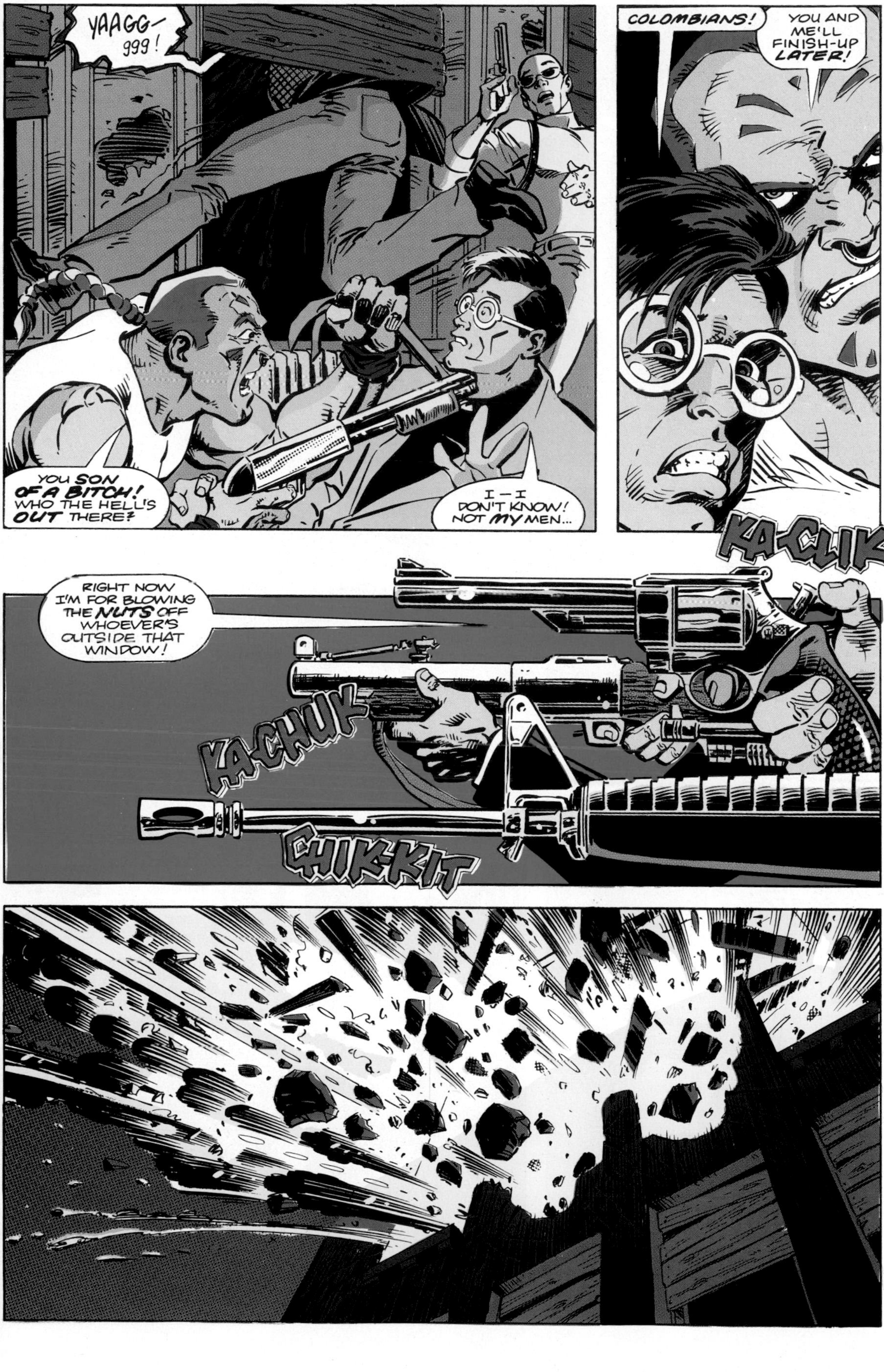
YAAGG-ggg!
YOU SON OF A BITCH! WHO THE HELL'S OUT THERE?
I—I DON'T KNOW! NOT MY MEN...
COLOMBIANS!
YOU AND ME'LL FINISH-UP LATER!
KA-CLIK
RIGHT NOW I'M FOR BLOWING THE NUTS OFF WHOEVER'S OUTSIDE THAT WINDOW!
KA-CHUK
CHIK-KIT

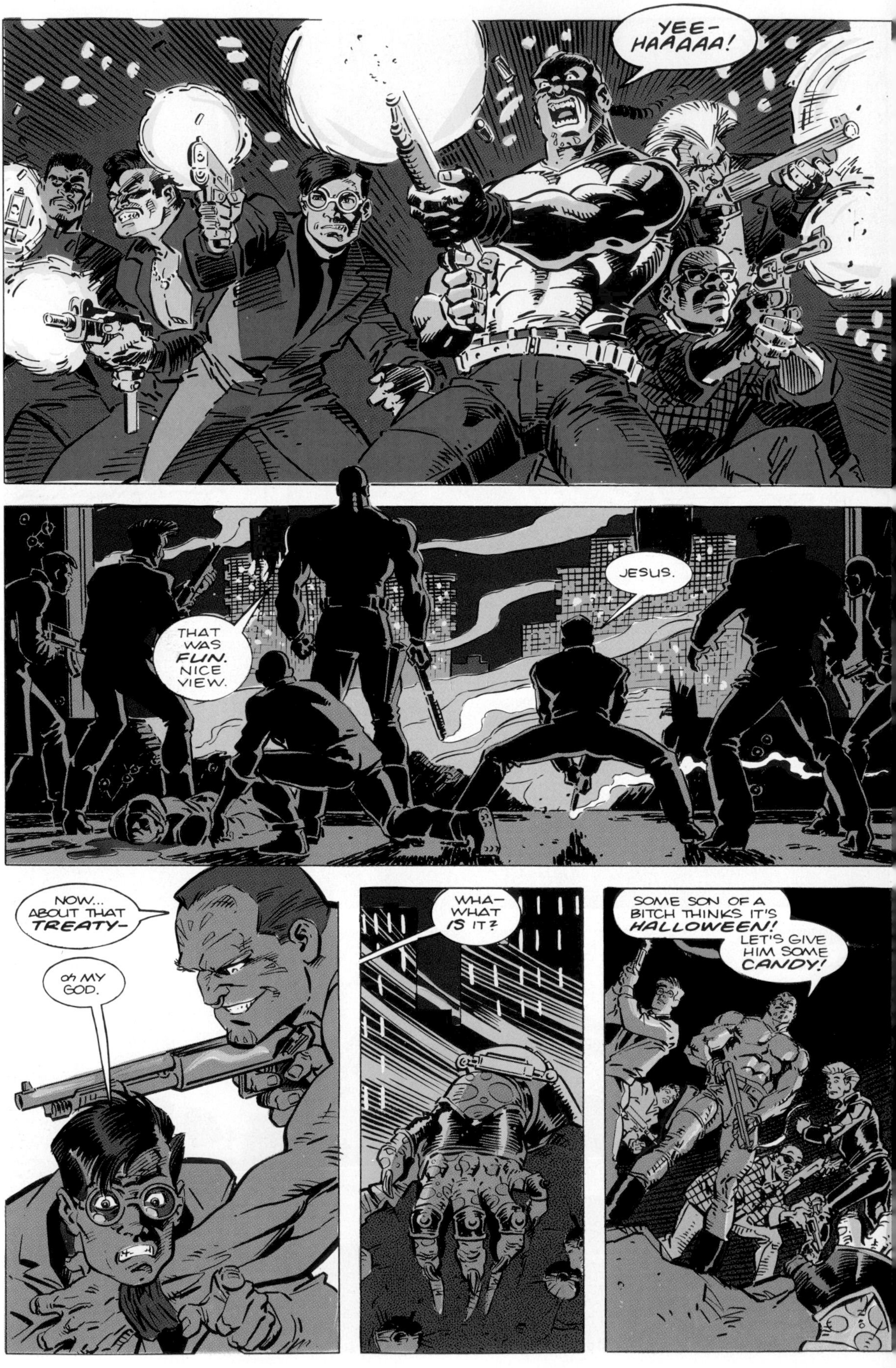
YEE-HAAAAAA!
THAT WAS FUN. NICE VIEW.
JESUS.
NOW... ABOUT THAT TREATY-
OH MY GOD.
WHA-WHAT IS IT?
SOME SON OF A BITCH THINKS IT'S HALLOWEEN!
LET'S GIVE HIM SOME CANDY!

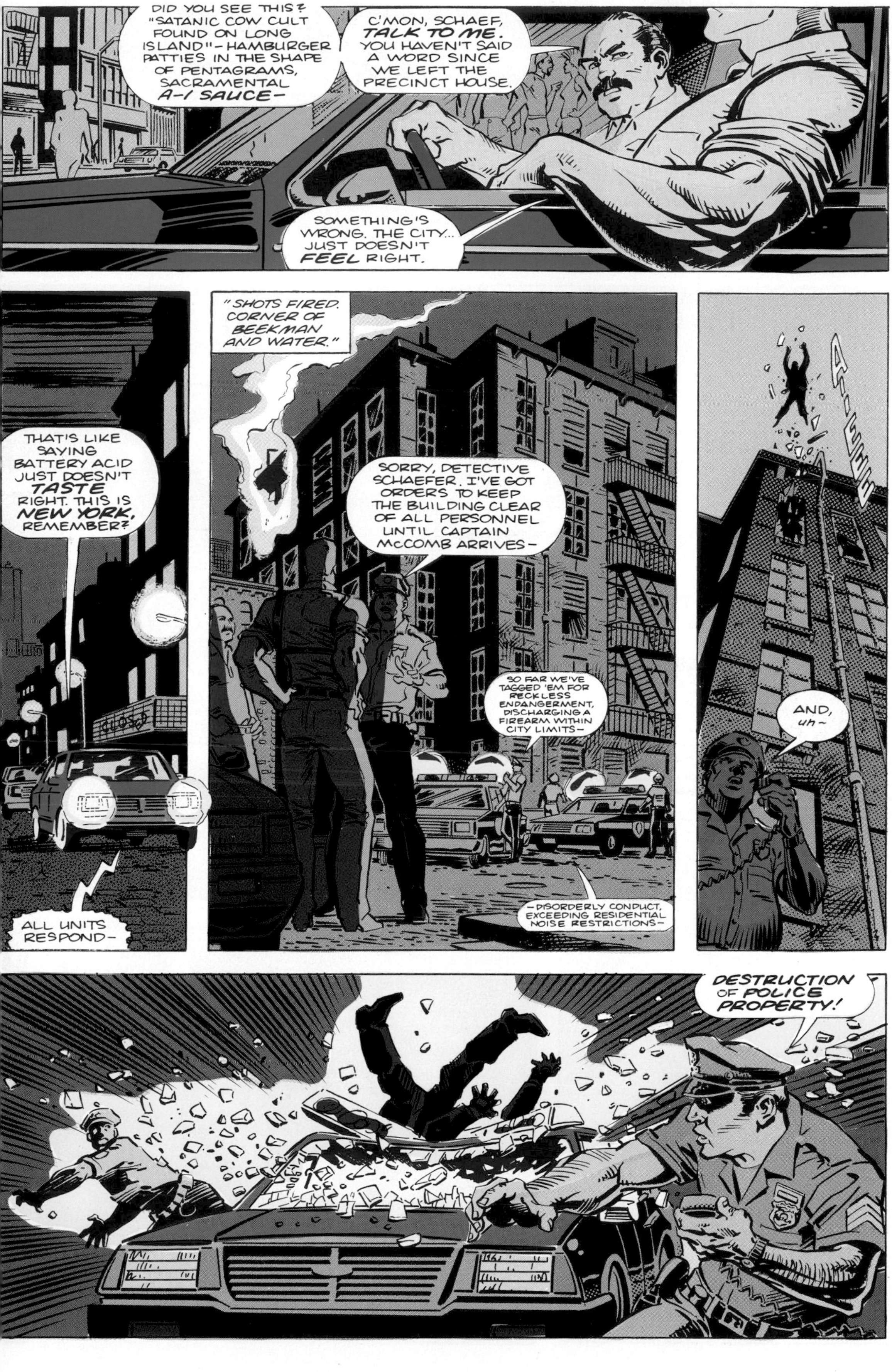
DID YOU SEE THIS? "SATANIC COW CULT FOUND ON LONG ISLAND" - HAMBURGER PATTIES IN THE SHAPE OF PENTAGRAMS, SACRAMENTAL A-1 SAUCE-
C'MON, SCHAEF, TALK TO ME. YOU HAVEN'T SAID A WORD SINCE WE LEFT THE PRECINCT HOUSE.
SOMETHING'S WRONG. THE CITY... JUST DOESN'T FEEL RIGHT.
THAT'S LIKE SAYING BATTERY ACID JUST DOESN'T TASTE RIGHT. THIS IS NEW YORK, REMEMBER?
ALL UNITS RESPOND-
"SHOTS FIRED. CORNER OF BEEKMAN AND WATER."
SORRY, DETECTIVE SCHAEFER. I'VE GOT ORDERS TO KEEP THE BUILDING CLEAR OF ALL PERSONNEL UNTIL CAPTAIN McCOMB ARRIVES-
SO FAR WE'VE TAGGED 'EM FOR RECKLESS ENDANGERMENT, DISCHARGING A FIREARM WITHIN CITY LIMITS-
-DISORDERLY CONDUCT, EXCEEDING RESIDENTIAL NOISE RESTRICTIONS-
AND, uh-
A-EEEE
DESTRUCTION OF POLICE PROPERTY!

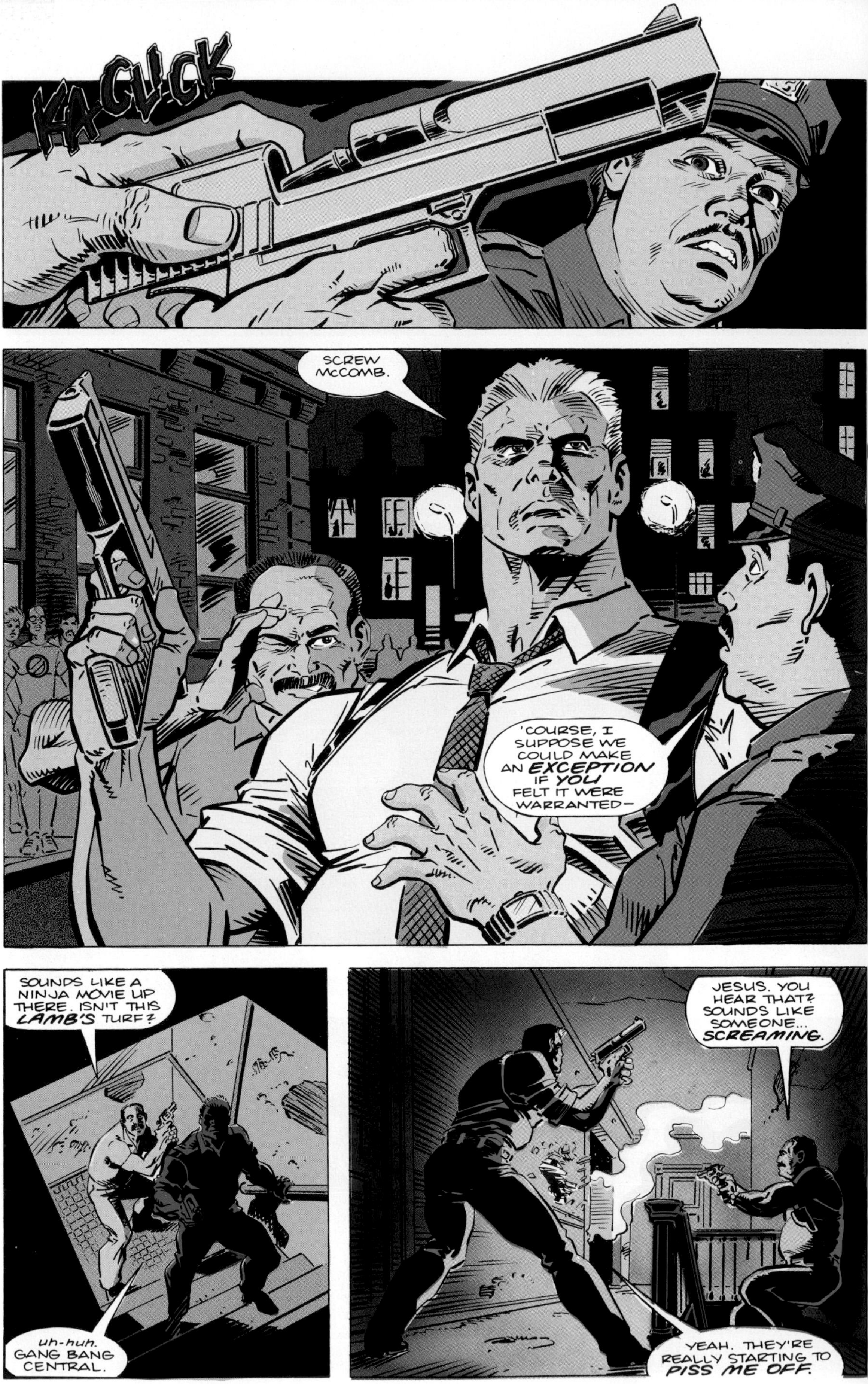
KA-CLICK
SCREW McCOMB.
'COURSE, I SUPPOSE WE COULD MAKE AN EXCEPTION IF YOU FELT IT WERE WARRANTED–
SOUNDS LIKE A NINJA MOVIE UP THERE. ISN'T THIS LAMB'S TURF?
uh-huh. GANG BANG CENTRAL.
JESUS. YOU HEAR THAT? SOUNDS LIKE SOMEONE... SCREAMING.
YEAH. THEY'RE REALLY STARTING TO PISS ME OFF.

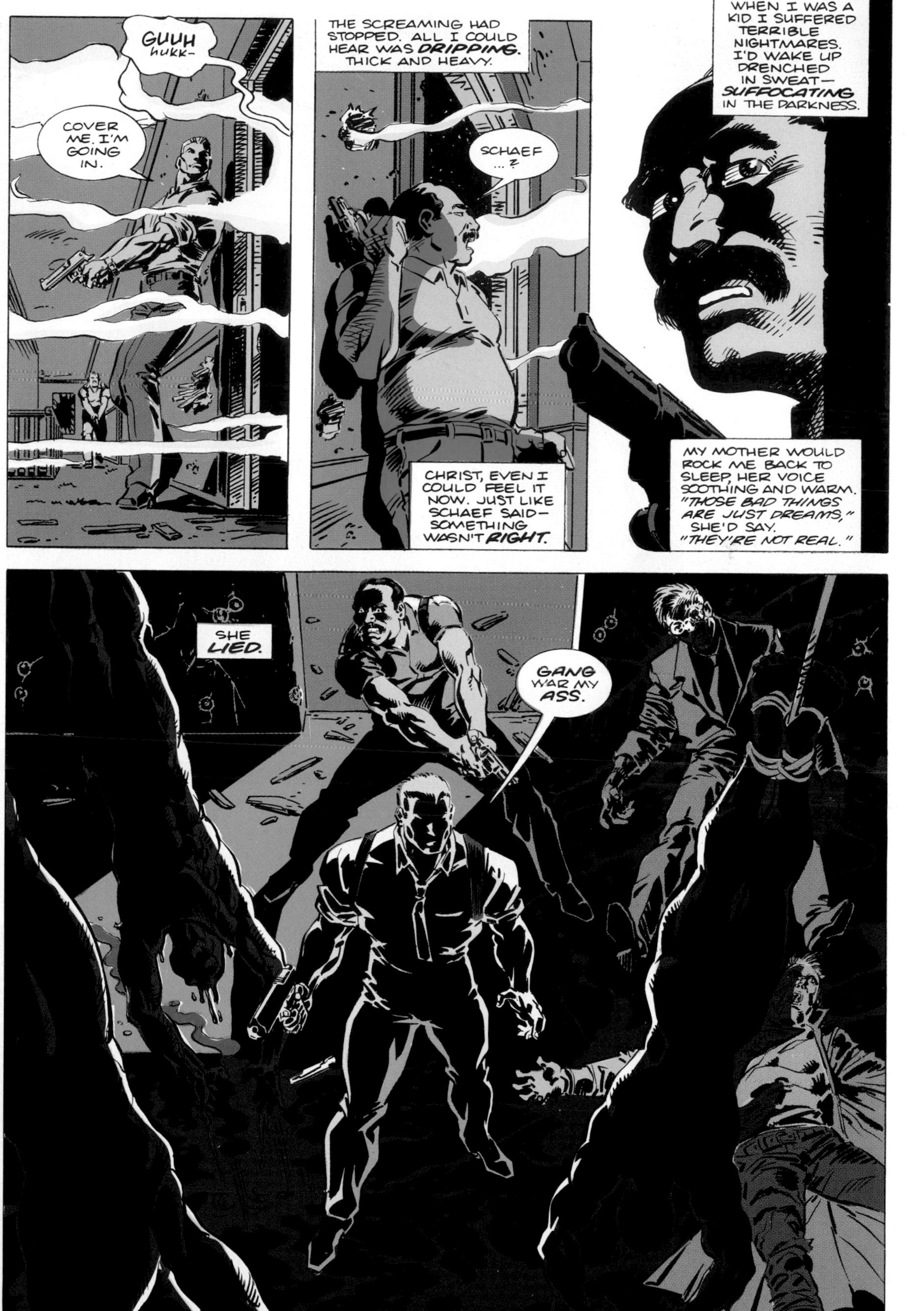
GUUH hukk-
COVER ME. I'M GOING IN.
THE SCREAMING HAD STOPPED. ALL I COULD HEAR WAS DRIPPING. THICK AND HEAVY.
SCHAEF ...?
CHRIST, EVEN I COULD FEEL IT NOW. JUST LIKE SCHAEF SAID— SOMETHING WASN'T RIGHT.
WHEN I WAS A KID I SUFFERED TERRIBLE NIGHTMARES. I'D WAKE UP DRENCHED IN SWEAT— SUFFOCATING IN THE DARKNESS.
MY MOTHER WOULD ROCK ME BACK TO SLEEP, HER VOICE SOOTHING AND WARM. "THOSE BAD THINGS ARE JUST DREAMS," SHE'D SAY. "THEY'RE NOT REAL."
SHE LIED.
GANG WAR MY ASS.

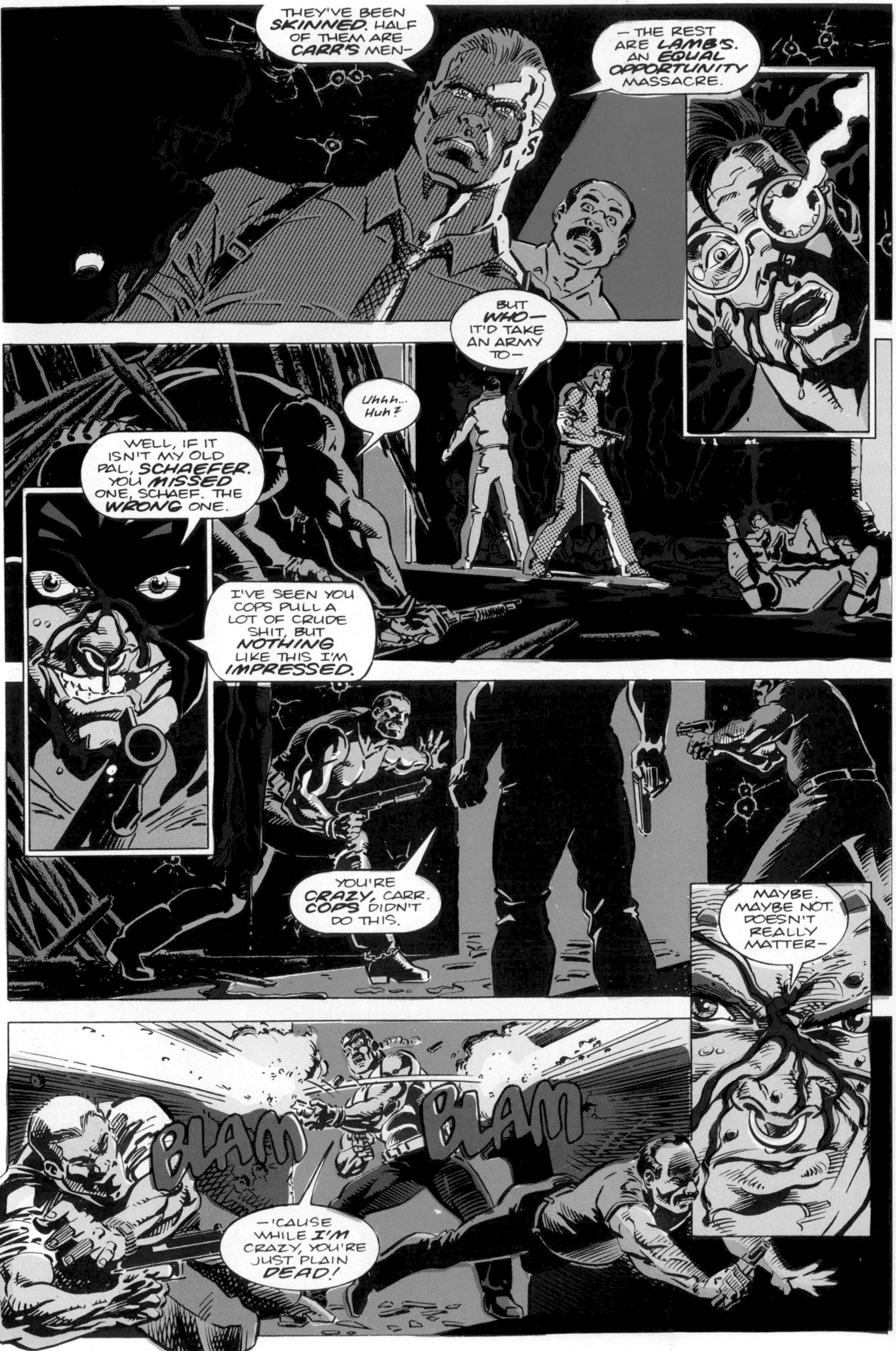
THEY'VE BEEN SKINNED. HALF OF THEM ARE CARR'S MEN-
—THE REST ARE LAMB'S. AN EQUAL OPPORTUNITY MASSACRE.
BUT WHO— IT'D TAKE AN ARMY TO—
Uhhh... Huh?
WELL, IF IT ISN'T MY OLD PAL, SCHAEFER. YOU MISSED ONE, SCHAEF. THE WRONG ONE.
I'VE SEEN YOU COPS PULL A LOT OF CRUDE SHIT, BUT NOTHING LIKE THIS. I'M IMPRESSED.
YOU'RE CRAZY, CARR. COPS DIDN'T DO THIS.
MAYBE. MAYBE NOT. DOESN'T REALLY MATTER—
BLAM
BLAM
—'CAUSE WHILE I'M CRAZY, YOU'RE JUST PLAIN DEAD!

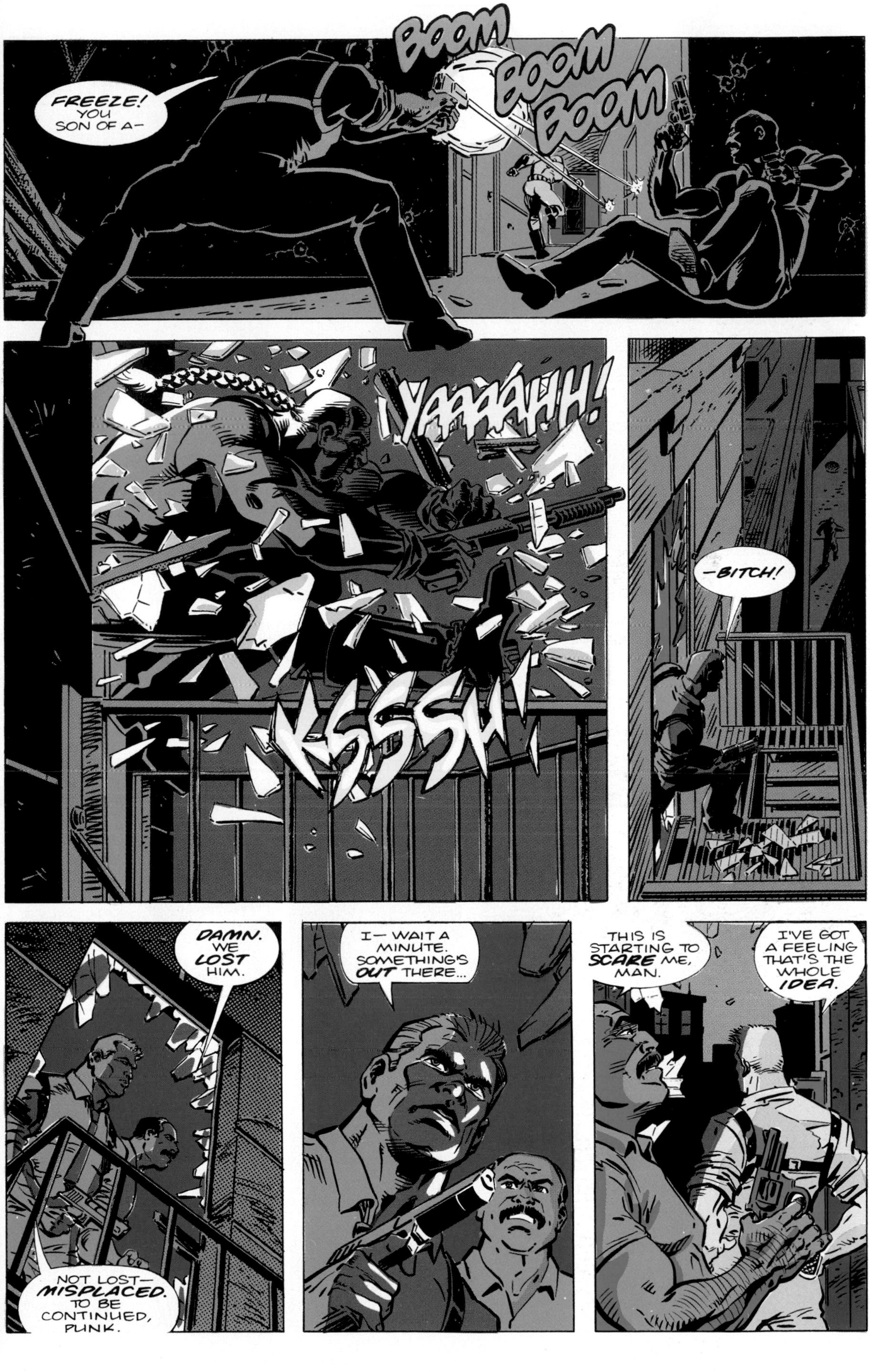

Boom
Boom
Boom
FREEZE! YOU SON OF A—
YAAAAHH!
KSSSH
—BITCH!
DAMN. WE LOST HIM.
NOT LOST— MISPLACED. TO BE CONTINUED, PUNK.
I— WAIT A MINUTE. SOMETHING'S OUT THERE...
THIS IS STARTING TO SCARE ME, MAN.
I'VE GOT A FEELING THAT'S THE WHOLE IDEA.

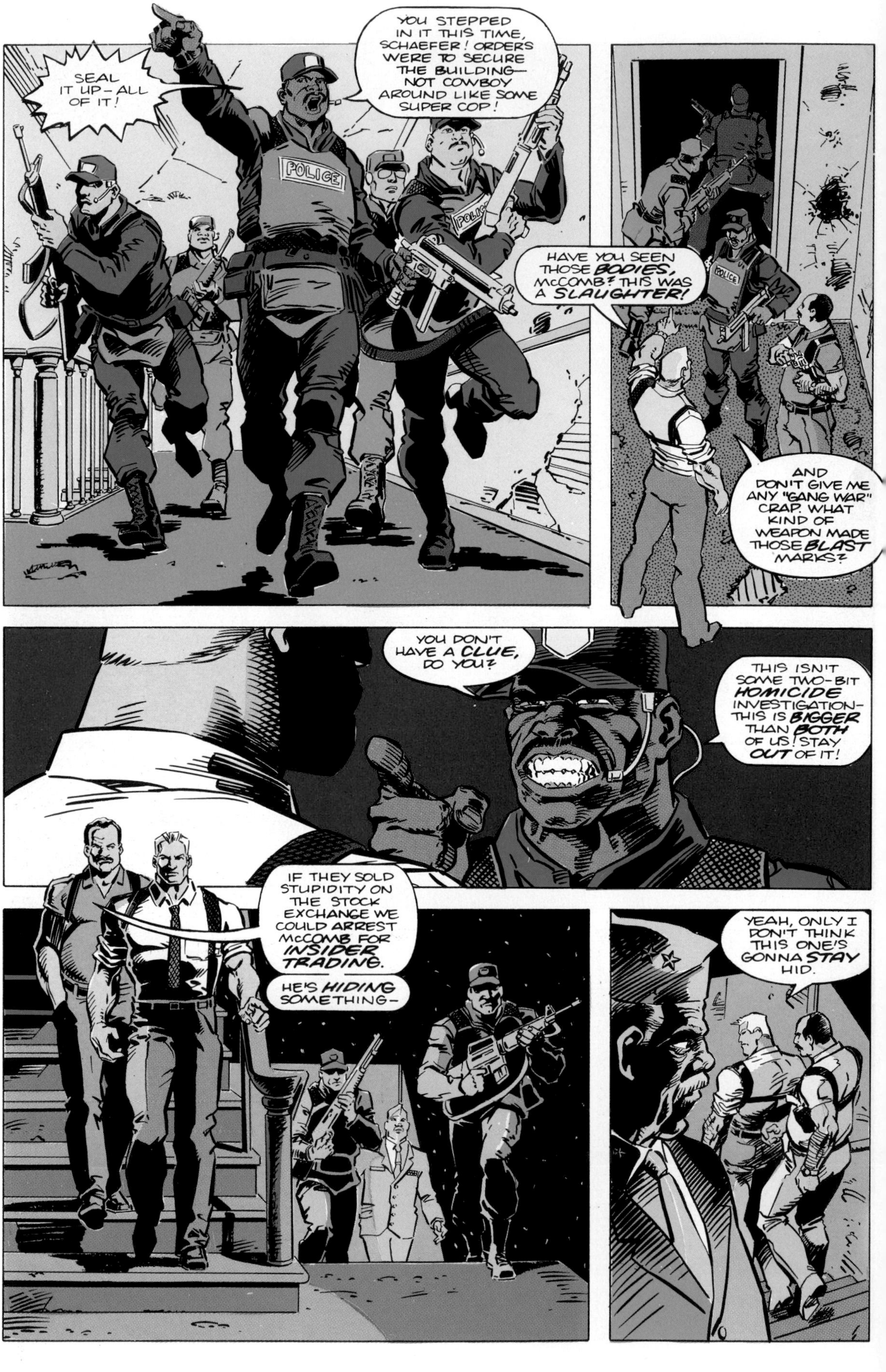
SEAL IT UP–ALL OF IT!
YOU STEPPED IN IT THIS TIME, SCHAEFER! ORDERS WERE TO SECURE THE BUILDING– NOT COWBOY AROUND LIKE SOME SUPER COP!
HAVE YOU SEEN THOSE BODIES, McCOMB? THIS WAS A SLAUGHTER!
AND DON'T GIVE ME ANY "GANG WAR" CRAP. WHAT KIND OF WEAPON MADE THOSE BLAST MARKS?
YOU DON'T HAVE A CLUE, DO YOU?
THIS ISN'T SOME TWO-BIT HOMICIDE INVESTIGATION– THIS IS BIGGER THAN BOTH OF US! STAY OUT OF IT!
IF THEY SOLD STUPIDITY ON THE STOCK EXCHANGE WE COULD ARREST McCOMB FOR INSIDER TRADING.
HE'S HIDING SOMETHING–
YEAH, ONLY I DON'T THINK THIS ONE'S GONNA STAY HID.

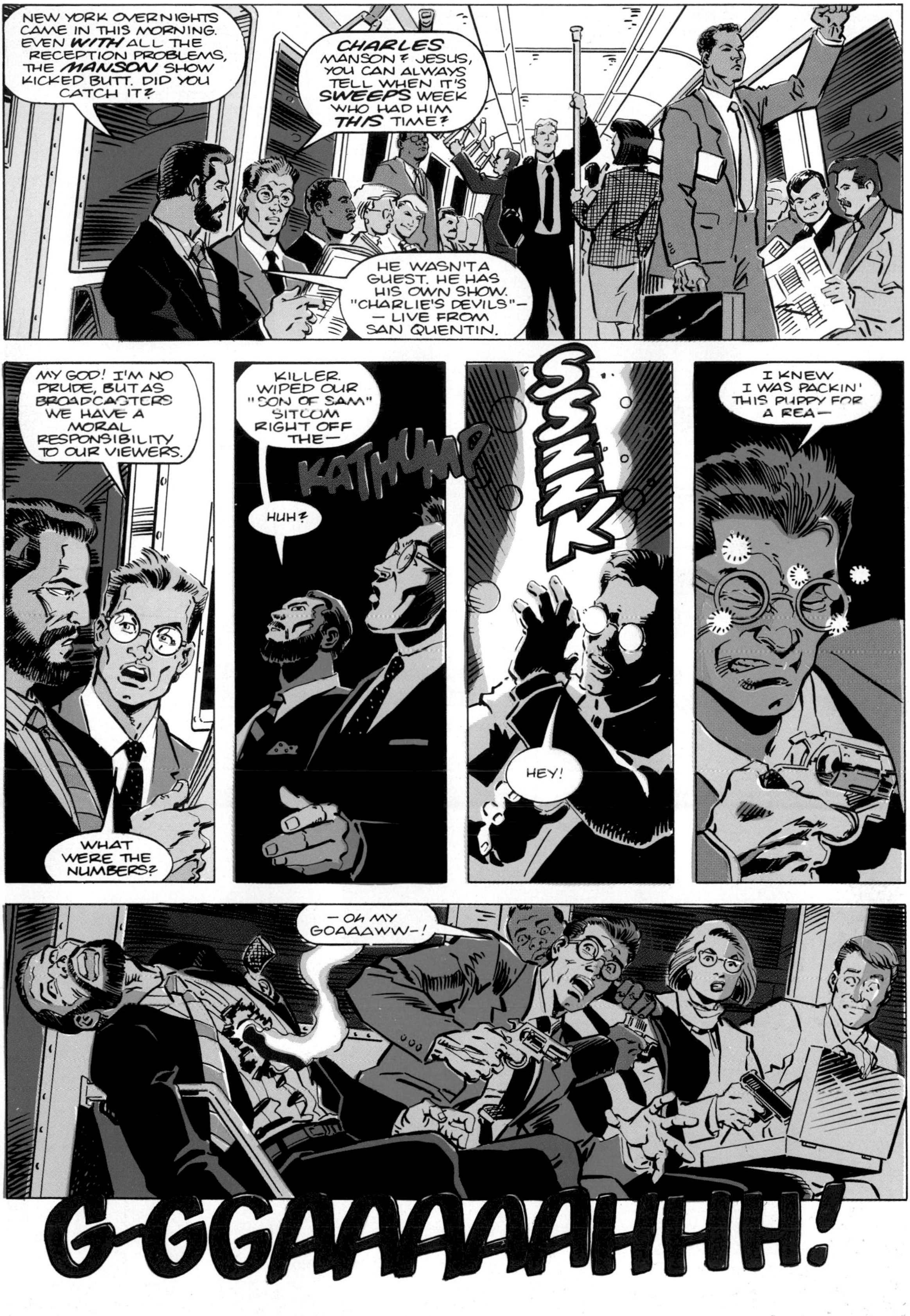
NEW YORK OVERNIGHTS CAME IN THIS MORNING. EVEN WITH ALL THE RECEPTION PROBLEMS, THE MANSON SHOW KICKED BUTT. DID YOU CATCH IT?
CHARLES MANSON? JESUS, YOU CAN ALWAYS TELL WHEN IT'S SWEEPS WEEK. WHO HAD HIM THIS TIME?
HE WASN'T A GUEST. HE HAS HIS OWN SHOW. "CHARLIE'S DEVILS"— — LIVE FROM SAN QUENTIN.
MY GOD! I'M NO PRUDE, BUT AS BROADCASTERS WE HAVE A MORAL RESPONSIBILITY TO OUR VIEWERS.
WHAT WERE THE NUMBERS?
KILLER. WIPED OUR "SON OF SAM" SITCOM RIGHT OFF THE—
KATHUMP
HUH?
SSNIKK
HEY!
I KNEW I WAS PACKIN' THIS PUPPY FOR A REA—
—OH MY GOAAAWW—!
G-GGAAAAAAHHHH!

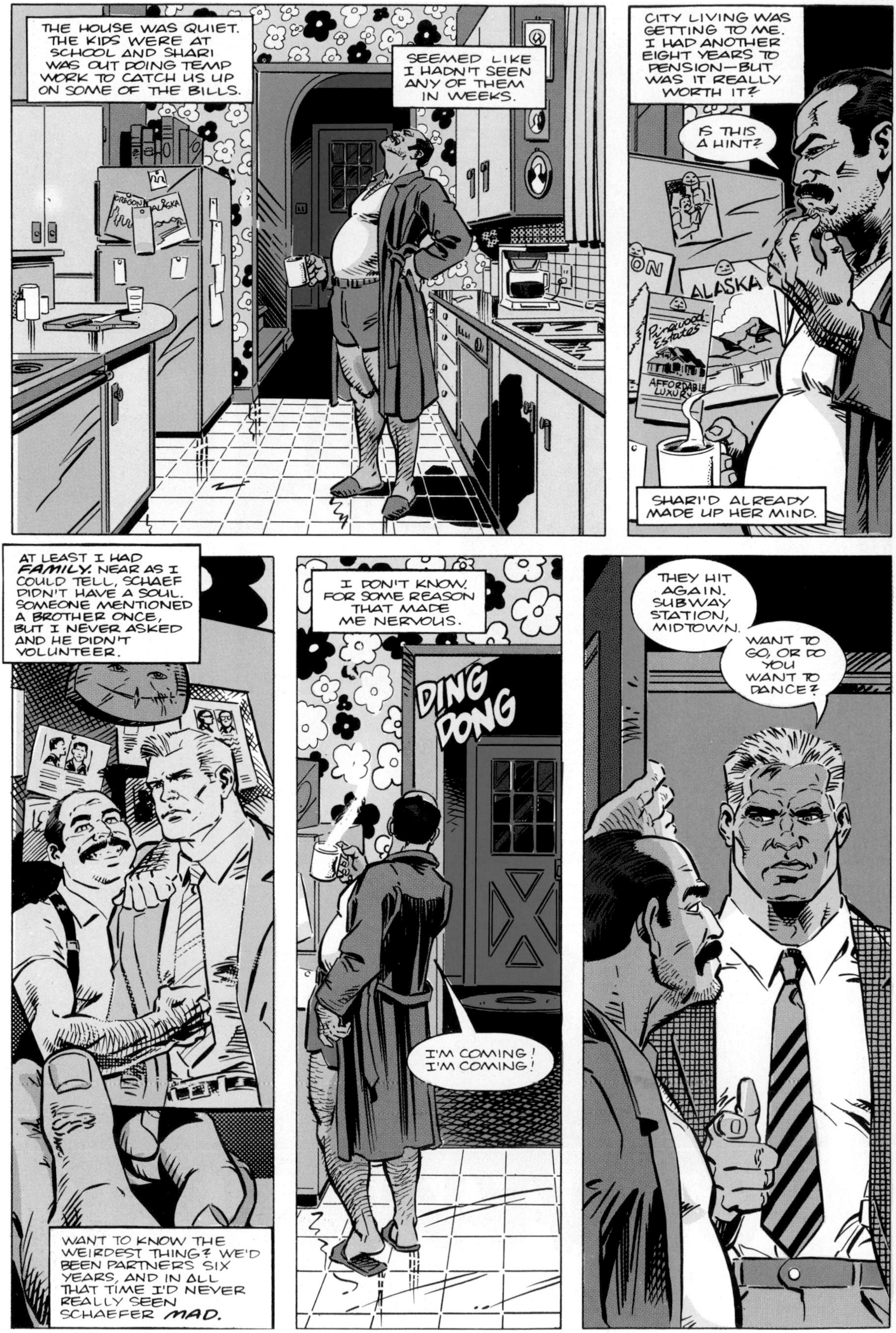

THE HOUSE WAS QUIET. THE KIDS WERE AT SCHOOL AND SHARI WAS OUT DOING TEMP WORK TO CATCH US UP ON SOME OF THE BILLS.
SEEMED LIKE I HADN'T SEEN ANY OF THEM IN WEEKS.
OREGON
ALASKA
CITY LIVING WAS GETTING TO ME. I HAD ANOTHER EIGHT YEARS TO PENSION—BUT WAS IT REALLY WORTH IT?
IS THIS A HINT?
ALASKA
Pinewood Estates
AFFORDABLE LUXURY
SHARI'D ALREADY MADE UP HER MIND.
AT LEAST I HAD FAMILY. NEAR AS I COULD TELL, SCHAEF DIDN'T HAVE A SOUL. SOMEONE MENTIONED A BROTHER ONCE, BUT I NEVER ASKED AND HE DIDN'T VOLUNTEER.
WANT TO KNOW THE WEIRDEST THING? WE'D BEEN PARTNERS SIX YEARS, AND IN ALL THAT TIME I'D NEVER REALLY SEEN SCHAEFER MAD.
I DON'T KNOW. FOR SOME REASON THAT MADE ME NERVOUS.
DING DONG
I'M COMING! I'M COMING!
THEY HIT AGAIN. SUBWAY STATION, MIDTOWN.
WANT TO GO, OR DO YOU WANT TO DANCE?

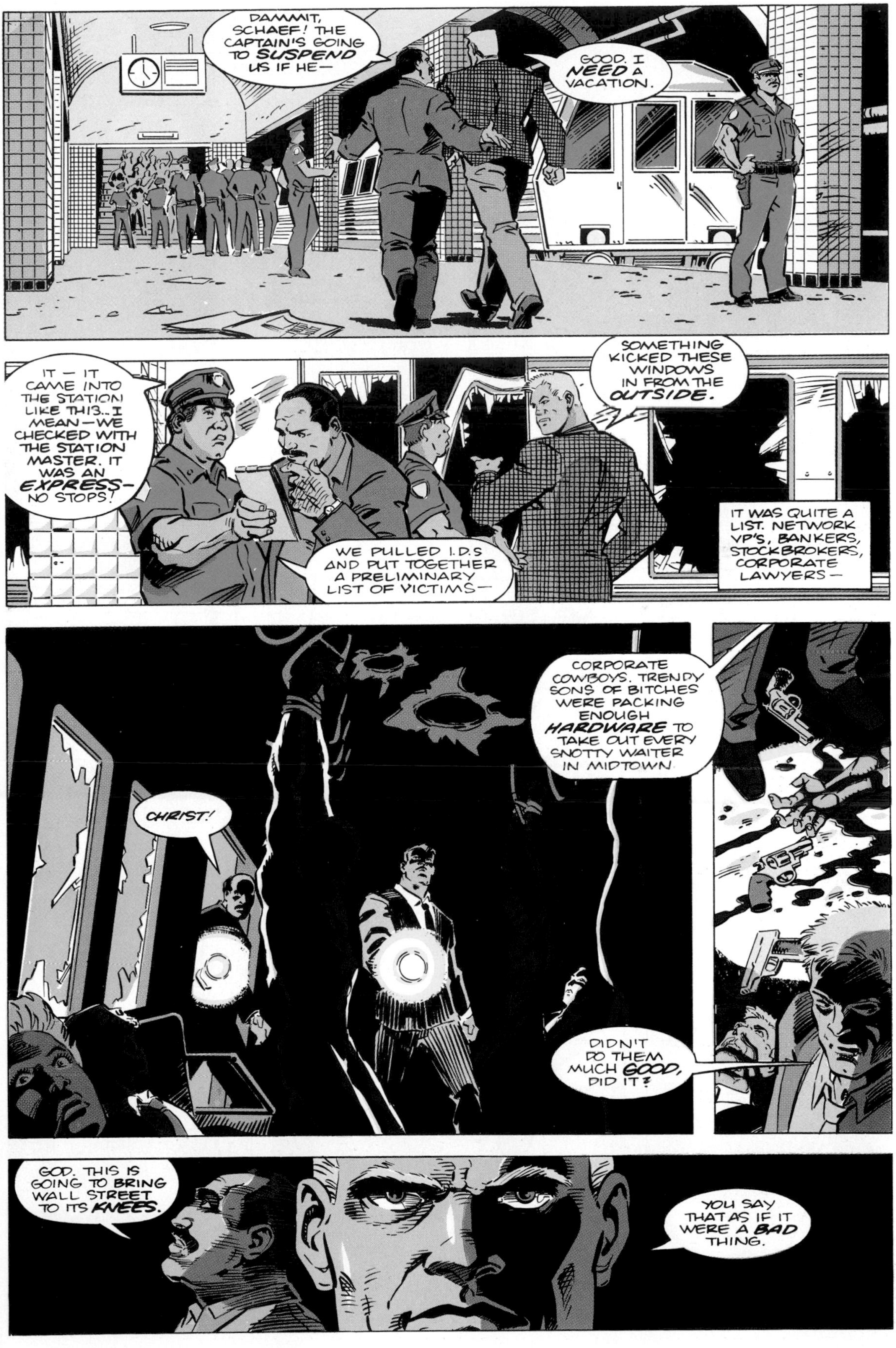
DAMMIT, SCHAEF! THE CAPTAIN'S GOING TO SUSPEND US IF HE—
GOOD. I NEED A VACATION.
IT — IT CAME INTO THE STATION LIKE THIS...I MEAN—WE CHECKED WITH THE STATION MASTER. IT WAS AN EXPRESS—NO STOPS!
SOMETHING KICKED THESE WINDOWS IN FROM THE OUTSIDE.
WE PULLED I.D.S AND PUT TOGETHER A PRELIMINARY LIST OF VICTIMS—
IT WAS QUITE A LIST. NETWORK VP'S, BANKERS, STOCKBROKERS, CORPORATE LAWYERS—
CORPORATE COWBOYS. TRENDY SONS OF BITCHES WERE PACKING ENOUGH HARDWARE TO TAKE OUT EVERY SNOTTY WAITER IN MIDTOWN.
CHRIST!
DIDN'T DO THEM MUCH GOOD, DID IT?
GOD. THIS IS GOING TO BRING WALL STREET TO ITS KNEES.
YOU SAY THAT AS IF IT WERE A BAD THING.

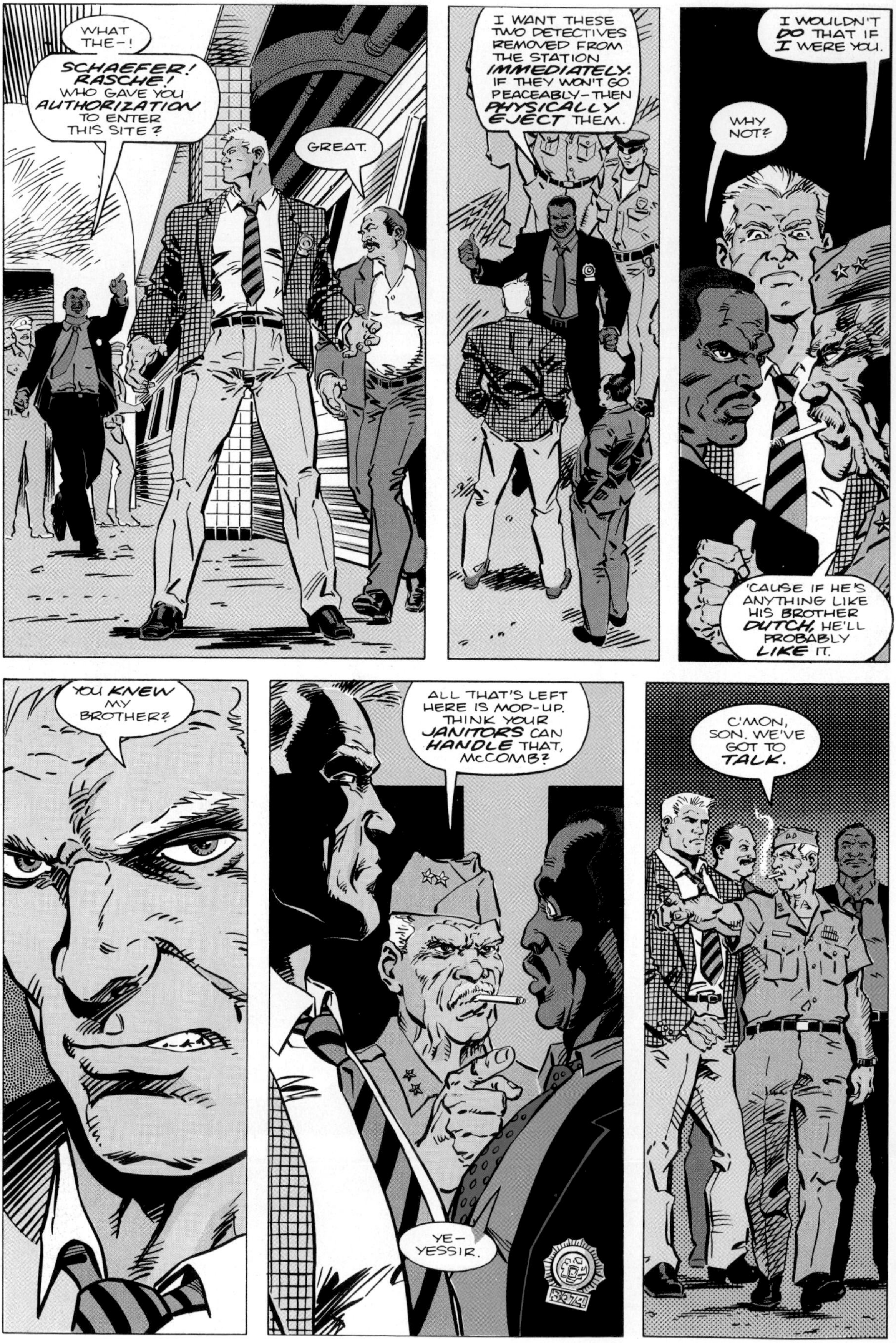
WHAT THE-!
SCHAEFER! RASCHE! WHO GAVE YOU AUTHORIZATION TO ENTER THIS SITE?
GREAT.
I WANT THESE TWO DETECTIVES REMOVED FROM THE STATION IMMEDIATELY. IF THEY WON'T GO PEACEABLY-THEN PHYSICALLY EJECT THEM.
I WOULDN'T DO THAT IF I WERE YOU.
WHY NOT?
'CAUSE IF HE'S ANYTHING LIKE HIS BROTHER DUTCH, HE'LL PROBABLY LIKE IT.
YOU KNEW MY BROTHER?
ALL THAT'S LEFT HERE IS MOP-UP. THINK YOUR JANITORS CAN HANDLE THAT, McCOMB?
YE-YESSIR.
C'MON, SON. WE'VE GOT TO TALK.

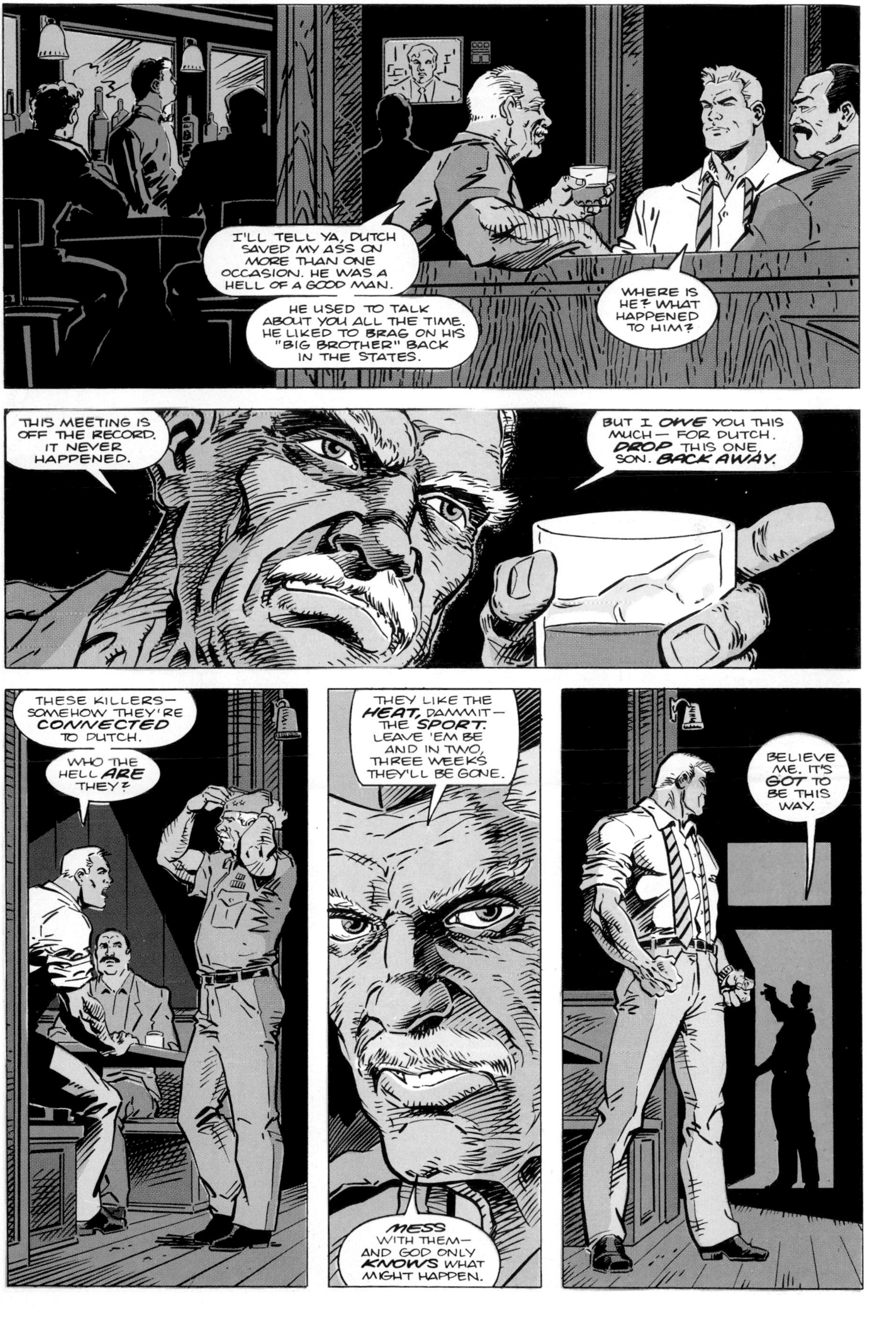
I'LL TELL YA, DUTCH SAVED MY ASS ON MORE THAN ONE OCCASION. HE WAS A HELL OF A GOOD MAN.
HE USED TO TALK ABOUT YOU ALL THE TIME. HE LIKED TO BRAG ON HIS "BIG BROTHER" BACK IN THE STATES.
WHERE IS HE? WHAT HAPPENED TO HIM?
THIS MEETING IS OFF THE RECORD. IT NEVER HAPPENED.
BUT I OWE YOU THIS MUCH— FOR DUTCH. DROP THIS ONE, SON. BACK AWAY.
THESE KILLERS— SOMEHOW THEY'RE CONNECTED TO DUTCH.
WHO THE HELL ARE THEY?
THEY LIKE THE HEAT, DAMMIT— THE SPORT. LEAVE 'EM BE AND IN TWO, THREE WEEKS THEY'LL BE GONE.
MESS WITH THEM— AND GOD ONLY KNOWS WHAT MIGHT HAPPEN.
BELIEVE ME. IT'S GOT TO BE THIS WAY.

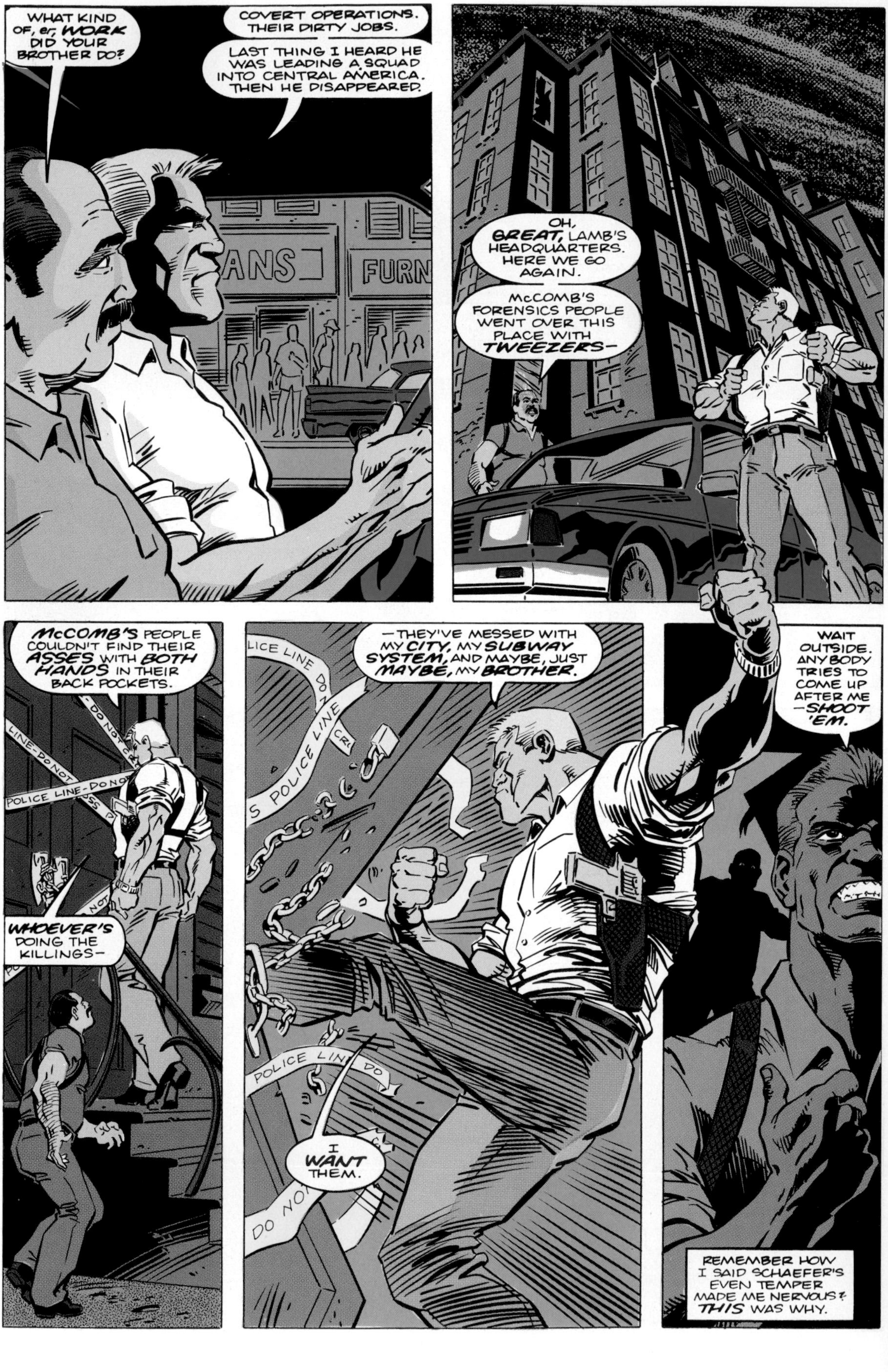
WHAT KIND OF, er, WORK DID YOUR BROTHER DO?
COVERT OPERATIONS. THEIR DIRTY JOBS.
LAST THING I HEARD HE WAS LEADING A SQUAD INTO CENTRAL AMERICA. THEN HE DISAPPEARED.
ANS
FURN
OH, GREAT, LAMB'S HEADQUARTERS. HERE WE GO AGAIN.
McCOMB'S FORENSICS PEOPLE WENT OVER THIS PLACE WITH TWEEZERS—
McCOMB'S PEOPLE COULDN'T FIND THEIR ASSES WITH BOTH HANDS IN THEIR BACK POCKETS.
POLICE LINE-DO NOT
WHOEVER'S DOING THE KILLINGS—
—THEY'VE MESSED WITH MY CITY, MY SUBWAY SYSTEM, AND MAYBE, JUST MAYBE, MY BROTHER.
POLICE LINE
I WANT THEM.
WAIT OUTSIDE. ANYBODY TRIES TO COME UP AFTER ME —SHOOT 'EM.
REMEMBER HOW I SAID SCHAEFER'S EVEN TEMPER MADE ME NERVOUS? THIS WAS WHY.

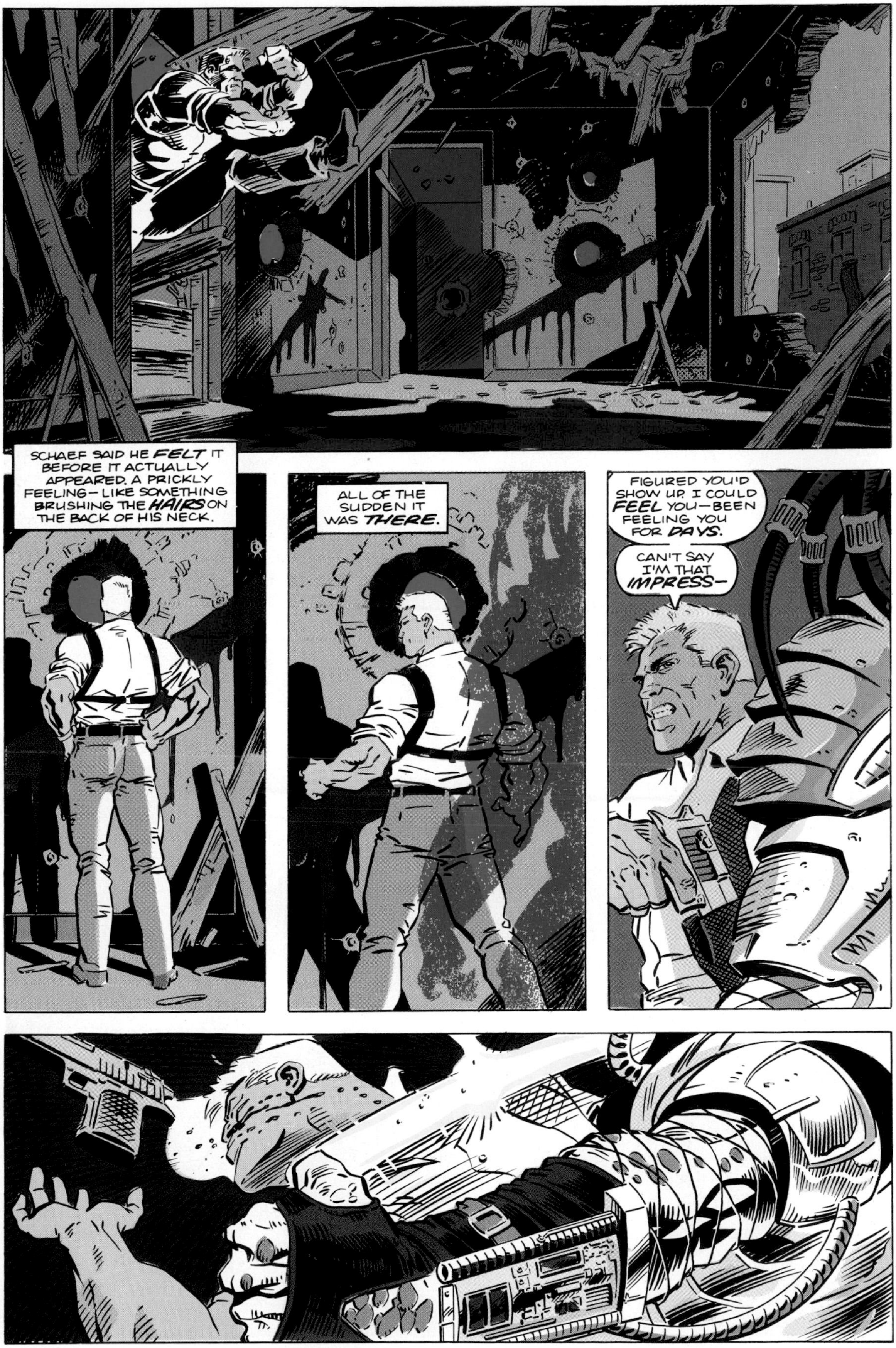
SCHAEF SAID HE FELT IT BEFORE IT ACTUALLY APPEARED. A PRICKLY FEELING-- LIKE SOMETHING BRUSHING THE HAIRS ON THE BACK OF HIS NECK.
ALL OF THE SUDDEN IT WAS THERE.
FIGURED YOU'D SHOW UP. I COULD FEEL YOU--BEEN FEELING YOU FOR DAYS.
CAN'T SAY I'M THAT IMPRESS--

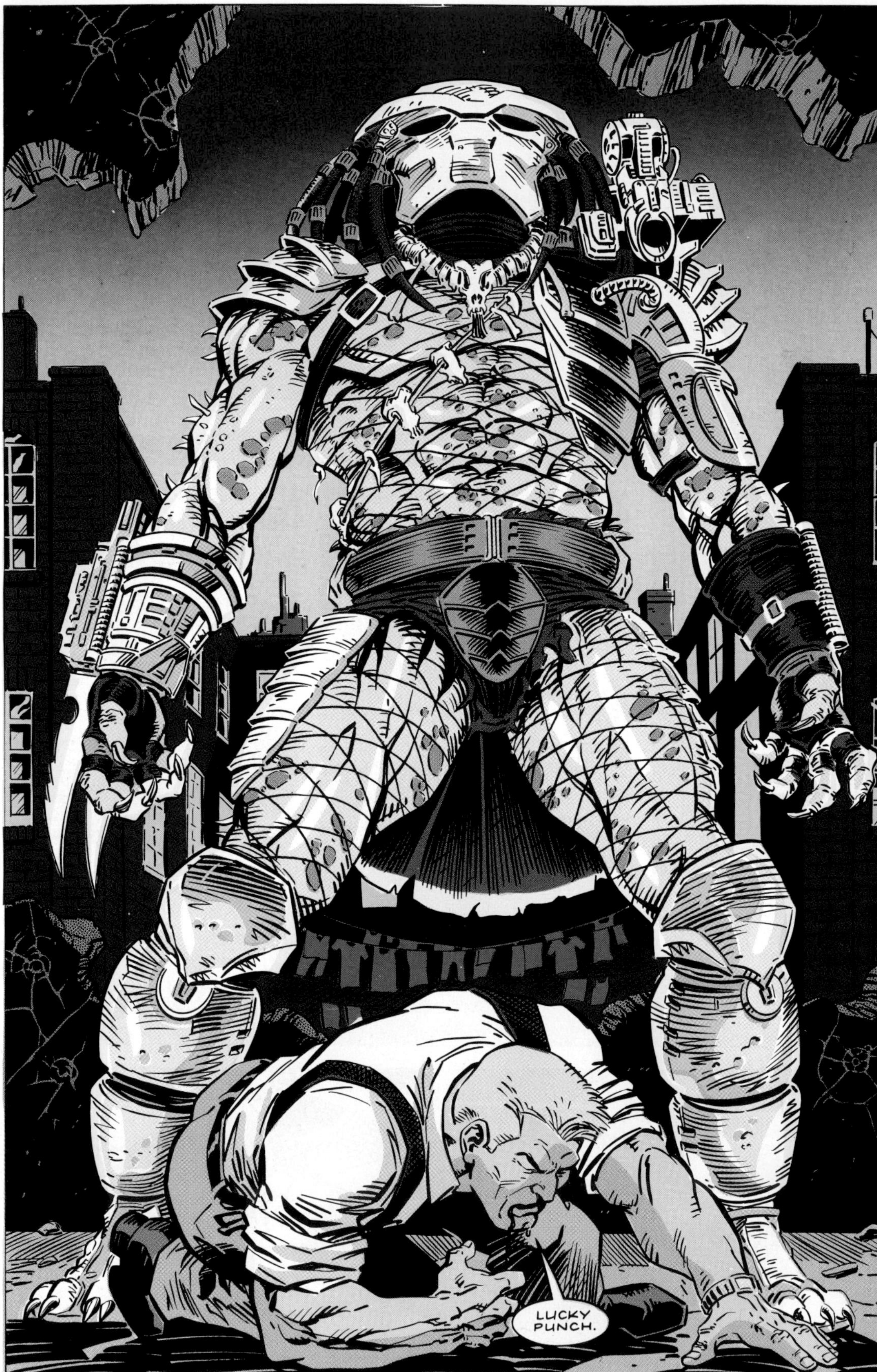
LUCKY PUNCH.

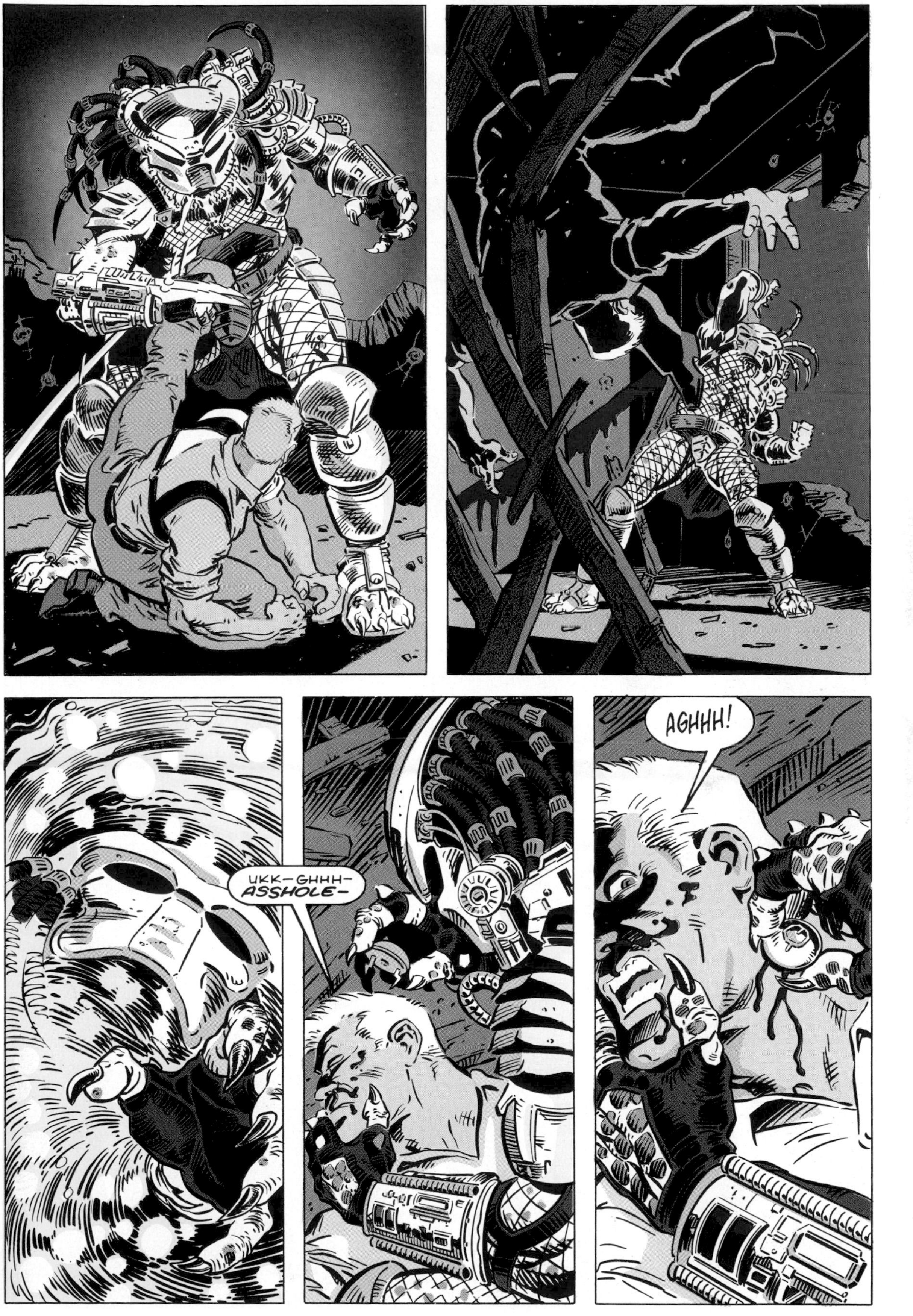
UKK-GHHH-
ASSHOLE-
AGHHH!

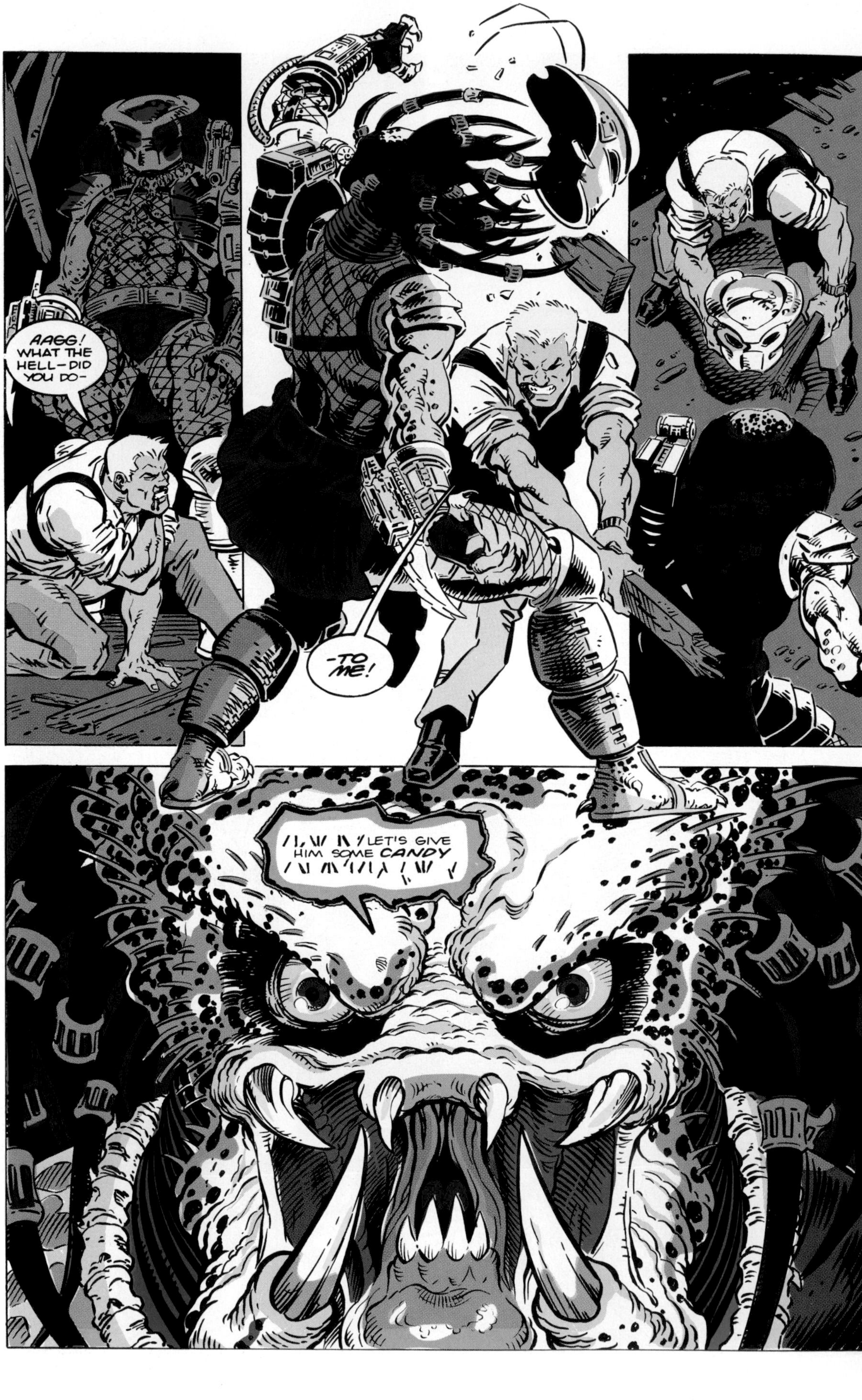
AAGG! WHAT THE HELL–DID YOU DO–
–TO ME!
LET'S GIVE HIM SOME CANDY

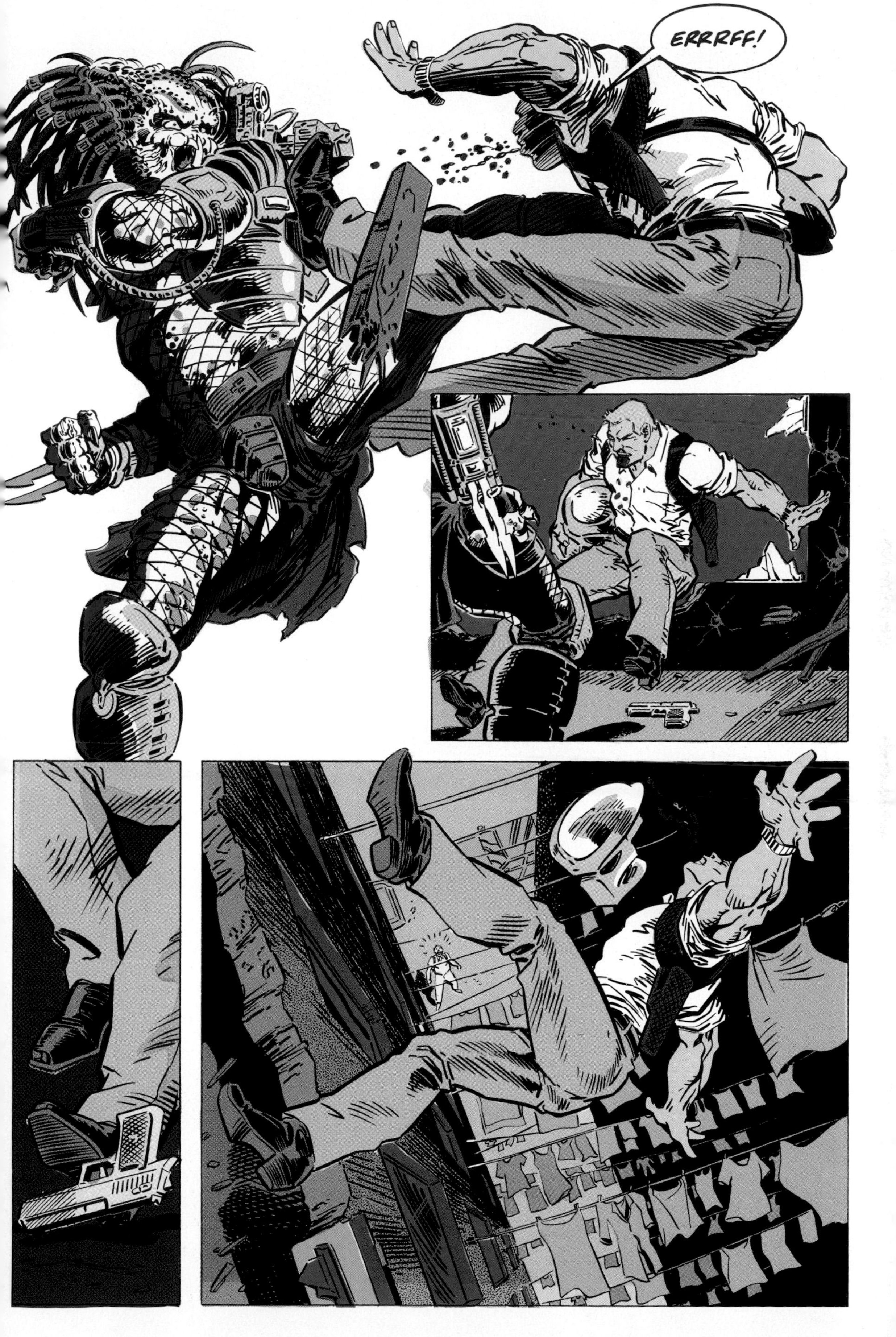
ERRRFF!

CHAPTER 2

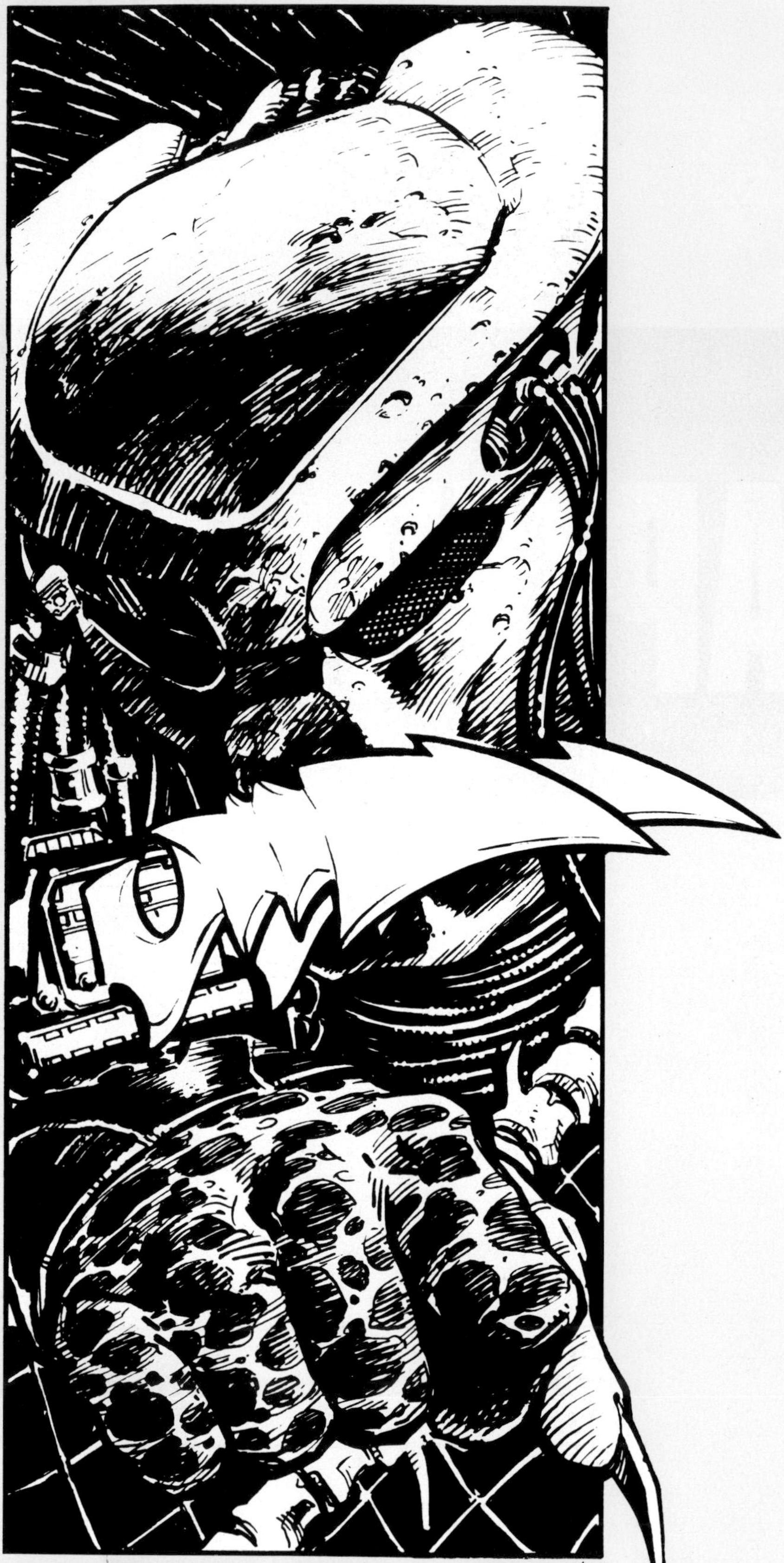

COPS IN NEW YORK TEND TO GET *USED* TO THINGS.

POLICE LINE - DO NOT CROSS POLICE LIN
NOT CR
LINE
POLICE LINE - DO NOT CRO
O NOT CROSS
OT CROSS

LIKE THE TIME SOME LIVE-WIRE TIED A COW TO THE CHAIRMAN OF *"FEDERAL BEEF"* AND PITCHED 'EM BOTH OFF THE TOP OF THE CHRYSLER BUILDING.

WAIT OUTSIDE. ANYBODY TRIES TO COME UP AFTER ME-- *SHOOT 'EM.*

DAMMIT, SCHAEF, THE *FORENSICS* PEOPLE WENT OVER THIS PLACE WIT . *TWEEZERS*-- WI AT DO YOU THINK : OU'RE GOING TO--

IT WAS SUPPOSED TO BE SOME SORT OF *PROTEST* AGAINST CHEMICALLY TREATED MEAT, BUT WHEN THAT JERSEY PANCAKED INTO LEXINGTON AVENUE, ALL *HELL* BROKE LOOSE.

CITY SANITATION MUST HAVE GONE THROUGH A DOZEN MOPS CLEANING UP THE MESS, BUT THEY DIDN'T CARE-- FREE STEAKS FOR CHRISTMAS.

THE POINT IS, THAT'S THE *JOB.* YOU LEARN TO *DEAL* WITH IT.

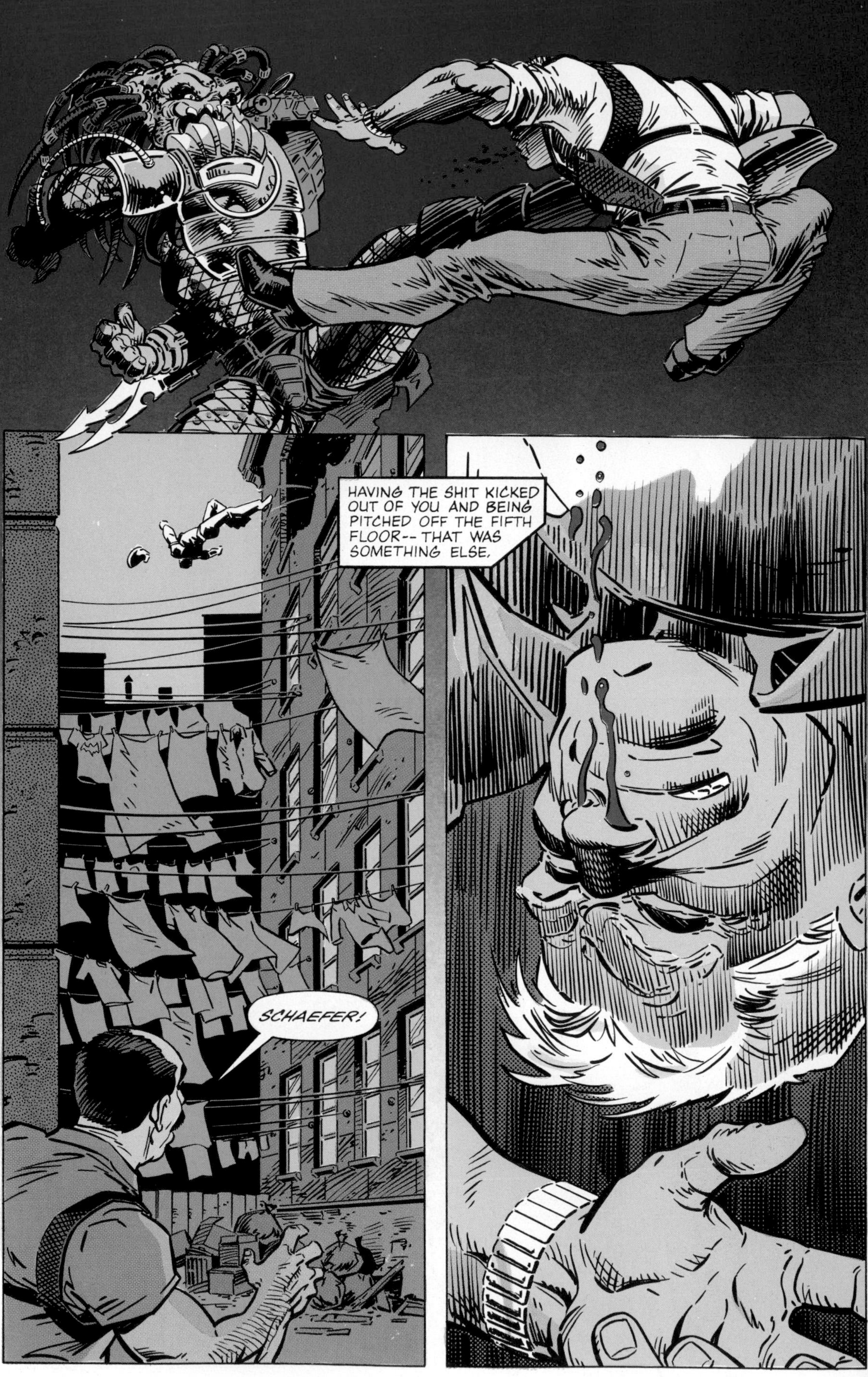
HAVING THE SHIT KICKED OUT OF YOU AND BEING PITCHED OFF THE FIFTH FLOOR-- THAT WAS SOMETHING ELSE.
SCHAEFER!

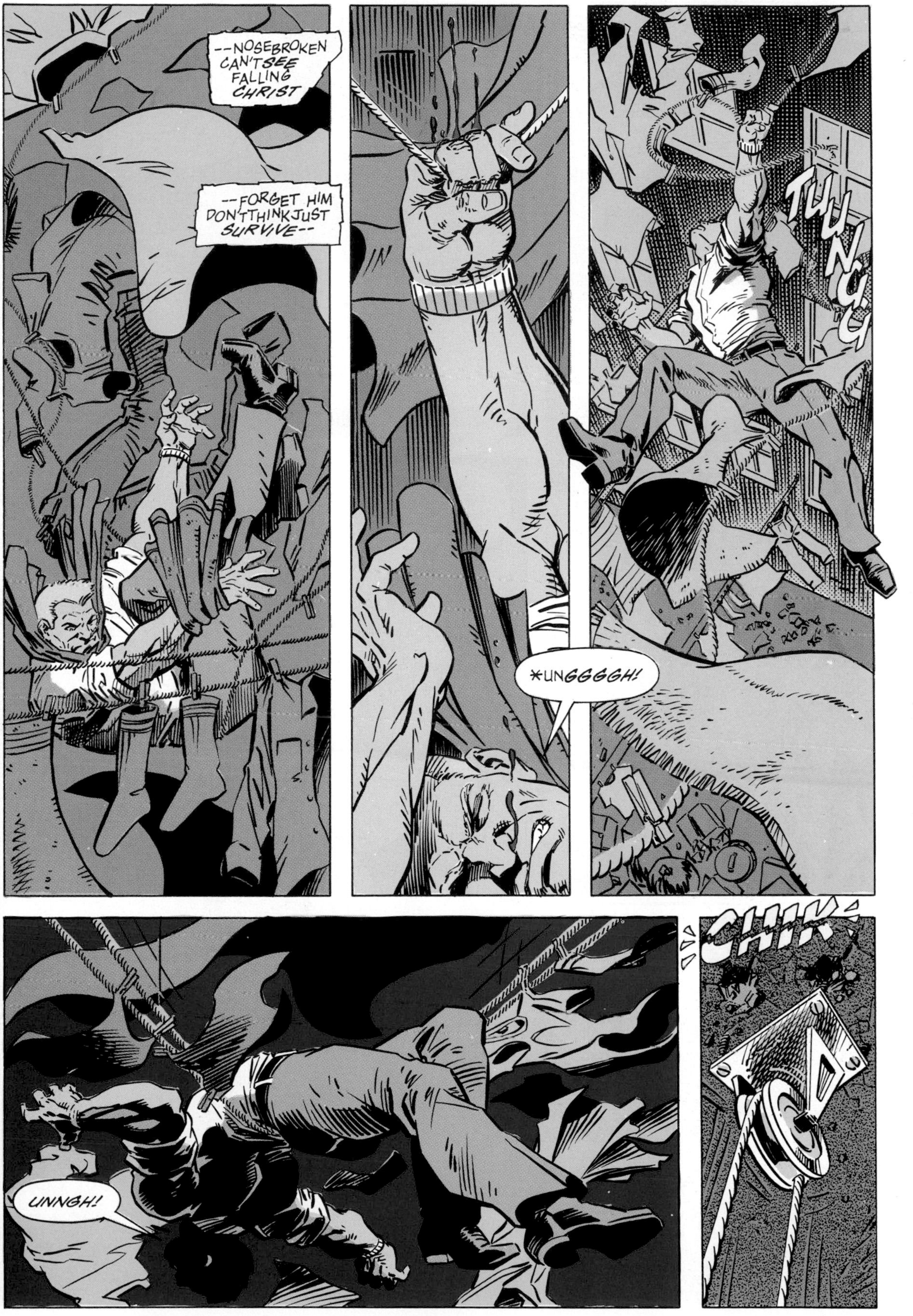
--NOSEBROKEN CAN'T SEE FALLING CHRIST
--FORGET HIM DON'T THINK JUST SURVIVE--
*UNGGGGH!
TUUNGG
UNNGH!
CHIK

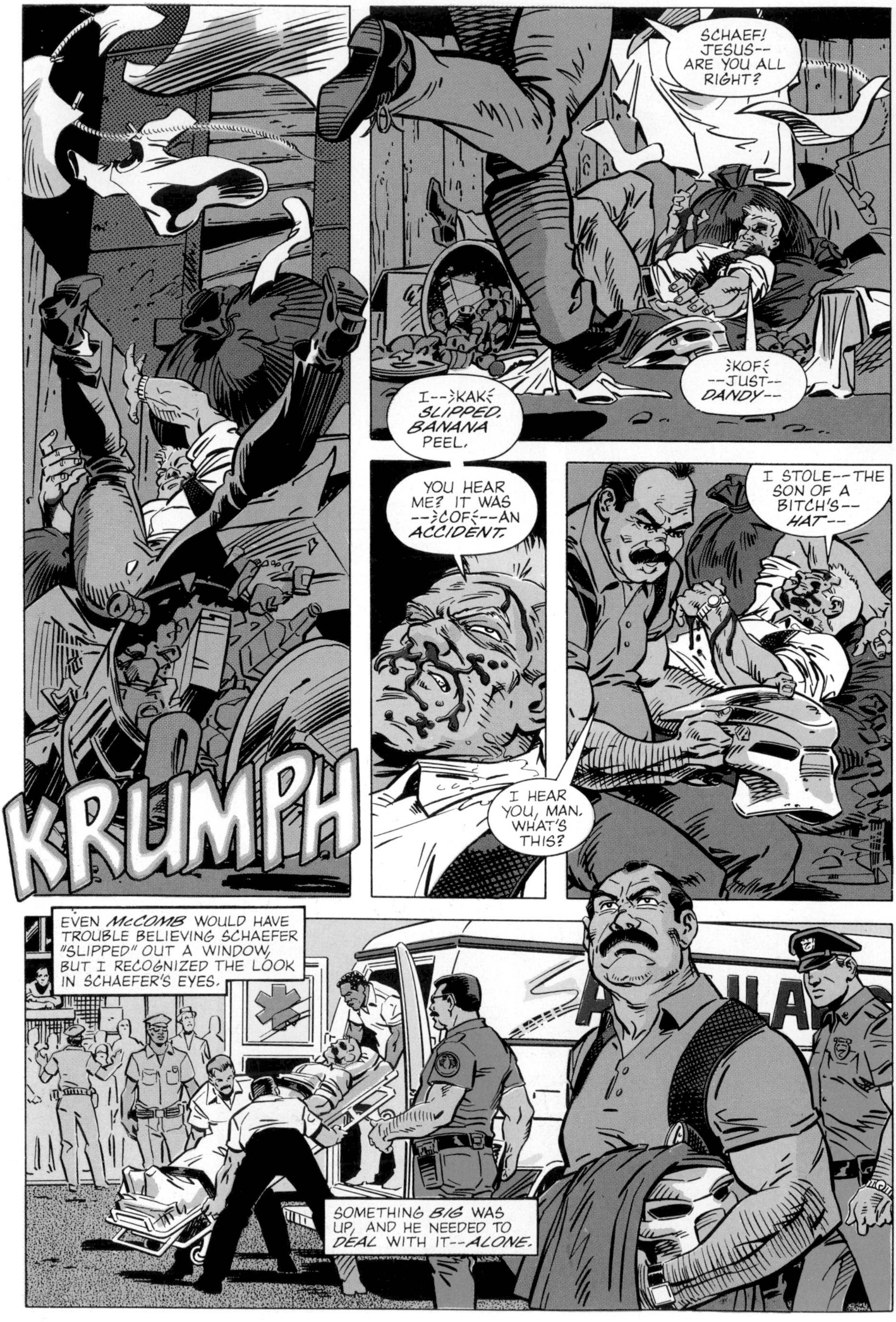
KRUMPH
SCHAEF! JESUS-- ARE YOU ALL RIGHT?
KOF --JUST-- DANDY--
I-- KAK SLIPPED. BANANA PEEL.
YOU HEAR ME? IT WAS --COF--AN ACCIDENT.
I HEAR YOU, MAN. WHAT'S THIS?
I STOLE--THE SON OF A BITCH'S--HAT--
EVEN McCOMB WOULD HAVE TROUBLE BELIEVING SCHAEFER "SLIPPED" OUT A WINDOW, BUT I RECOGNIZED THE LOOK IN SCHAEFER'S EYES.
SOMETHING BIG WAS UP, AND HE NEEDED TO DEAL WITH IT--ALONE.

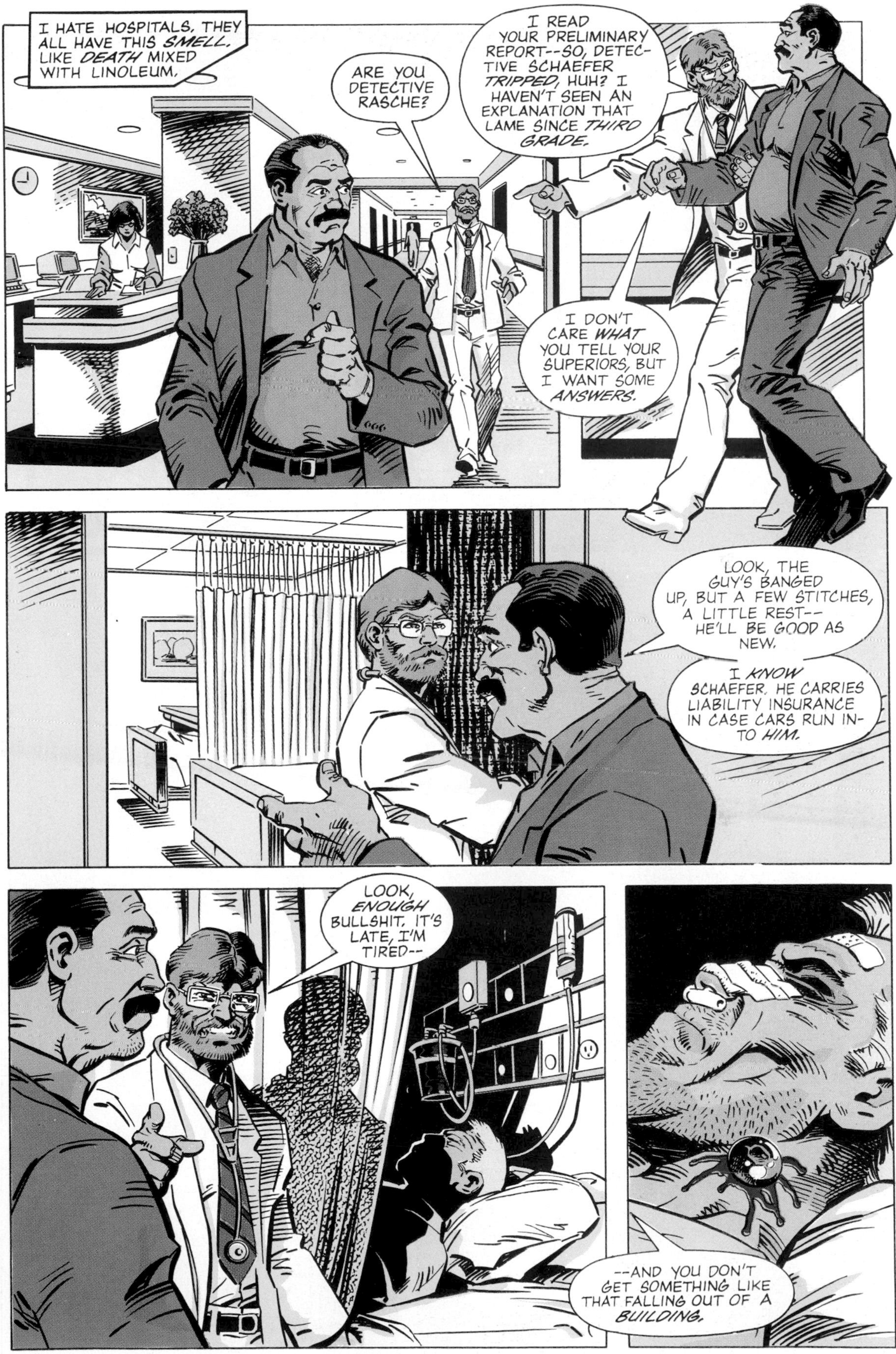
I HATE HOSPITALS. THEY ALL HAVE THIS SMELL. LIKE DEATH MIXED WITH LINOLEUM.
ARE YOU DETECTIVE RASCHE?
I READ YOUR PRELIMINARY REPORT--SO, DETECTIVE SCHAEFER TRIPPED, HUH? I HAVEN'T SEEN AN EXPLANATION THAT LAME SINCE THIRD GRADE.
I DON'T CARE WHAT YOU TELL YOUR SUPERIORS, BUT I WANT SOME ANSWERS.
LOOK, THE GUY'S BANGED UP, BUT A FEW STITCHES, A LITTLE REST-- HE'LL BE GOOD AS NEW.
I KNOW SCHAEFER. HE CARRIES LIABILITY INSURANCE IN CASE CARS RUN INTO HIM.
LOOK, ENOUGH BULLSHIT. IT'S LATE, I'M TIRED--
--AND YOU DON'T GET SOMETHING LIKE THAT FALLING OUT OF A BUILDING.

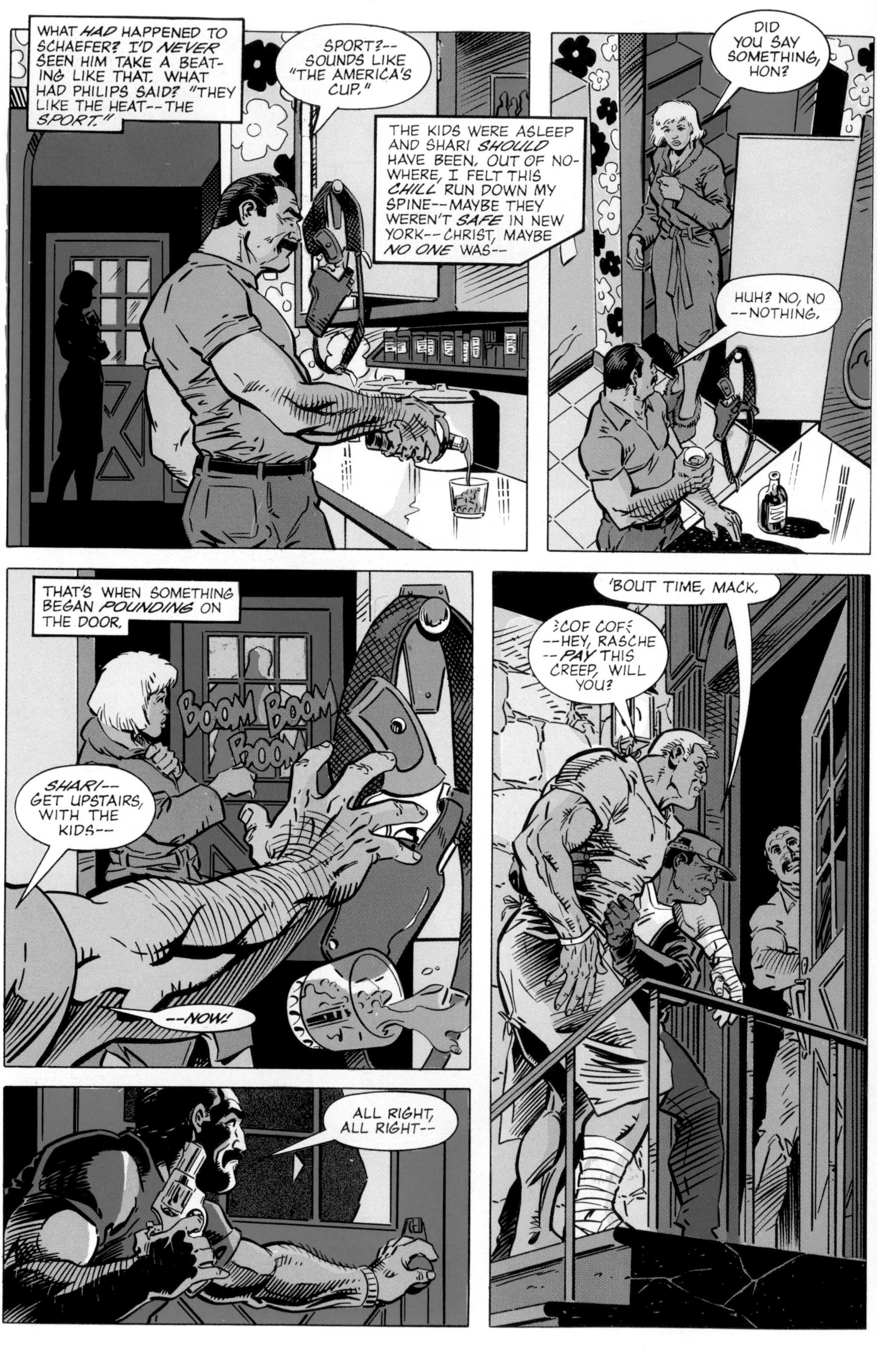
WHAT HAD HAPPENED TO SCHAEFER? I'D NEVER SEEN HIM TAKE A BEATING LIKE THAT. WHAT HAD PHILIPS SAID? "THEY LIKE THE HEAT--THE SPORT."
SPORT?-- SOUNDS LIKE "THE AMERICA'S CUP."
THE KIDS WERE ASLEEP AND SHARI SHOULD HAVE BEEN. OUT OF NOWHERE, I FELT THIS CHILL RUN DOWN MY SPINE--MAYBE THEY WEREN'T SAFE IN NEW YORK--CHRIST, MAYBE NO ONE WAS--
DID YOU SAY SOMETHING, HON?
HUH? NO, NO --NOTHING.
THAT'S WHEN SOMETHING BEGAN POUNDING ON THE DOOR.
BOOM BOOM BOOM
SHARI-- GET UPSTAIRS, WITH THE KIDS--
--NOW!
ALL RIGHT, ALL RIGHT--
'BOUT TIME, MACK.
COF COF --HEY, RASCHE --PAY THIS CREEP, WILL YOU?

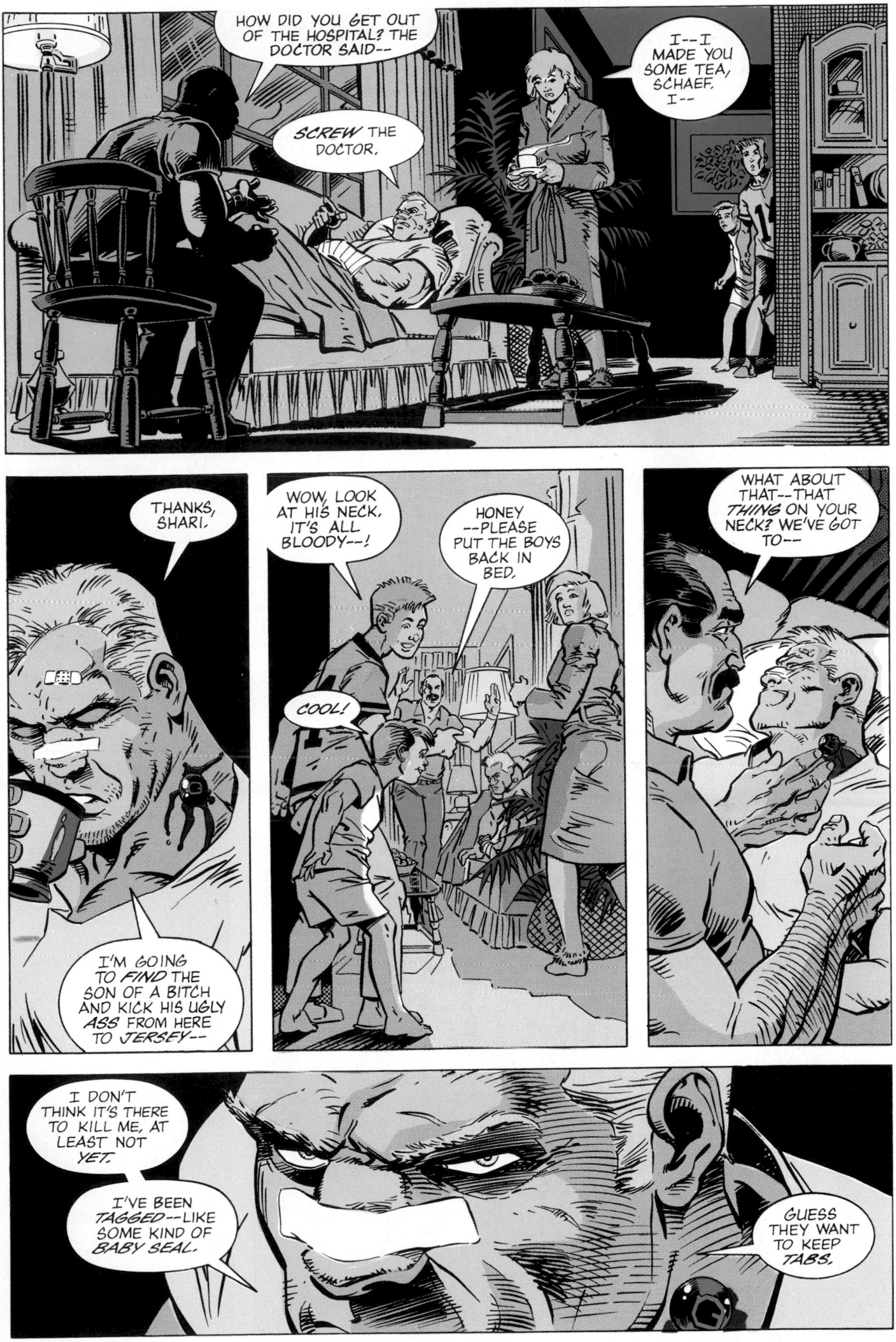

HOW DID YOU GET OUT OF THE HOSPITAL? THE DOCTOR SAID--
SCREW THE DOCTOR.
I--I MADE YOU SOME TEA, SCHAEF. I--
THANKS, SHARI.
I'M GOING TO FIND THE SON OF A BITCH AND KICK HIS UGLY ASS FROM HERE TO JERSEY--
WOW, LOOK AT HIS NECK. IT'S ALL BLOODY--!
HONEY --PLEASE PUT THE BOYS BACK IN BED.
COOL!
WHAT ABOUT THAT--THAT THING ON YOUR NECK? WE'VE GOT TO--
I DON'T THINK IT'S THERE TO KILL ME, AT LEAST NOT YET.
I'VE BEEN TAGGED--LIKE SOME KIND OF BABY SEAL.
GUESS THEY WANT TO KEEP TABS.

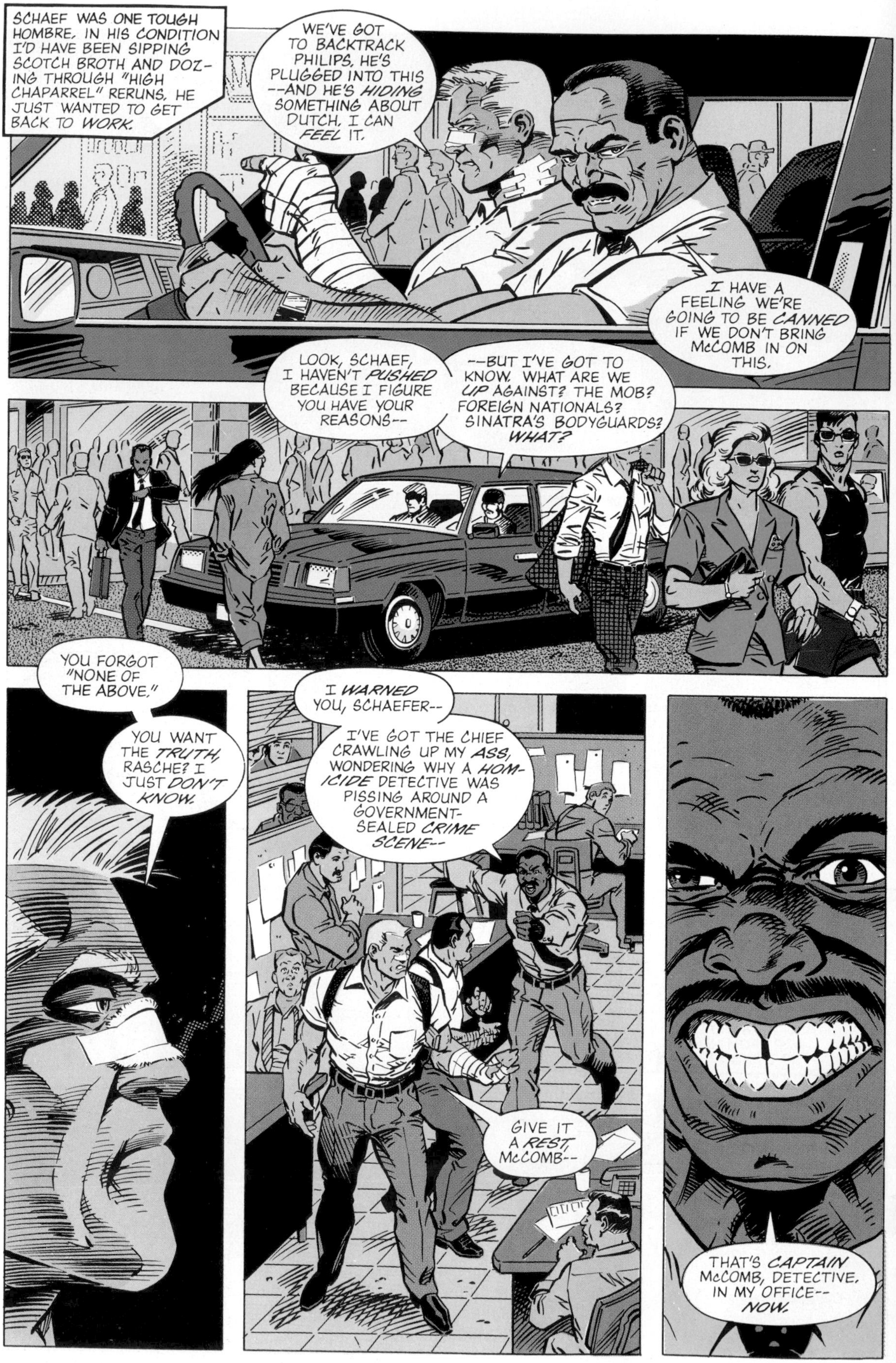
SCHAEF WAS ONE TOUGH HOMBRE. IN HIS CONDITION I'D HAVE BEEN SIPPING SCOTCH BROTH AND DOZING THROUGH "HIGH CHAPARREL" RERUNS. HE JUST WANTED TO GET BACK TO WORK.
WE'VE GOT TO BACKTRACK PHILIPS. HE'S PLUGGED INTO THIS --AND HE'S HIDING SOMETHING ABOUT DUTCH. I CAN FEEL IT.
I HAVE A FEELING WE'RE GOING TO BE CANNED IF WE DON'T BRING McCOMB IN ON THIS.
LOOK, SCHAEF, I HAVEN'T PUSHED BECAUSE I FIGURE YOU HAVE YOUR REASONS--
--BUT I'VE GOT TO KNOW. WHAT ARE WE UP AGAINST? THE MOB? FOREIGN NATIONALS? SINATRA'S BODYGUARDS? WHAT?
YOU FORGOT "NONE OF THE ABOVE."
YOU WANT THE TRUTH, RASCHE? I JUST DON'T KNOW.
I WARNED YOU, SCHAEFER--
I'VE GOT THE CHIEF CRAWLING UP MY ASS, WONDERING WHY A HOMICIDE DETECTIVE WAS PISSING AROUND A GOVERNMENT-SEALED CRIME SCENE--
GIVE IT A REST, McCOMB--
THAT'S CAPTAIN McCOMB, DETECTIVE. IN MY OFFICE--NOW.

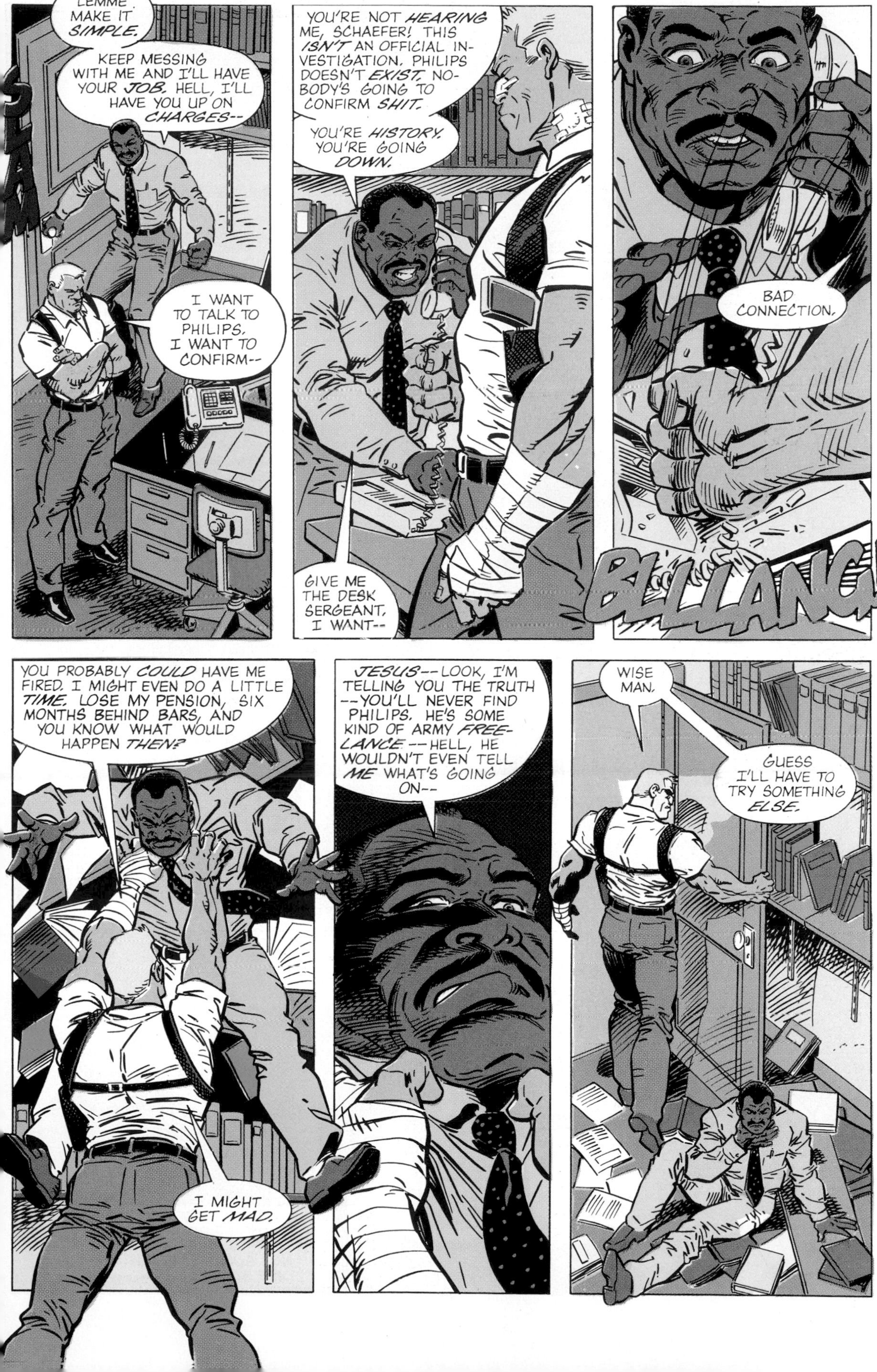
SLAM
LEMME MAKE IT SIMPLE.
KEEP MESSING WITH ME AND I'LL HAVE YOUR JOB. HELL, I'LL HAVE YOU UP ON CHARGES--
I WANT TO TALK TO PHILIPS. I WANT TO CONFIRM--
YOU'RE NOT HEARING ME, SCHAEFER! THIS ISN'T AN OFFICIAL INVESTIGATION. PHILIPS DOESN'T EXIST. NOBODY'S GOING TO CONFIRM SHIT.
YOU'RE HISTORY. YOU'RE GOING DOWN.
GIVE ME THE DESK SERGEANT. I WANT--
BAD CONNECTION.
BLLLANG!
YOU PROBABLY COULD HAVE ME FIRED. I MIGHT EVEN DO A LITTLE TIME. LOSE MY PENSION. SIX MONTHS BEHIND BARS, AND YOU KNOW WHAT WOULD HAPPEN THEN?
I MIGHT GET MAD.
JESUS--LOOK, I'M TELLING YOU THE TRUTH--YOU'LL NEVER FIND PHILIPS. HE'S SOME KIND OF ARMY FREE-LANCE.--HELL, HE WOULDN'T EVEN TELL ME WHAT'S GOING ON--
WISE MAN.
GUESS I'LL HAVE TO TRY SOMETHING ELSE.

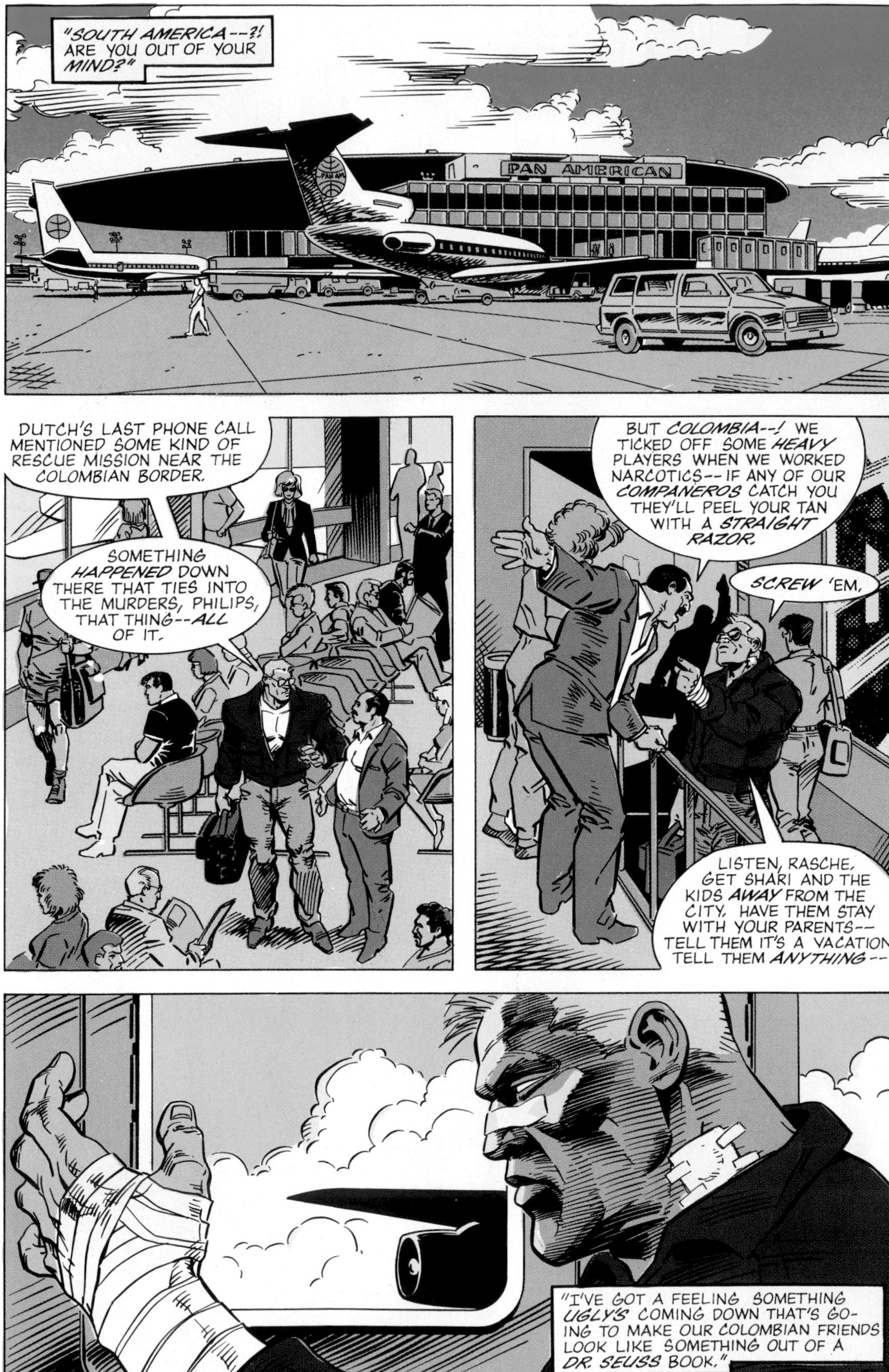
"SOUTH AMERICA--?! ARE YOU OUT OF YOUR MIND?"
PAN AMERICAN
DUTCH'S LAST PHONE CALL MENTIONED SOME KIND OF RESCUE MISSION NEAR THE COLOMBIAN BORDER.
SOMETHING HAPPENED DOWN THERE THAT TIES INTO THE MURDERS, PHILIPS, THAT THING--ALL OF IT.
BUT COLOMBIA--! WE TICKED OFF SOME HEAVY PLAYERS WHEN WE WORKED NARCOTICS--IF ANY OF OUR COMPANEROS CATCH YOU THEY'LL PEEL YOUR TAN WITH A STRAIGHT RAZOR.
SCREW 'EM.
LISTEN, RASCHE, GET SHARI AND THE KIDS AWAY FROM THE CITY. HAVE THEM STAY WITH YOUR PARENTS--TELL THEM IT'S A VACATION, TELL THEM ANYTHING--
"I'VE GOT A FEELING SOMETHING UGLY'S COMING DOWN THAT'S GOING TO MAKE OUR COLOMBIAN FRIENDS LOOK LIKE SOMETHING OUT OF A DR. SEUSS BOOK."

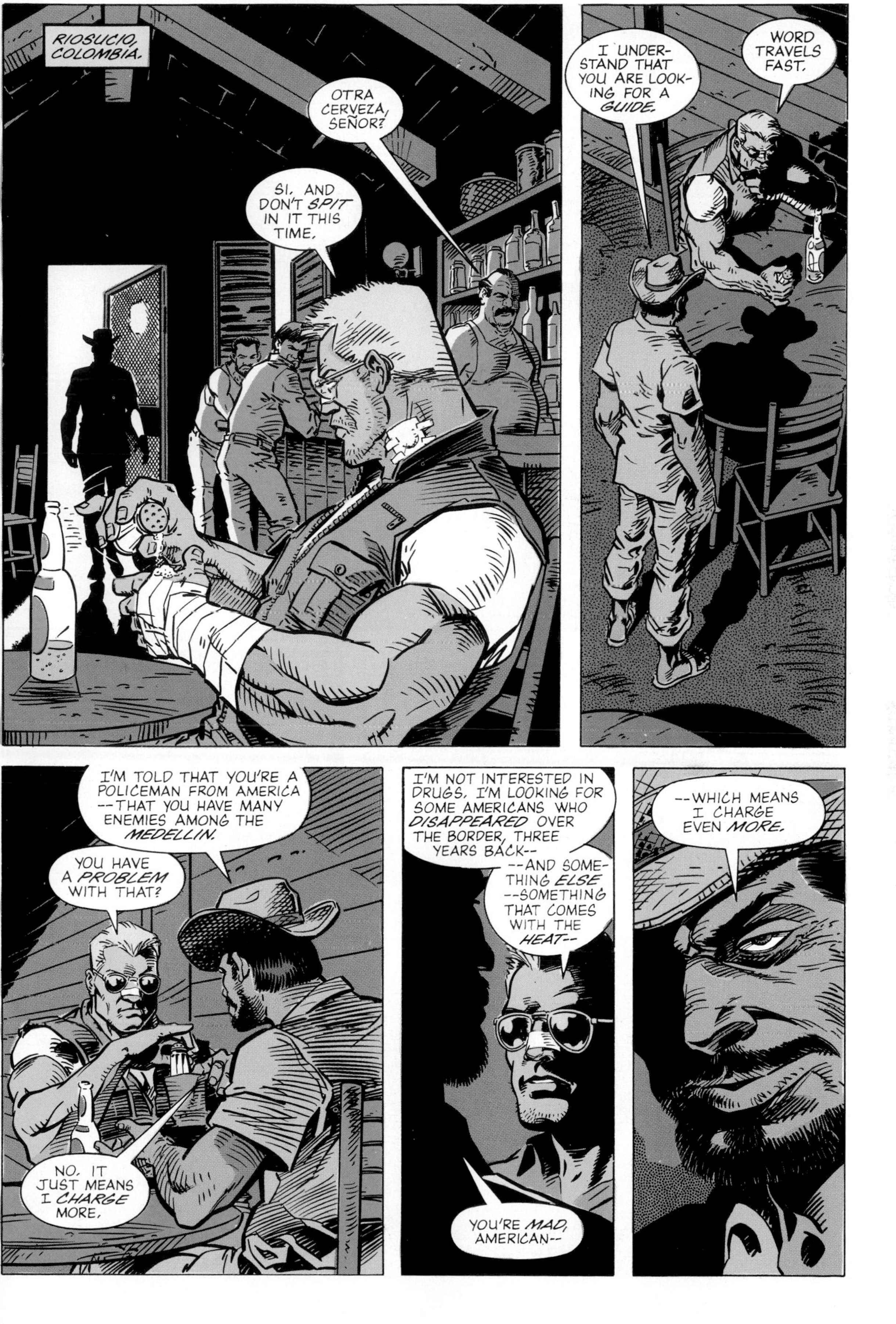
RIOSUCIO, COLOMBIA.
OTRA CERVEZA, SEÑOR?
SI. AND DON'T SPIT IN IT THIS TIME.
I UNDERSTAND THAT YOU ARE LOOKING FOR A GUIDE.
WORD TRAVELS FAST.
I'M TOLD THAT YOU'RE A POLICEMAN FROM AMERICA --THAT YOU HAVE MANY ENEMIES AMONG THE MEDELLIN.
YOU HAVE A PROBLEM WITH THAT?
NO. IT JUST MEANS I CHARGE MORE.
I'M NOT INTERESTED IN DRUGS. I'M LOOKING FOR SOME AMERICANS WHO DISAPPEARED OVER THE BORDER, THREE YEARS BACK--
--AND SOMETHING ELSE --SOMETHING THAT COMES WITH THE HEAT--
YOU'RE MAD, AMERICAN--
--WHICH MEANS I CHARGE EVEN MORE.

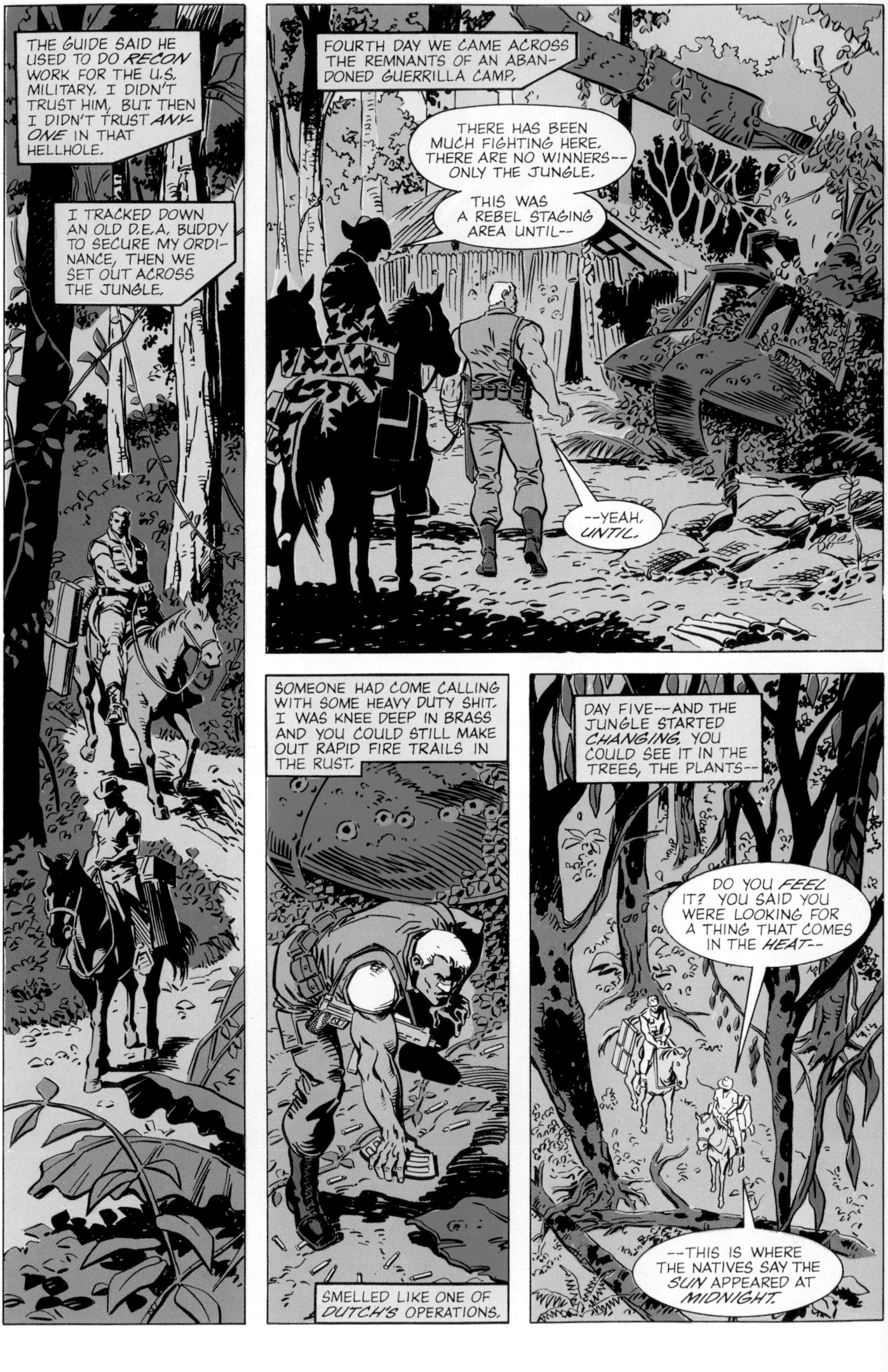
THE GUIDE SAID HE USED TO DO RECON WORK FOR THE U.S. MILITARY. I DIDN'T TRUST HIM, BUT THEN I DIDN'T TRUST ANYONE IN THAT HELLHOLE.
I TRACKED DOWN AN OLD D.E.A. BUDDY TO SECURE MY ORDINANCE, THEN WE SET OUT ACROSS THE JUNGLE.
FOURTH DAY WE CAME ACROSS THE REMNANTS OF AN ABANDONED GUERRILLA CAMP.
THERE HAS BEEN MUCH FIGHTING HERE. THERE ARE NO WINNERS-- ONLY THE JUNGLE.
THIS WAS A REBEL STAGING AREA UNTIL--
--YEAH, UNTIL.
SOMEONE HAD COME CALLING WITH SOME HEAVY DUTY SHIT. I WAS KNEE DEEP IN BRASS AND YOU COULD STILL MAKE OUT RAPID FIRE TRAILS IN THE RUST.
SMELLED LIKE ONE OF DUTCH'S OPERATIONS.
DAY FIVE--AND THE JUNGLE STARTED CHANGING. YOU COULD SEE IT IN THE TREES, THE PLANTS--
DO YOU FEEL IT? YOU SAID YOU WERE LOOKING FOR A THING THAT COMES IN THE HEAT--
--THIS IS WHERE THE NATIVES SAY THE SUN APPEARED AT MIDNIGHT.

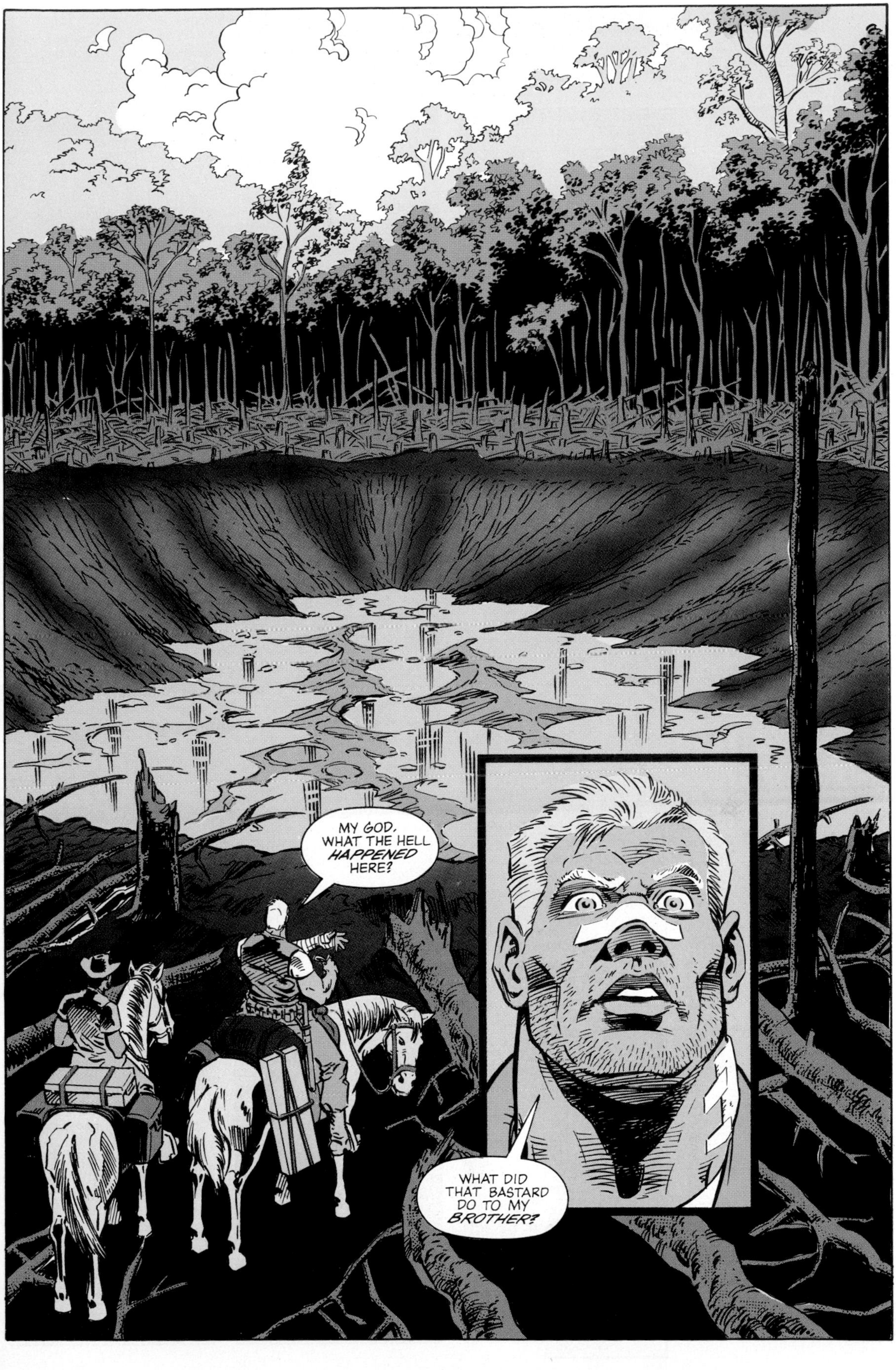
MY GOD, WHAT THE HELL HAPPENED HERE?
WHAT DID THAT BASTARD DO TO MY BROTHER?

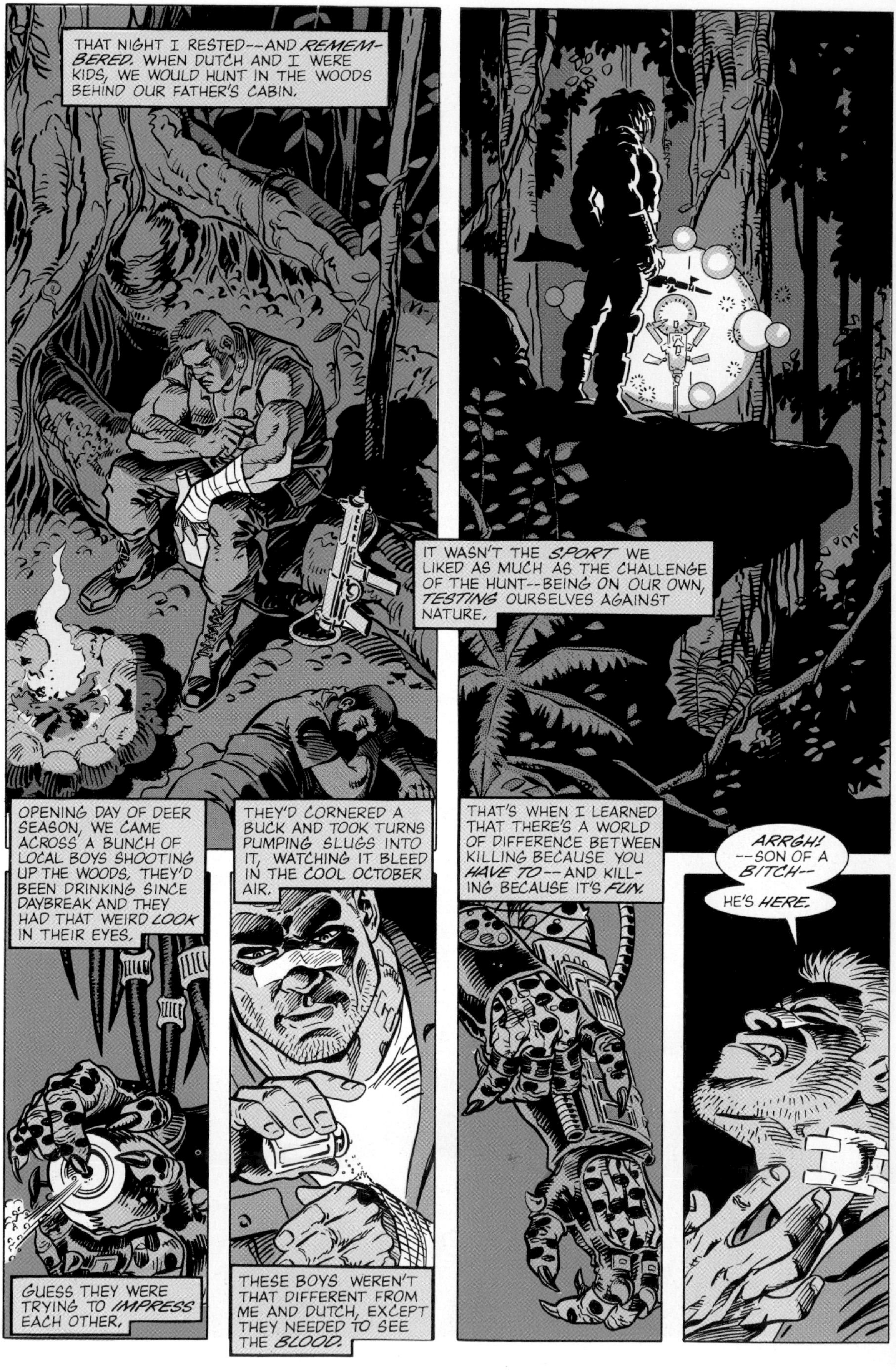
THAT NIGHT I RESTED--AND REMEMBERED. WHEN DUTCH AND I WERE KIDS, WE WOULD HUNT IN THE WOODS BEHIND OUR FATHER'S CABIN.
IT WASN'T THE SPORT WE LIKED AS MUCH AS THE CHALLENGE OF THE HUNT--BEING ON OUR OWN, TESTING OURSELVES AGAINST NATURE.
OPENING DAY OF DEER SEASON, WE CAME ACROSS A BUNCH OF LOCAL BOYS SHOOTING UP THE WOODS. THEY'D BEEN DRINKING SINCE DAYBREAK AND THEY HAD THAT WEIRD LOOK IN THEIR EYES.
GUESS THEY WERE TRYING TO IMPRESS EACH OTHER.
THEY'D CORNERED A BUCK AND TOOK TURNS PUMPING SLUGS INTO IT, WATCHING IT BLEED IN THE COOL OCTOBER AIR.
THESE BOYS WEREN'T THAT DIFFERENT FROM ME AND DUTCH, EXCEPT THEY NEEDED TO SEE THE BLOOD.
THAT'S WHEN I LEARNED THAT THERE'S A WORLD OF DIFFERENCE BETWEEN KILLING BECAUSE YOU HAVE TO--AND KILLING BECAUSE IT'S FUN.
ARRGH! --SON OF A BITCH--
HE'S HERE.

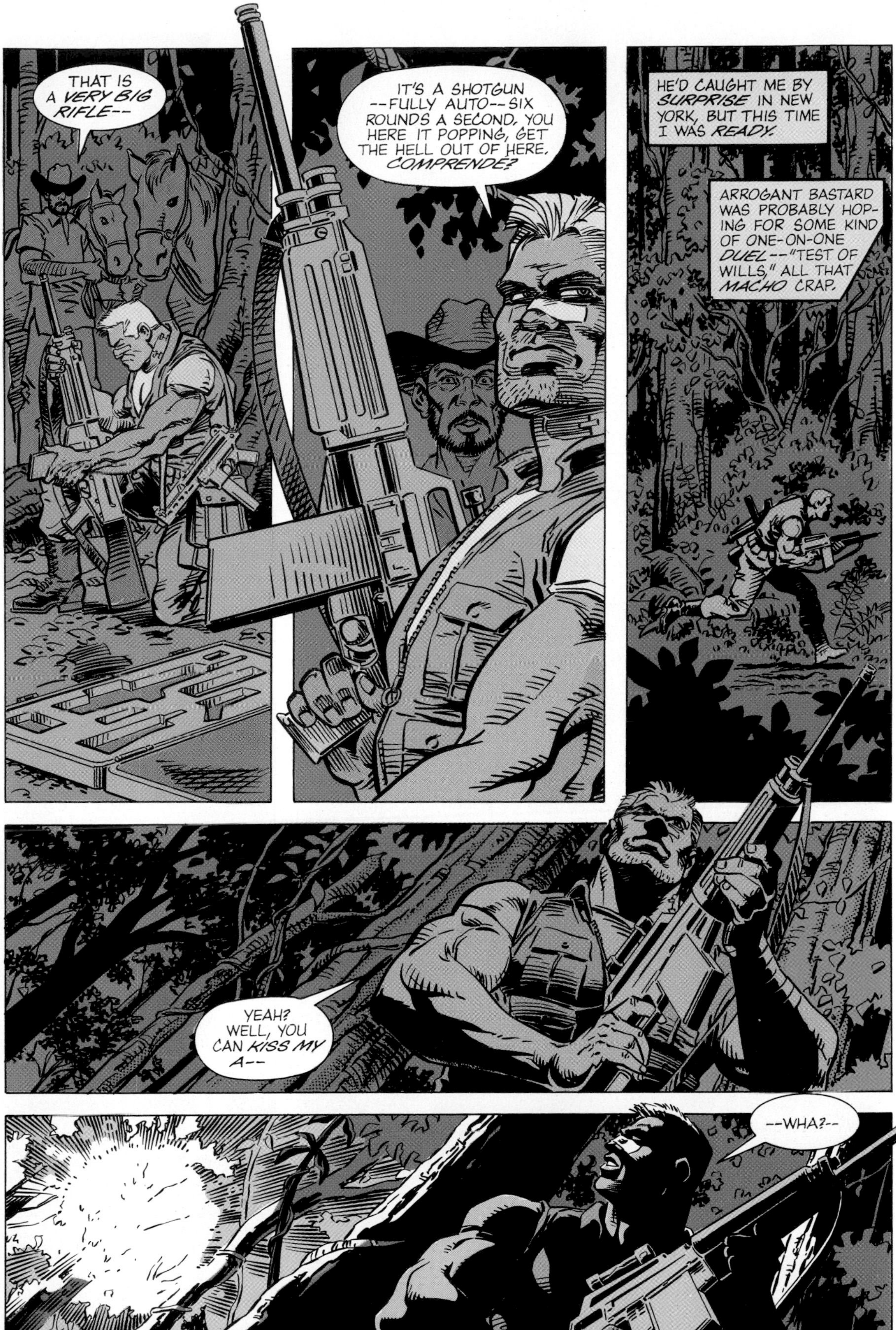
THAT IS A VERY BIG RIFLE--
IT'S A SHOTGUN --FULLY AUTO--SIX ROUNDS A SECOND, YOU HERE IT POPPING, GET THE HELL OUT OF HERE, COMPRENDE?
HE'D CAUGHT ME BY SURPRISE IN NEW YORK, BUT THIS TIME I WAS READY.
ARROGANT BASTARD WAS PROBABLY HOPING FOR SOME KIND OF ONE-ON-ONE DUEL--"TEST OF WILLS," ALL THAT MACHO CRAP.
YEAH? WELL, YOU CAN KISS MY A--
--WHA?--

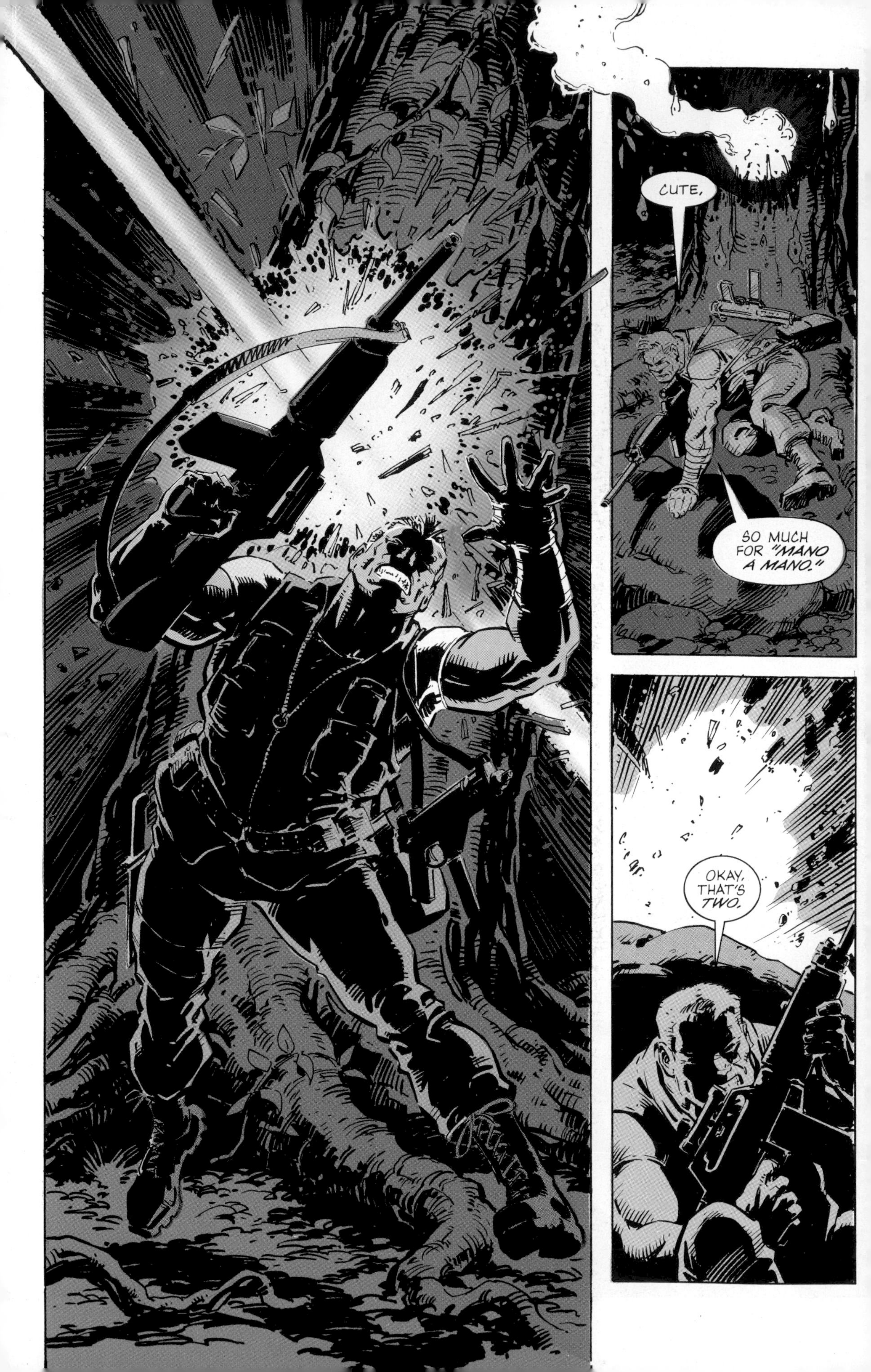
CUTE,
SO MUCH FOR "MANO A MANO."
OKAY, THAT'S TWO.

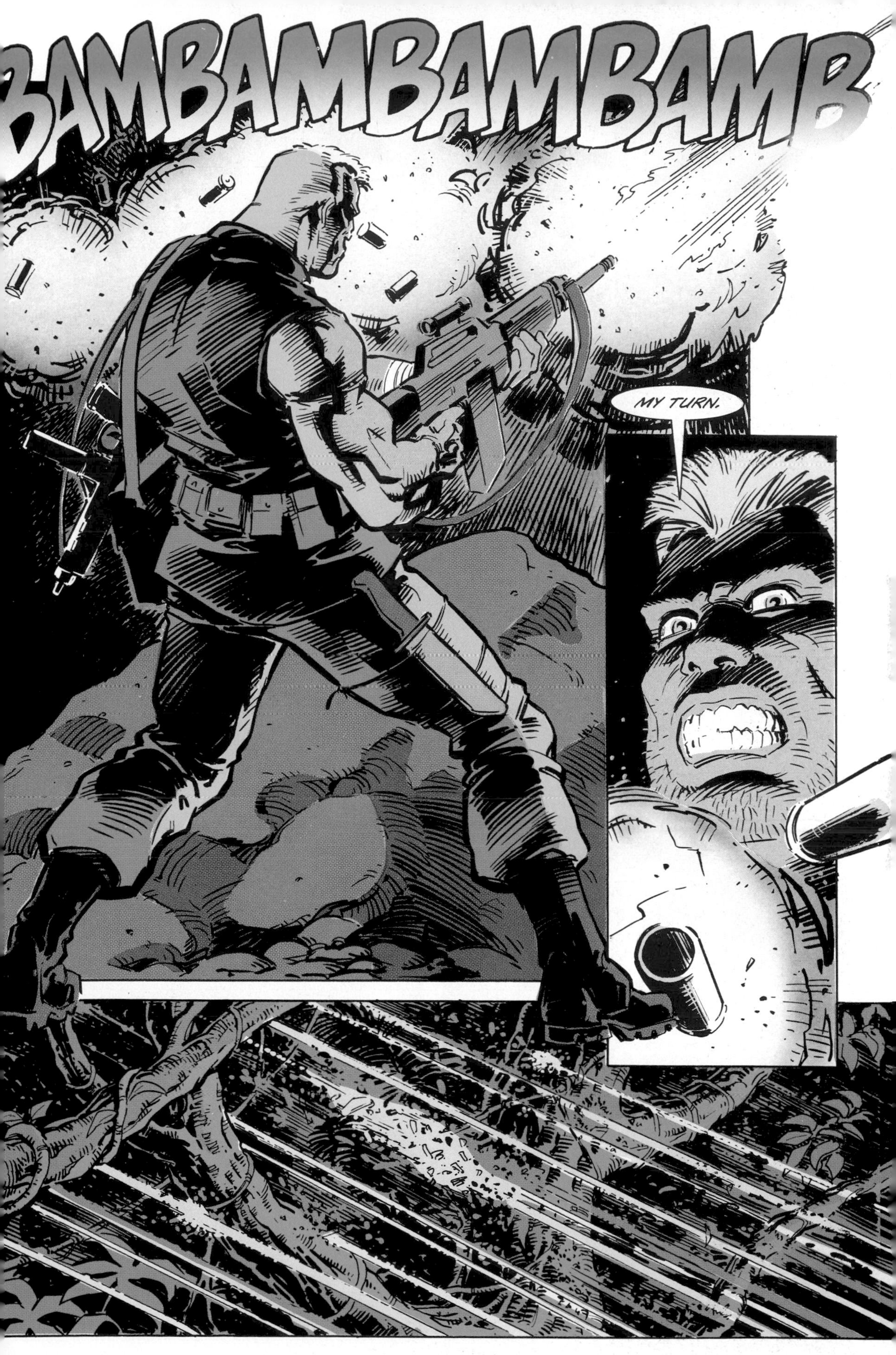
BAMBAMBAMBAMB
MY TURN.

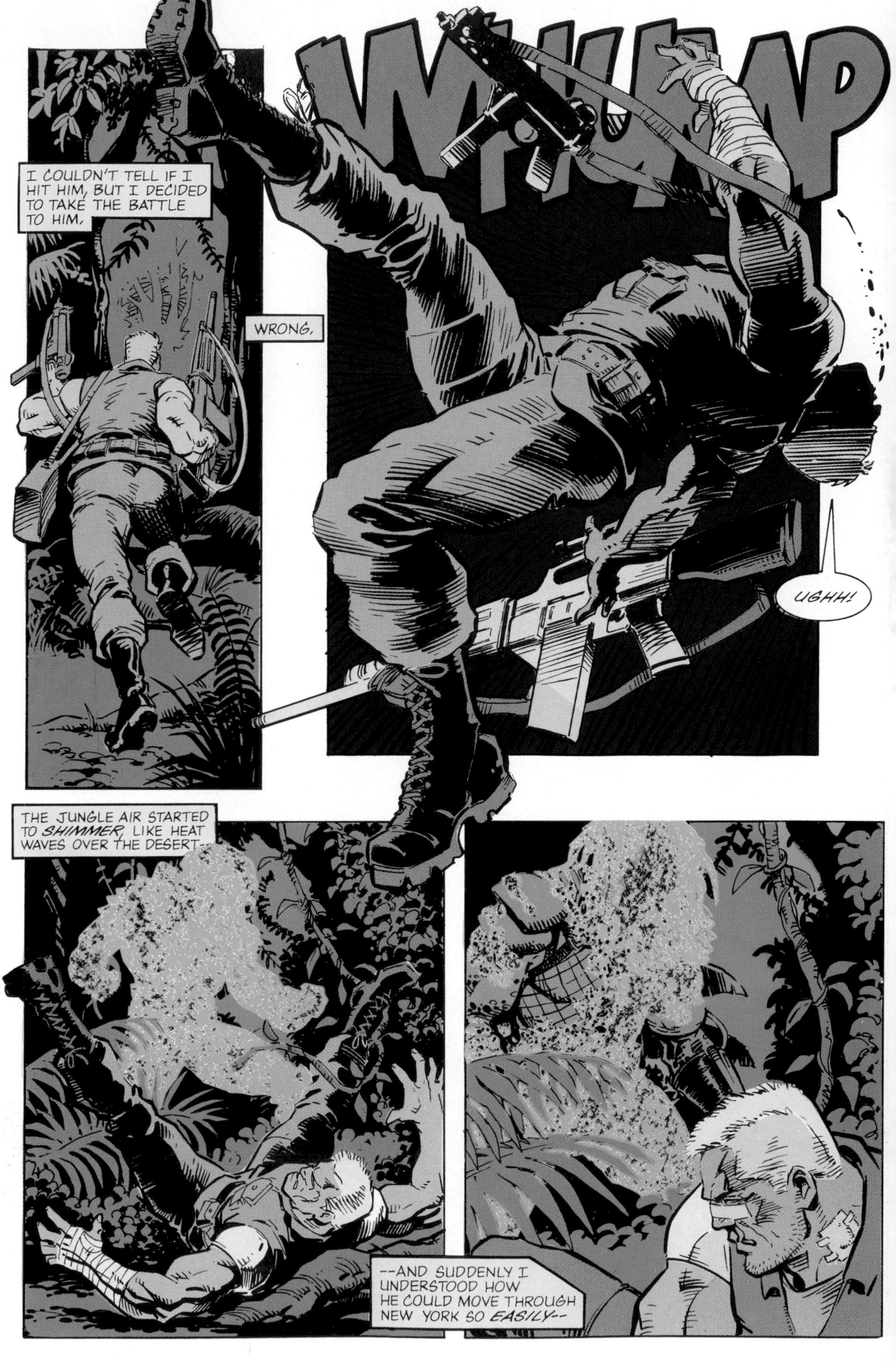
I COULDN'T TELL IF I HIT HIM, BUT I DECIDED TO TAKE THE BATTLE TO HIM,
WRONG.
WHAP
UGHH!
THE JUNGLE AIR STARTED TO SHIMMER, LIKE HEAT WAVES OVER THE DESERT--
--AND SUDDENLY I UNDERSTOOD HOW HE COULD MOVE THROUGH NEW YORK SO EASILY--

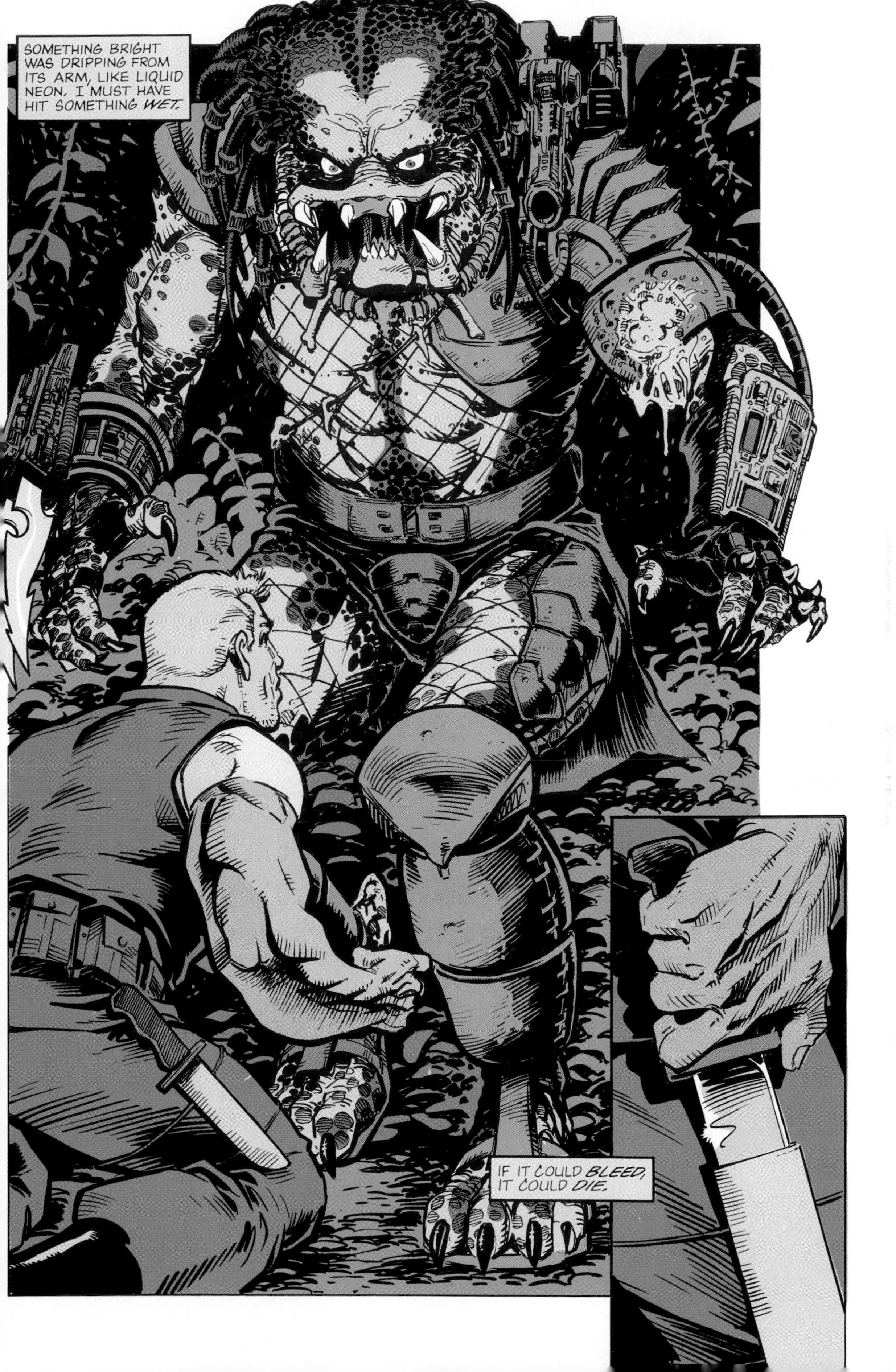
SOMETHING BRIGHT WAS DRIPPING FROM ITS ARM, LIKE LIQUID NEON. I MUST HAVE HIT SOMETHING WET.
IF IT COULD BLEED, IT COULD DIE.

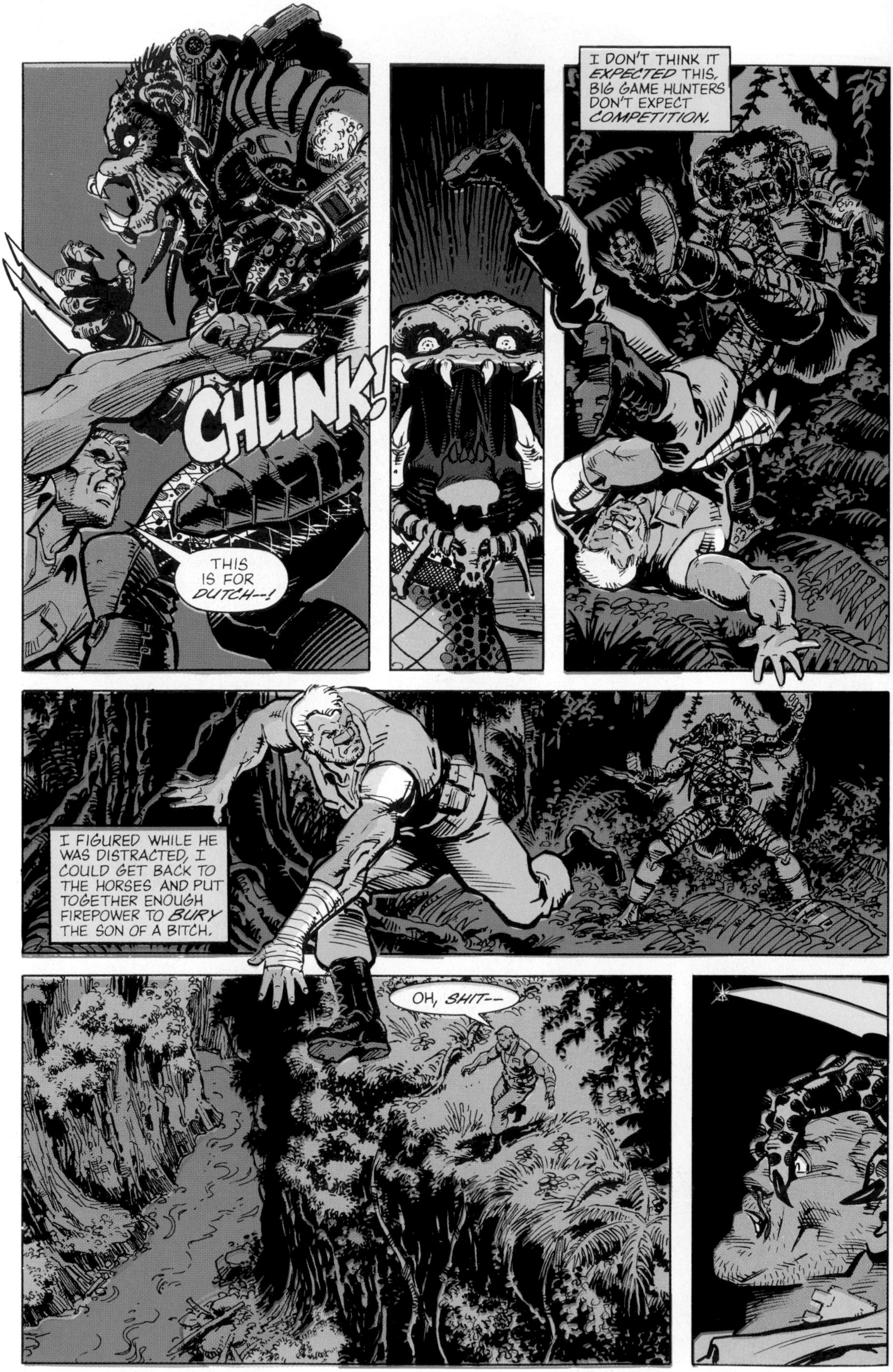
I DON'T THINK IT EXPECTED THIS. BIG GAME HUNTERS DON'T EXPECT COMPETITION.
CHUNK!
THIS IS FOR DUTCH--!
I FIGURED WHILE HE WAS DISTRACTED, I COULD GET BACK TO THE HORSES AND PUT TOGETHER ENOUGH FIREPOWER TO BURY THE SON OF A BITCH.
OH, SHIT--

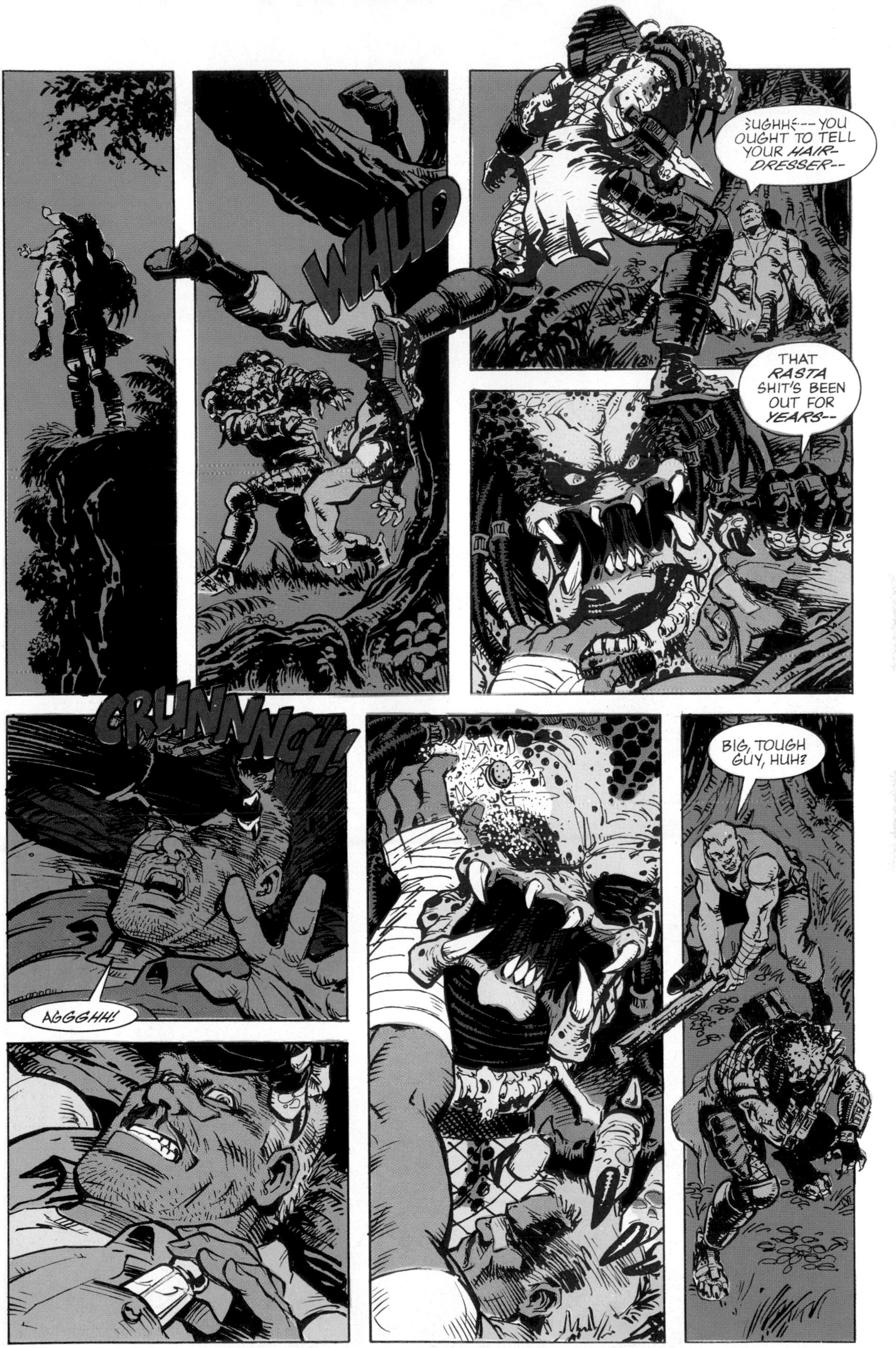
WHUD
UGHH--YOU OUGHT TO TELL YOUR HAIR-DRESSER--
THAT RASTA SHIT'S BEEN OUT FOR YEARS--
CRUNNNCH!
AGGGHH!
BIG, TOUGH GUY, HUH?

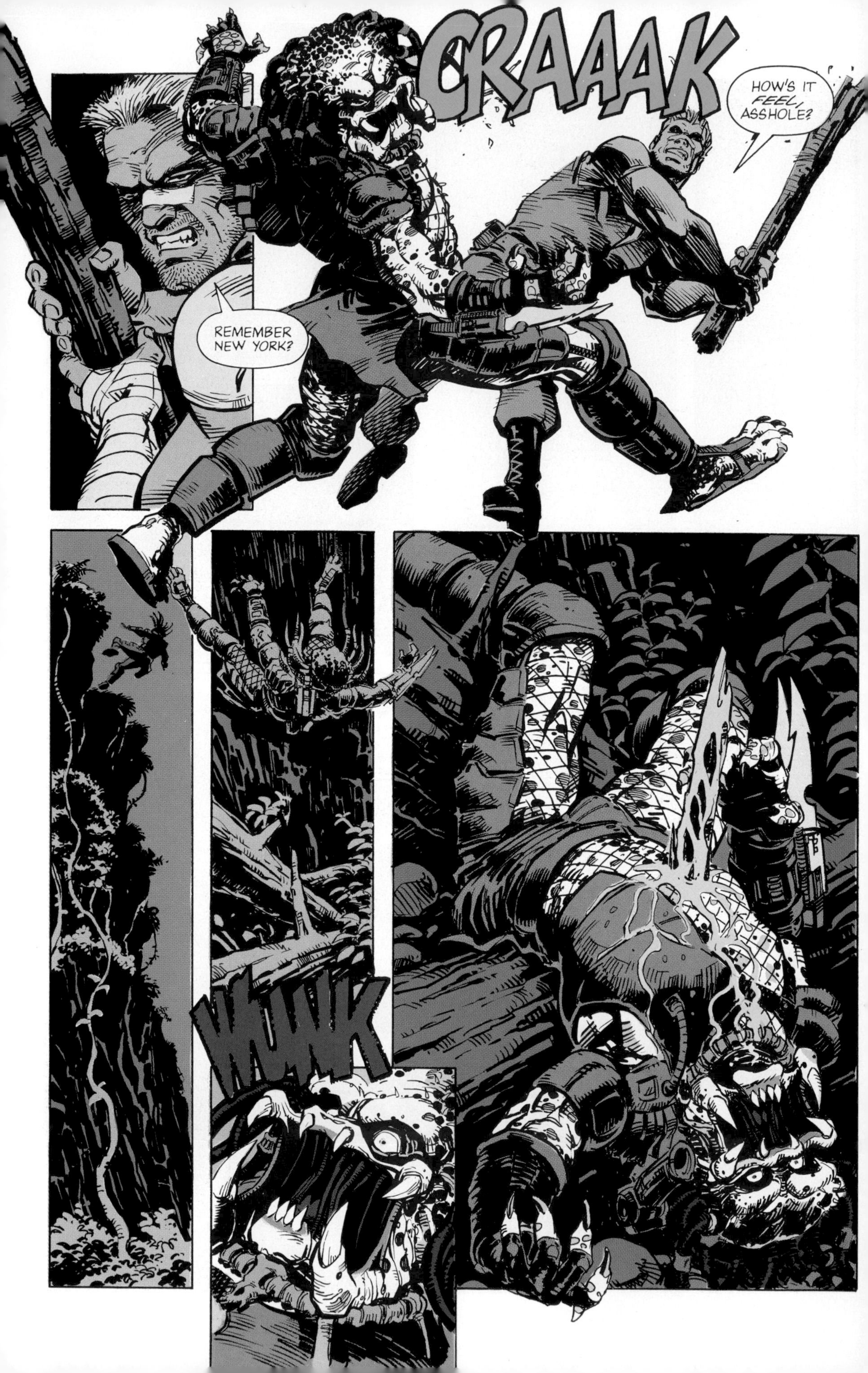
CRAAAK
REMEMBER NEW YORK?
HOW'S IT FEEL, ASSHOLE?
WUNK

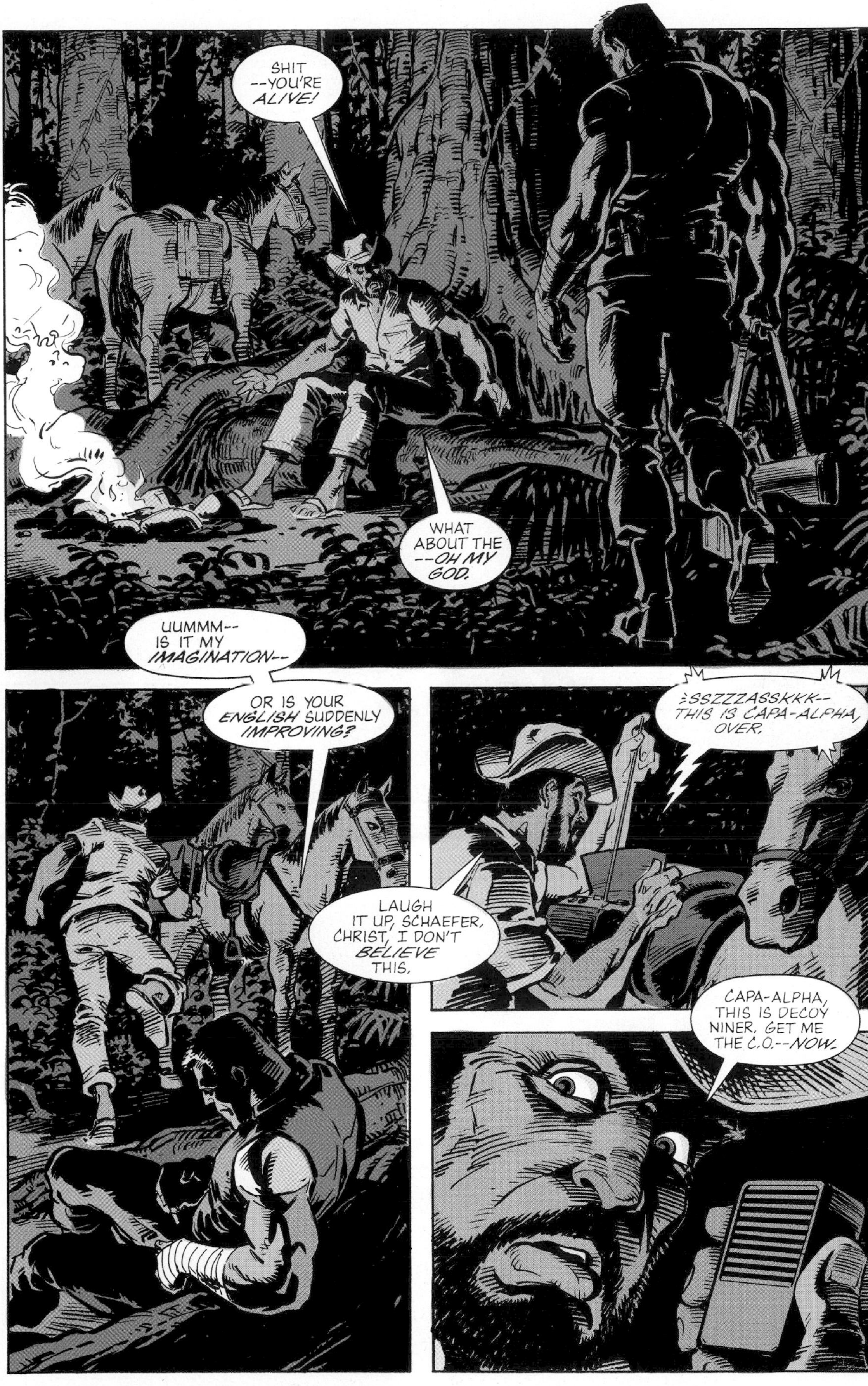
SHIT --YOU'RE ALIVE!
WHAT ABOUT THE --OH MY GOD.
UUMMM-- IS IT MY IMAGINATION--
OR IS YOUR ENGLISH SUDDENLY IMPROVING?
LAUGH IT UP, SCHAEFER. CHRIST, I DON'T BELIEVE THIS.
=SSZZZASSKKK-- THIS IS CAPA-ALPHA, OVER.
CAPA-ALPHA, THIS IS DECOY NINER. GET ME THE C.O.--NOW.

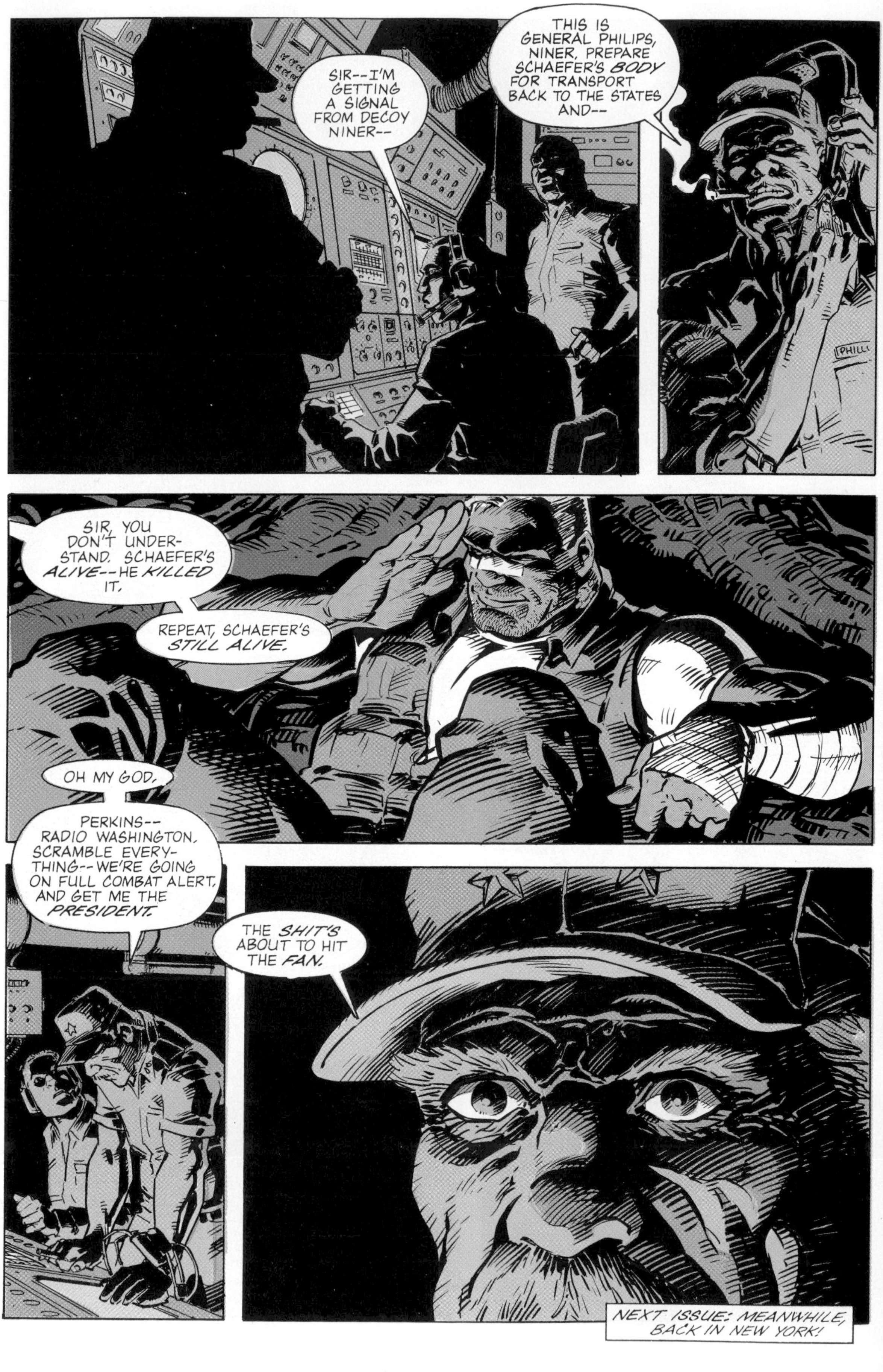
SIR--I'M GETTING A SIGNAL FROM DECOY NINER--
THIS IS GENERAL PHILIPS, NINER. PREPARE SCHAEFER'S BODY FOR TRANSPORT BACK TO THE STATES AND--
PHILL
SIR, YOU DON'T UNDER-STAND. SCHAEFER'S ALIVE--HE KILLED IT.
REPEAT, SCHAEFER'S STILL ALIVE.
OH MY GOD.
PERKINS--RADIO WASHINGTON. SCRAMBLE EVERY-THING--WE'RE GOING ON FULL COMBAT ALERT. AND GET ME THE PRESIDENT.
THE SHIT'S ABOUT TO HIT THE FAN.
NEXT ISSUE: MEANWHILE, BACK IN NEW YORK!

1

2

CHAPTER 3

4

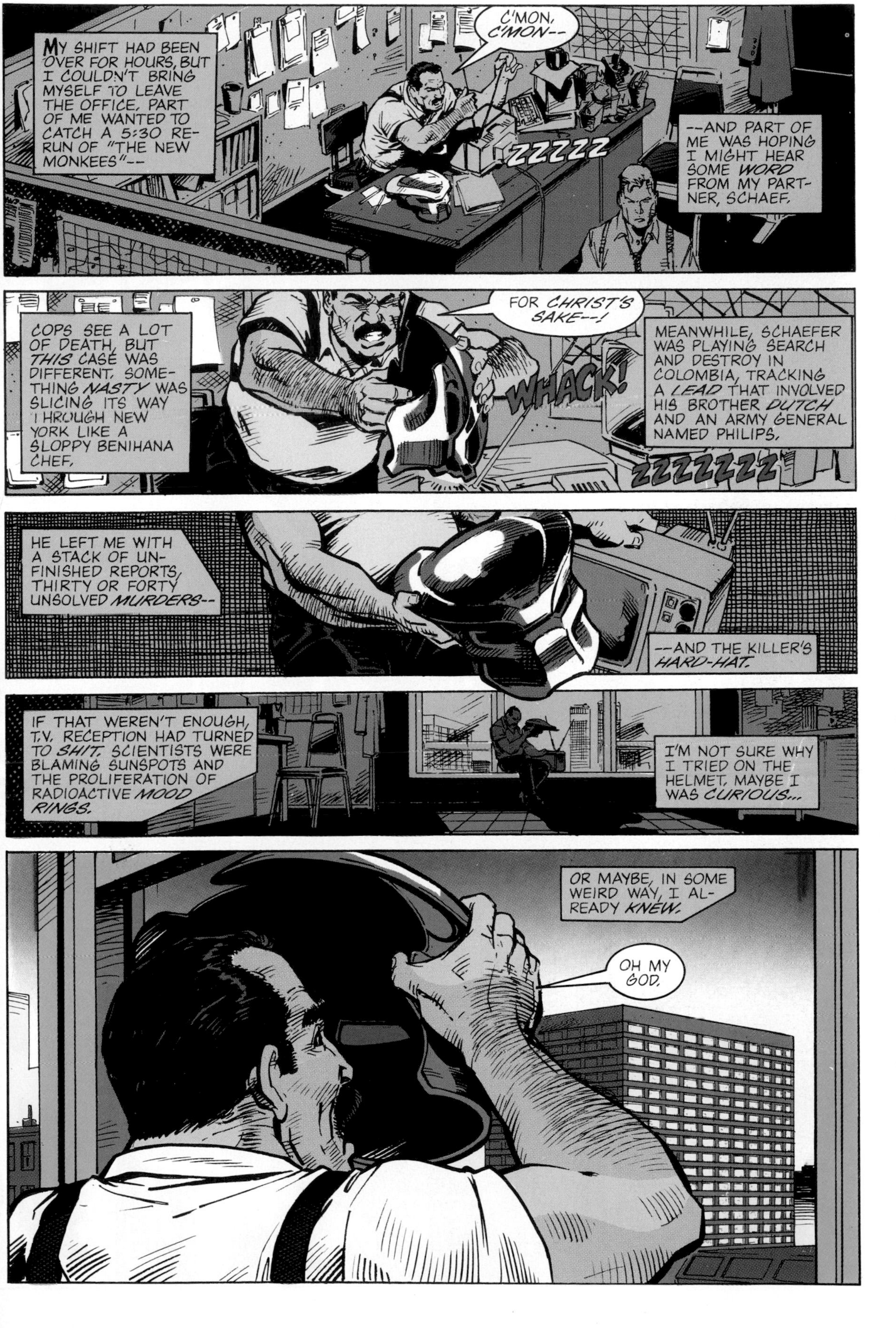
MY SHIFT HAD BEEN OVER FOR HOURS, BUT I COULDN'T BRING MYSELF TO LEAVE THE OFFICE. PART OF ME WANTED TO CATCH A 5:30 RE-RUN OF "THE NEW MONKEES"--
C'MON, C'MON--
ZZZZZ
--AND PART OF ME WAS HOPING I MIGHT HEAR SOME WORD FROM MY PARTNER, SCHAEF.
COPS SEE A LOT OF DEATH, BUT THIS CASE WAS DIFFERENT. SOMETHING NASTY WAS SLICING ITS WAY THROUGH NEW YORK LIKE A SLOPPY BENIHANA CHEF.
FOR CHRIST'S SAKE--!
WHACK!
MEANWHILE, SCHAEFER WAS PLAYING SEARCH AND DESTROY IN COLOMBIA, TRACKING A LEAD THAT INVOLVED HIS BROTHER DUTCH AND AN ARMY GENERAL NAMED PHILIPS.
ZZZZZZZ
HE LEFT ME WITH A STACK OF UNFINISHED REPORTS, THIRTY OR FORTY UNSOLVED MURDERS--
--AND THE KILLER'S HARD-HAT.
IF THAT WEREN'T ENOUGH, T.V. RECEPTION HAD TURNED TO SHIT. SCIENTISTS WERE BLAMING SUNSPOTS AND THE PROLIFERATION OF RADIOACTIVE MOOD RINGS.
I'M NOT SURE WHY I TRIED ON THE HELMET. MAYBE I WAS CURIOUS...
OR MAYBE, IN SOME WEIRD WAY, I ALREADY KNEW.
OH MY GOD.

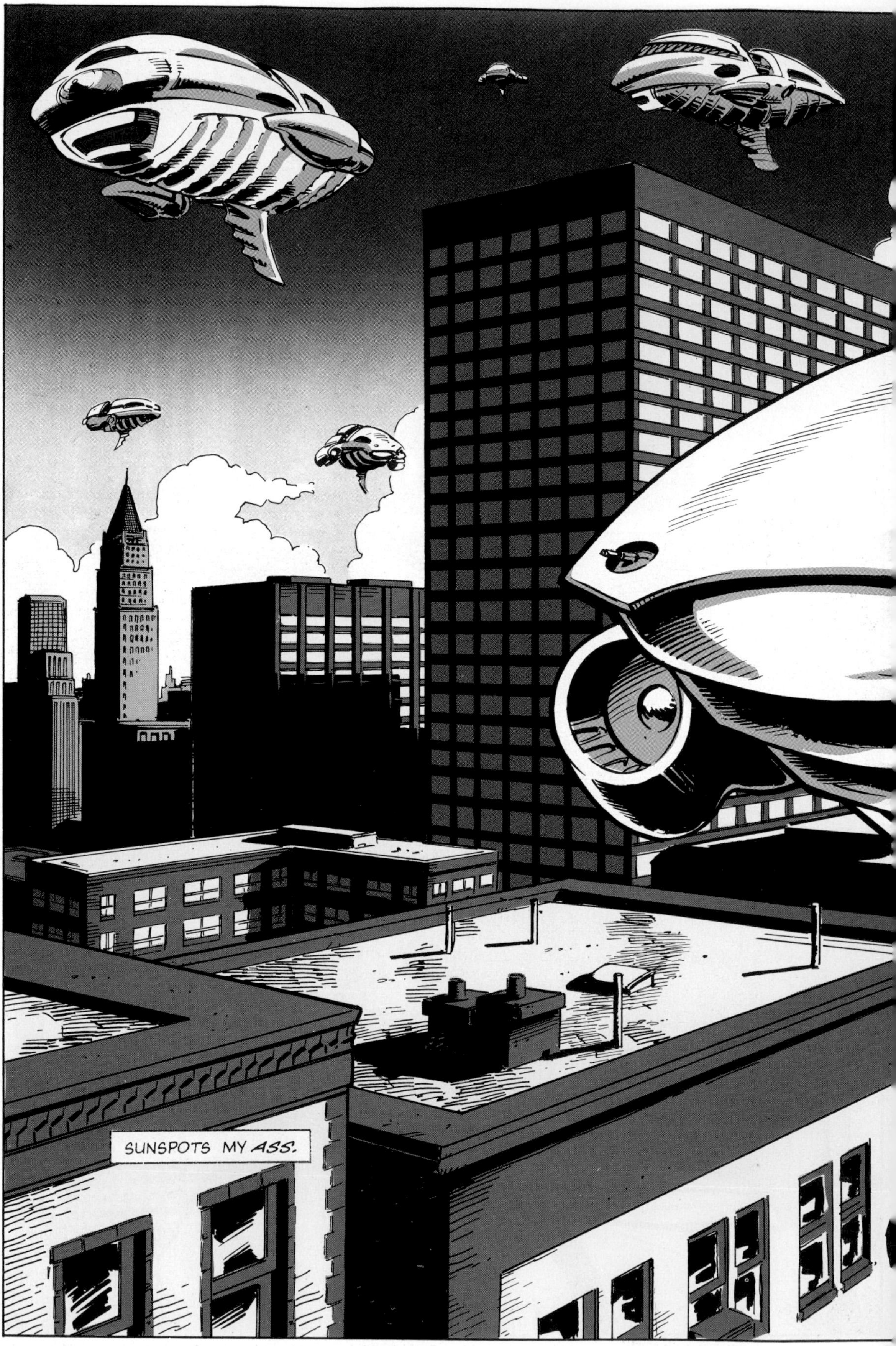
SUNSPOTS MY ASS.

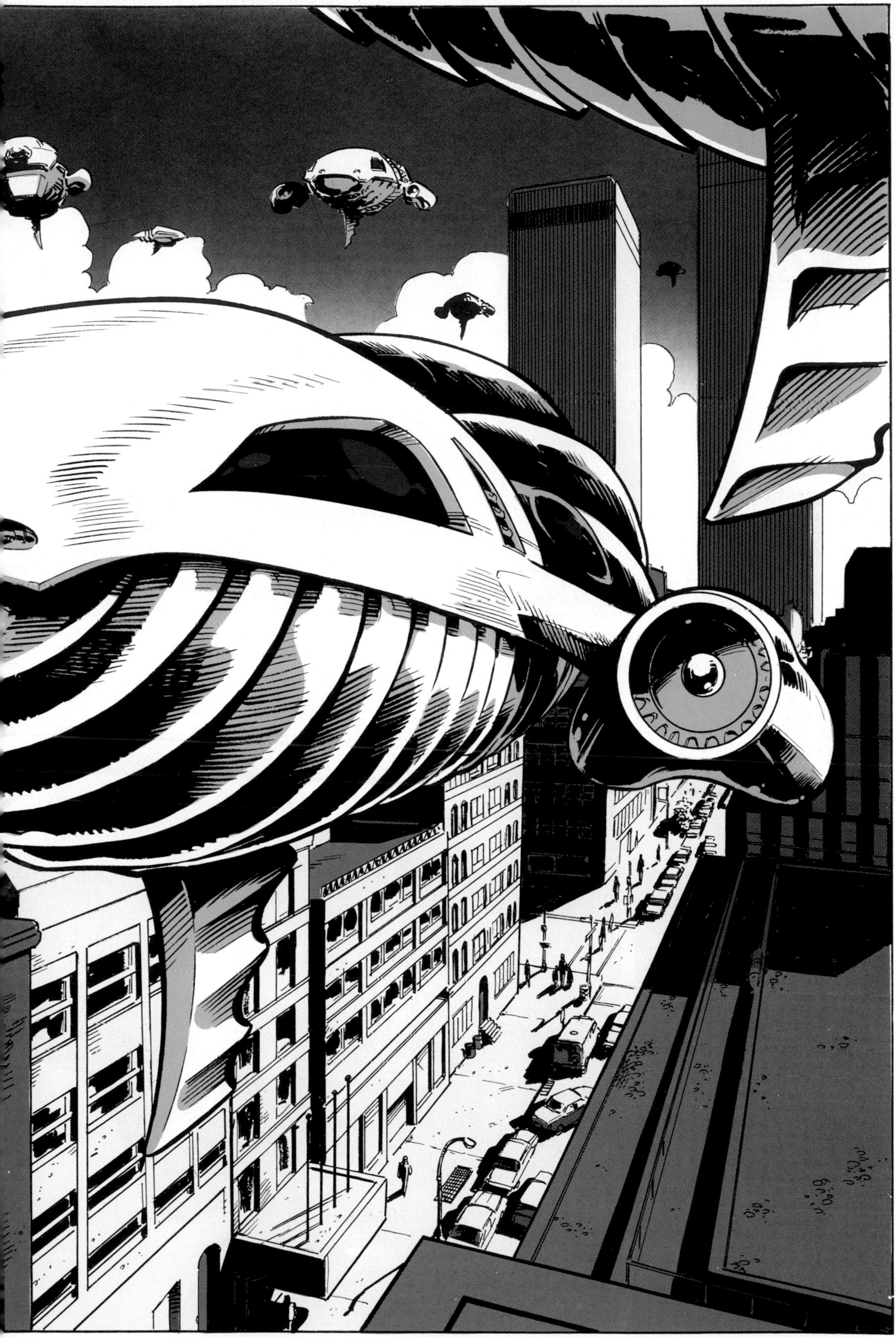

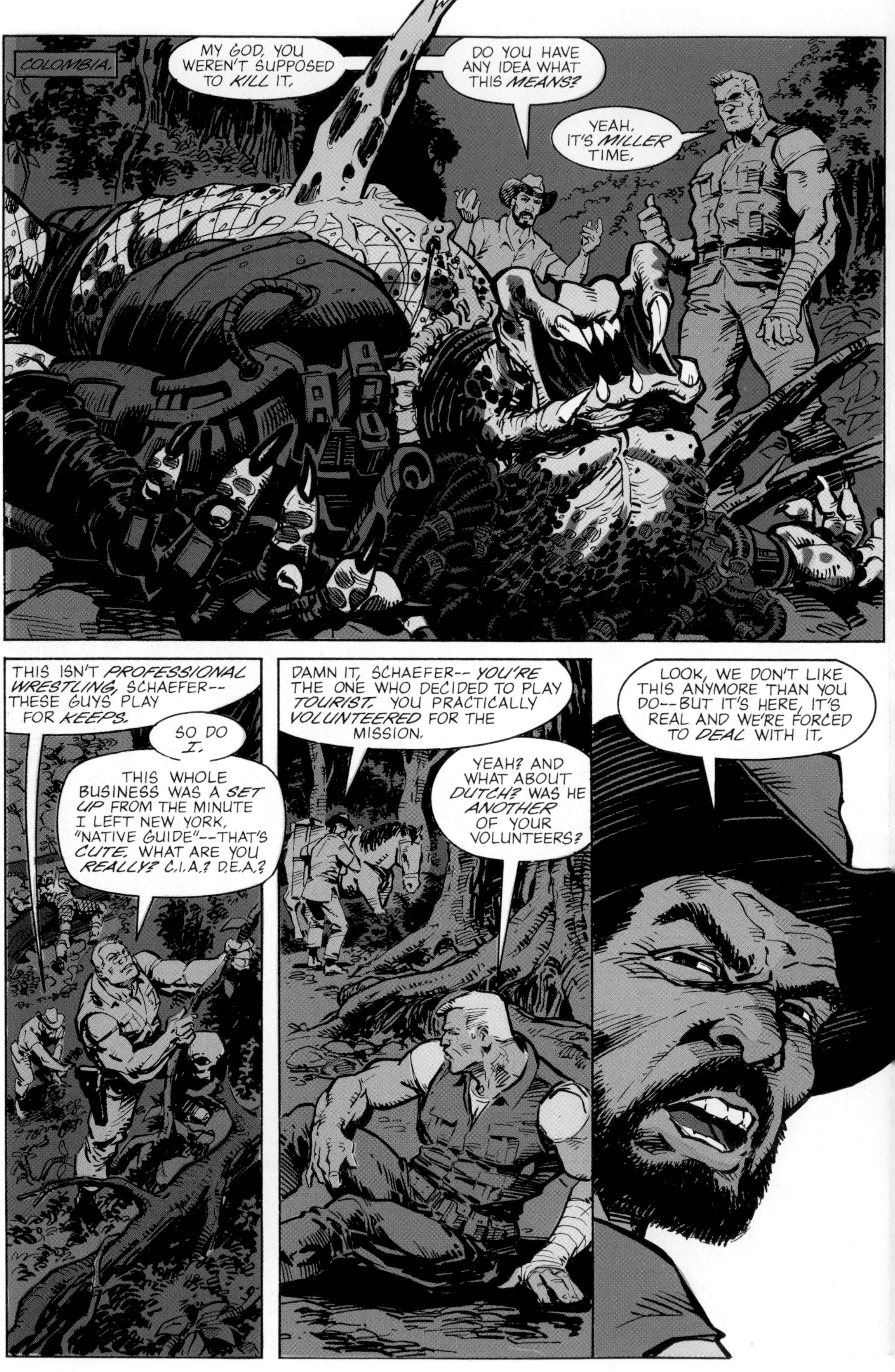
COLOMBIA.
MY GOD, YOU WEREN'T SUPPOSED TO KILL IT.
DO YOU HAVE ANY IDEA WHAT THIS MEANS?
YEAH, IT'S MILLER TIME.
THIS ISN'T PROFESSIONAL WRESTLING, SCHAEFER-- THESE GUYS PLAY FOR KEEPS.
SO DO I.
THIS WHOLE BUSINESS WAS A SET UP FROM THE MINUTE I LEFT NEW YORK. "NATIVE GUIDE"--THAT'S CUTE. WHAT ARE YOU REALLY? C.I.A.? D.E.A.?
DAMN IT, SCHAEFER-- YOU'RE THE ONE WHO DECIDED TO PLAY TOURIST. YOU PRACTICALLY VOLUNTEERED FOR THE MISSION.
YEAH? AND WHAT ABOUT DUTCH? WAS HE ANOTHER OF YOUR VOLUNTEERS?
LOOK, WE DON'T LIKE THIS ANYMORE THAN YOU DO--BUT IT'S HERE, IT'S REAL AND WE'RE FORCED TO DEAL WITH IT.

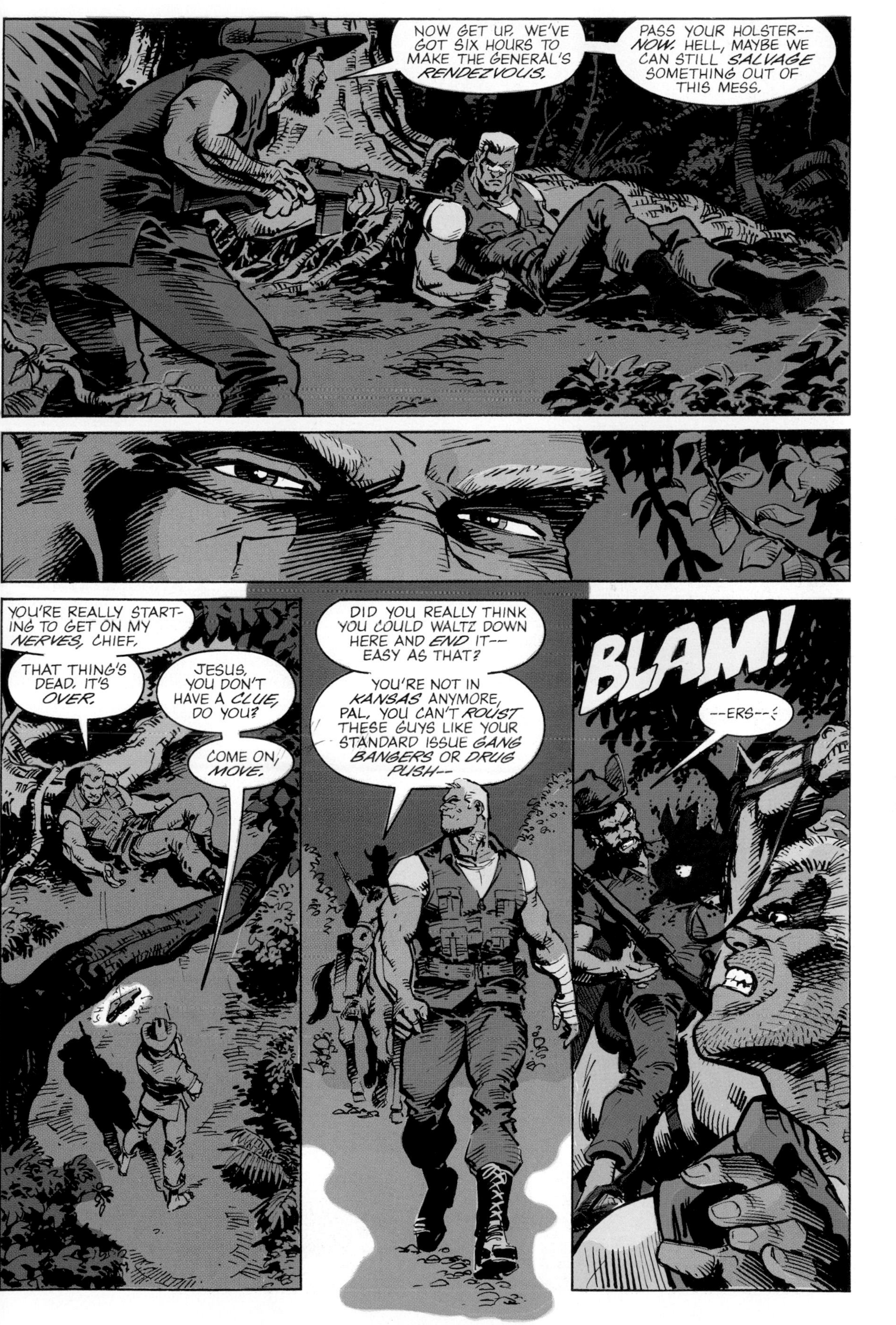
NOW GET UP. WE'VE GOT SIX HOURS TO MAKE THE GENERAL'S RENDEZVOUS.
PASS YOUR HOLSTER-- NOW. HELL, MAYBE WE CAN STILL SALVAGE SOMETHING OUT OF THIS MESS.
YOU'RE REALLY STARTING TO GET ON MY NERVES, CHIEF.
THAT THING'S DEAD. IT'S OVER.
JESUS, YOU DON'T HAVE A CLUE, DO YOU?
COME ON, MOVE.
DID YOU REALLY THINK YOU COULD WALTZ DOWN HERE AND END IT-- EASY AS THAT?
YOU'RE NOT IN KANSAS ANYMORE, PAL. YOU CAN'T ROUST THESE GUYS LIKE YOUR STANDARD ISSUE GANG BANGERS OR DRUG PUSH--
BLAM!
--ERS--!

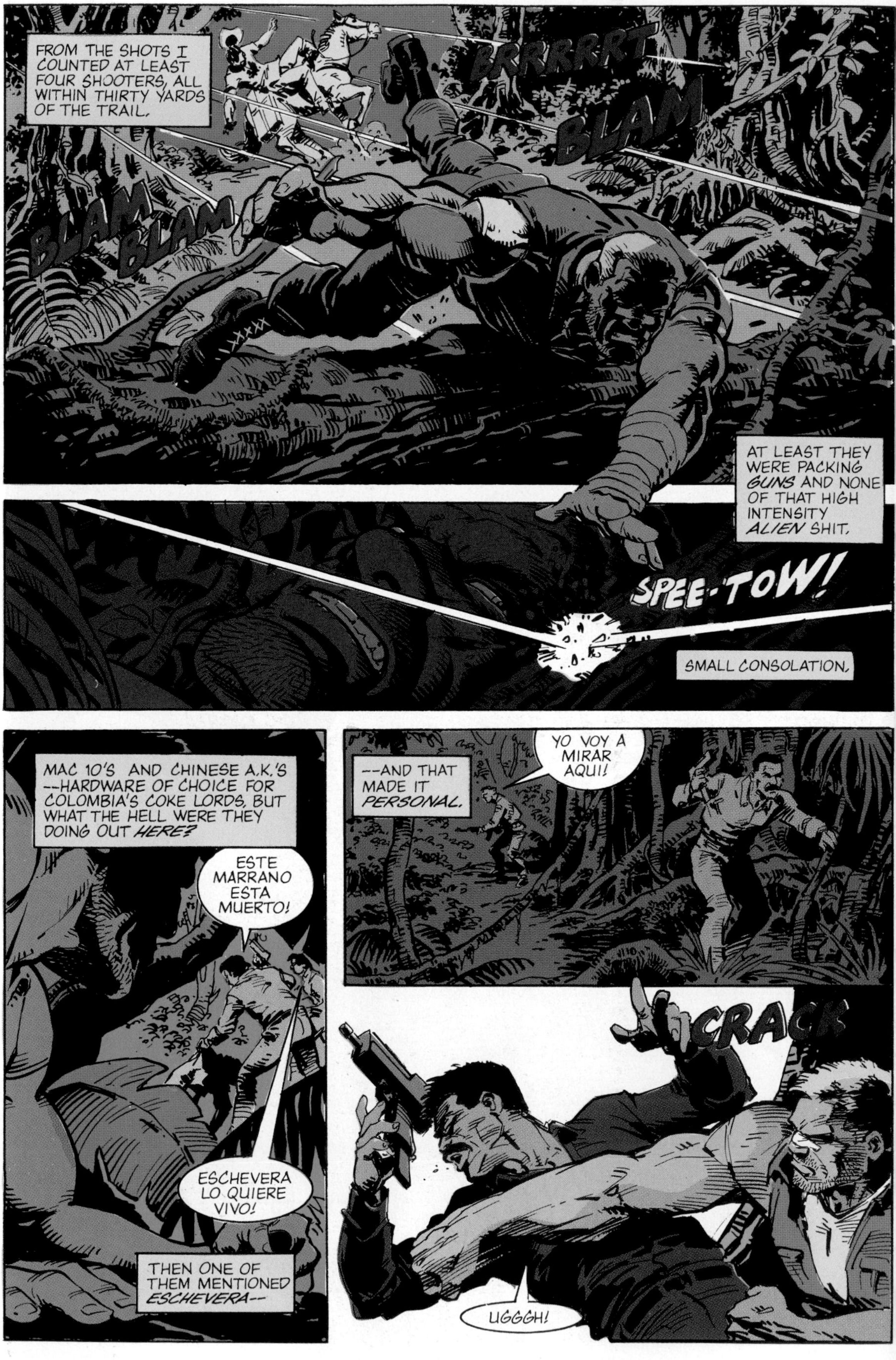
FROM THE SHOTS I COUNTED AT LEAST FOUR SHOOTERS, ALL WITHIN THIRTY YARDS OF THE TRAIL.
BRRRRRT
BLAM
BLAM BLAM
AT LEAST THEY WERE PACKING GUNS AND NONE OF THAT HIGH INTENSITY ALIEN SHIT.
SPEE-TOW!
SMALL CONSOLATION.
MAC 10'S AND CHINESE A.K.'S --HARDWARE OF CHOICE FOR COLOMBIA'S COKE LORDS, BUT WHAT THE HELL WERE THEY DOING OUT HERE?
ESTE MARRANO ESTA MUERTO!
ESCHEVERA LO QUIERE VIVO!
THEN ONE OF THEM MENTIONED ESCHEVERA--
--AND THAT MADE IT PERSONAL.
YO VOY A MIRAR AQUI!
CRACK
UGGGH!

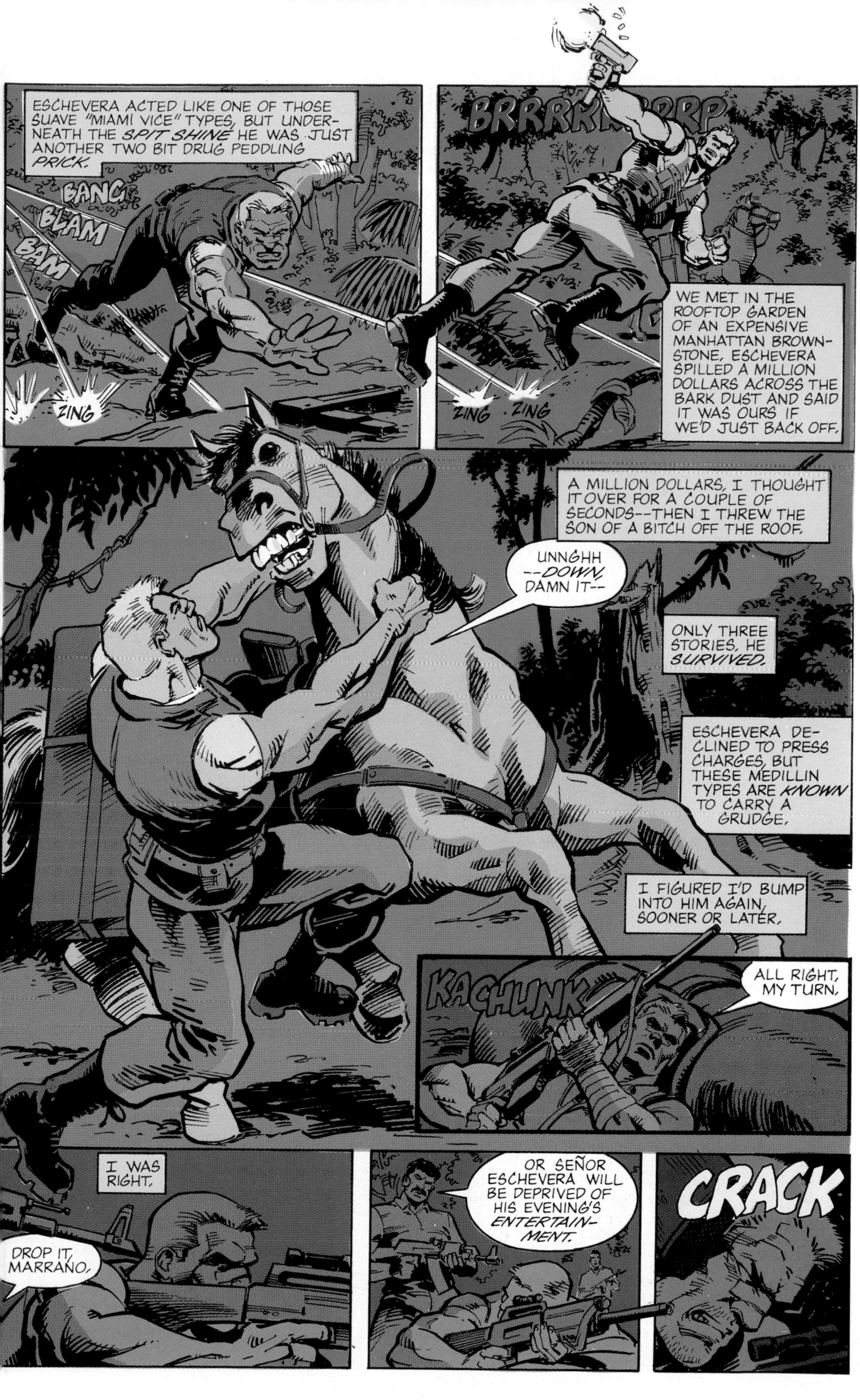
ESCHEVERA ACTED LIKE ONE OF THOSE SUAVE "MIAMI VICE" TYPES, BUT UNDERNEATH THE *SPIT SHINE* HE WAS JUST ANOTHER TWO BIT DRUG PEDDLING *PRICK.*
BANG
BLAM
BAM
ZING
BRRRRRRRRP
WE MET IN THE ROOFTOP GARDEN OF AN EXPENSIVE MANHATTAN BROWNSTONE. ESCHEVERA SPILLED A MILLION DOLLARS ACROSS THE BARK DUST AND SAID IT WAS OURS IF WE'D JUST BACK OFF.
ZING ZING
A MILLION DOLLARS. I THOUGHT IT OVER FOR A COUPLE OF SECONDS--THEN I THREW THE SON OF A BITCH OFF THE ROOF.
UNNGHH --*DOWN,* DAMN IT--
ONLY THREE STORIES. HE *SURVIVED.*
ESCHEVERA DECLINED TO PRESS CHARGES, BUT THESE MEDILLIN TYPES ARE *KNOWN* TO CARRY A GRUDGE.
I FIGURED I'D BUMP INTO HIM AGAIN, SOONER OR LATER.
KACHUNK
ALL RIGHT, MY TURN.
I WAS RIGHT.
DROP IT, MARRANO.
OR SEÑOR ESCHEVERA WILL BE DEPRIVED OF HIS EVENING'S *ENTERTAINMENT.*
CRACK

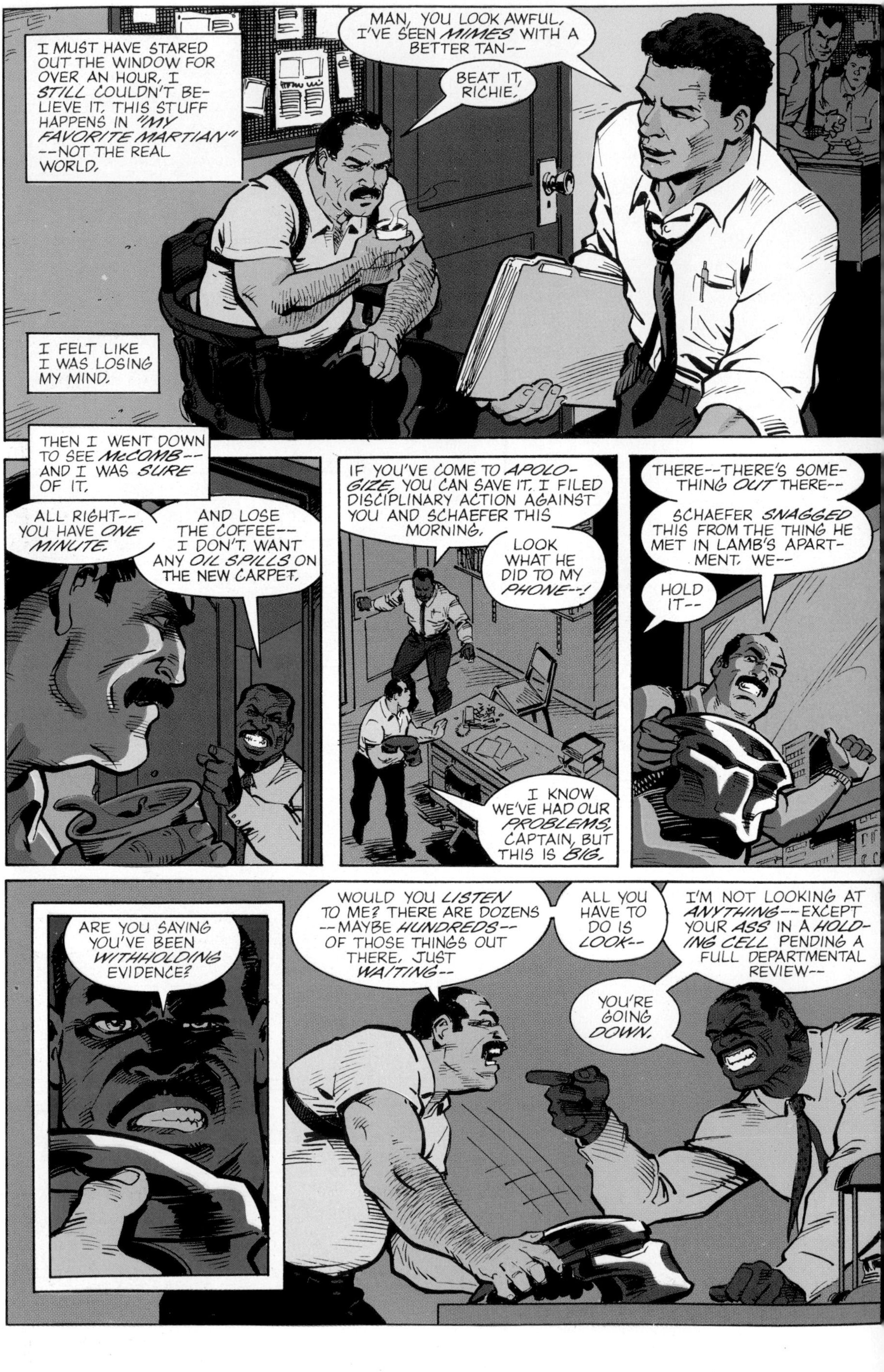
I MUST HAVE STARED OUT THE WINDOW FOR OVER AN HOUR. I STILL COULDN'T BELIEVE IT. THIS STUFF HAPPENS IN "MY FAVORITE MARTIAN" --NOT THE REAL WORLD.
MAN, YOU LOOK AWFUL. I'VE SEEN MIMES WITH A BETTER TAN--
BEAT IT, RICHIE.
I FELT LIKE I WAS LOSING MY MIND.
THEN I WENT DOWN TO SEE McCOMB-- AND I WAS SURE OF IT.
ALL RIGHT-- YOU HAVE ONE MINUTE.
AND LOSE THE COFFEE-- I DON'T WANT ANY OIL SPILLS ON THE NEW CARPET.
IF YOU'VE COME TO APOLOGIZE, YOU CAN SAVE IT. I FILED DISCIPLINARY ACTION AGAINST YOU AND SCHAEFER THIS MORNING.
LOOK WHAT HE DID TO MY PHONE--!
I KNOW WE'VE HAD OUR PROBLEMS, CAPTAIN, BUT THIS IS BIG.
THERE--THERE'S SOMETHING OUT THERE--
SCHAEFER SNAGGED THIS FROM THE THING HE MET IN LAMB'S APARTMENT. WE--
HOLD IT--
ARE YOU SAYING YOU'VE BEEN WITHHOLDING EVIDENCE?
WOULD YOU LISTEN TO ME? THERE ARE DOZENS --MAYBE HUNDREDS-- OF THOSE THINGS OUT THERE, JUST WAITING--
ALL YOU HAVE TO DO IS LOOK--
I'M NOT LOOKING AT ANYTHING--EXCEPT YOUR ASS IN A HOLDING CELL PENDING A FULL DEPARTMENTAL REVIEW--
YOU'RE GOING DOWN.

FINE, I'LL HAVE MY LITTLE CHAT WITH THE *CHIEF*--

HEY-- YOU'RE NOT GOING *ANYWHERE!*

McCOMB HAD ALL THE GOOD SENSE OF AN *OPOSSUM* CROSSING A FOUR LANE *INTERSTATE.* NEW YORK WAS UNDER SIEGE AND HE WAS WORRIED ABOUT HIS *CARPET.*

JESUS, SCHAEFER-- WHERE ARE YOU WHEN I *NEED* YOU?

MY ONLY CHANCE WAS TAKING MY CASE TO McCOMB'S *SUPERIORS.*

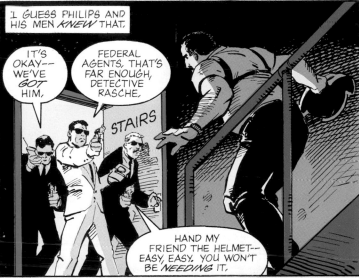

I GUESS PHILIPS AND HIS MEN *KNEW* THAT.

IT'S OKAY-- WE'VE *GOT* HIM.

FEDERAL AGENTS, THAT'S FAR ENOUGH, DETECTIVE RASCHE.

STAIRS

HAND MY FRIEND THE HELMET-- EASY, EASY. YOU WON'T BE *NEEDING* IT.

YOU HAVE TO BE *SHITTING* ME-- YOU CAN'T KIDNAP A *POLICE OFFICER* FROM THE MIDDLE OF A DOWNTOWN *PRECINCT HOUSE*--!

YOU'RE NOT *REGULAR* FEDS --WHO THE HELL *ARE* YOU?

THERE'S BEEN A *MANPOWER* SHORTAGE DUE TO THE CRISIS, WE'VE BEEN CALLED IN TO *ASSIST.*

PARKING

WE'RE *I.R.S.* --AUDITS AND REVIEW.

OH MY *GOD*--

--ACCOUNTANTS.

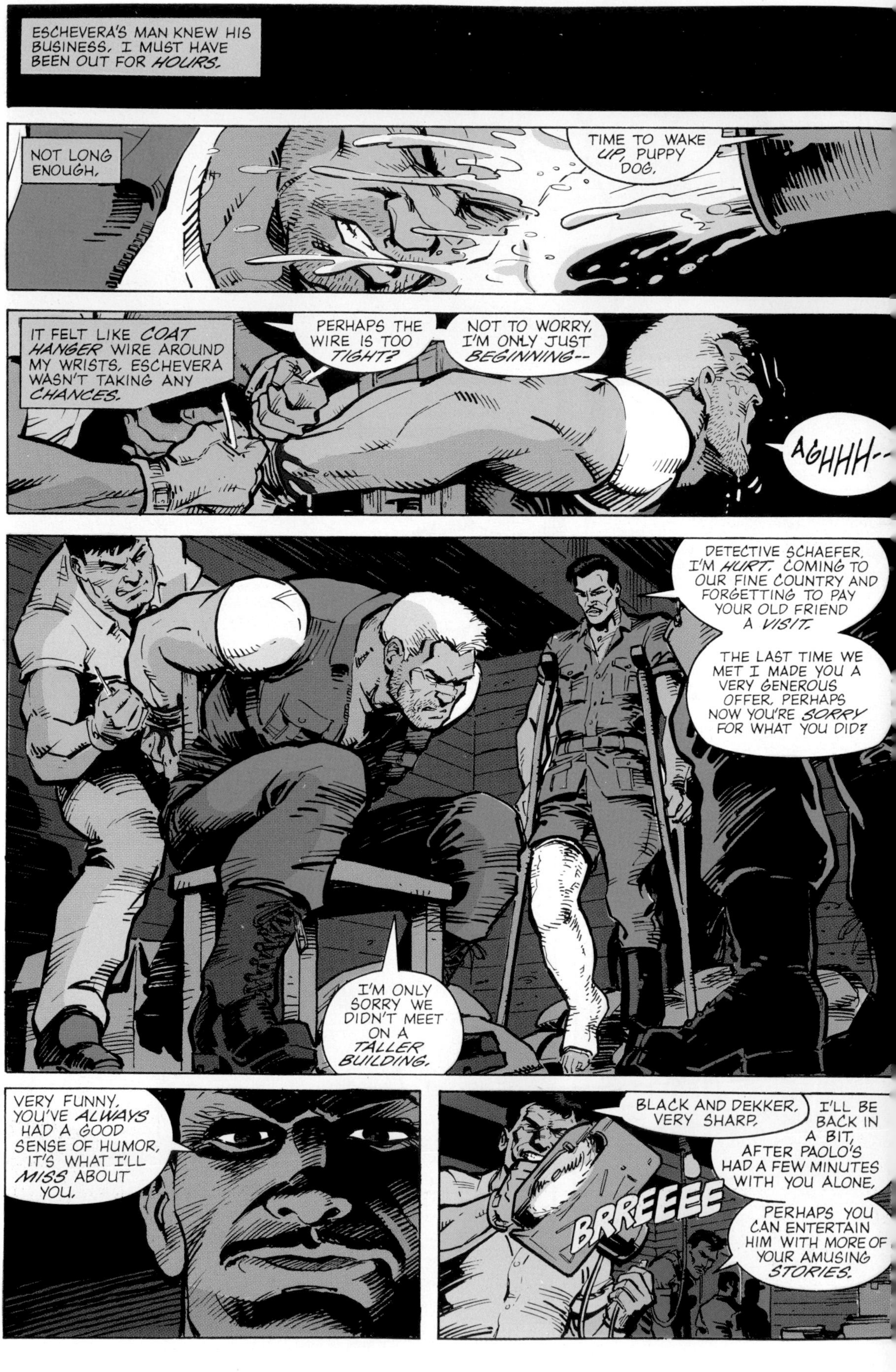
ESCHEVERA'S MAN KNEW HIS BUSINESS. I MUST HAVE BEEN OUT FOR HOURS.
NOT LONG ENOUGH.
TIME TO WAKE UP, PUPPY DOG.
IT FELT LIKE COAT HANGER WIRE AROUND MY WRISTS. ESCHEVERA WASN'T TAKING ANY CHANCES.
PERHAPS THE WIRE IS TOO TIGHT?
NOT TO WORRY. I'M ONLY JUST BEGINNING--
AGHHH--
DETECTIVE SCHAEFER, I'M HURT. COMING TO OUR FINE COUNTRY AND FORGETTING TO PAY YOUR OLD FRIEND A VISIT.
THE LAST TIME WE MET I MADE YOU A VERY GENEROUS OFFER. PERHAPS NOW YOU'RE SORRY FOR WHAT YOU DID?
I'M ONLY SORRY WE DIDN'T MEET ON A TALLER BUILDING.
VERY FUNNY. YOU'VE ALWAYS HAD A GOOD SENSE OF HUMOR. IT'S WHAT I'LL MISS ABOUT YOU.
BLACK AND DEKKER. VERY SHARP.
I'LL BE BACK IN A BIT, AFTER PAOLO'S HAD A FEW MINUTES WITH YOU ALONE.
BRREEEE
PERHAPS YOU CAN ENTERTAIN HIM WITH MORE OF YOUR AMUSING STORIES.

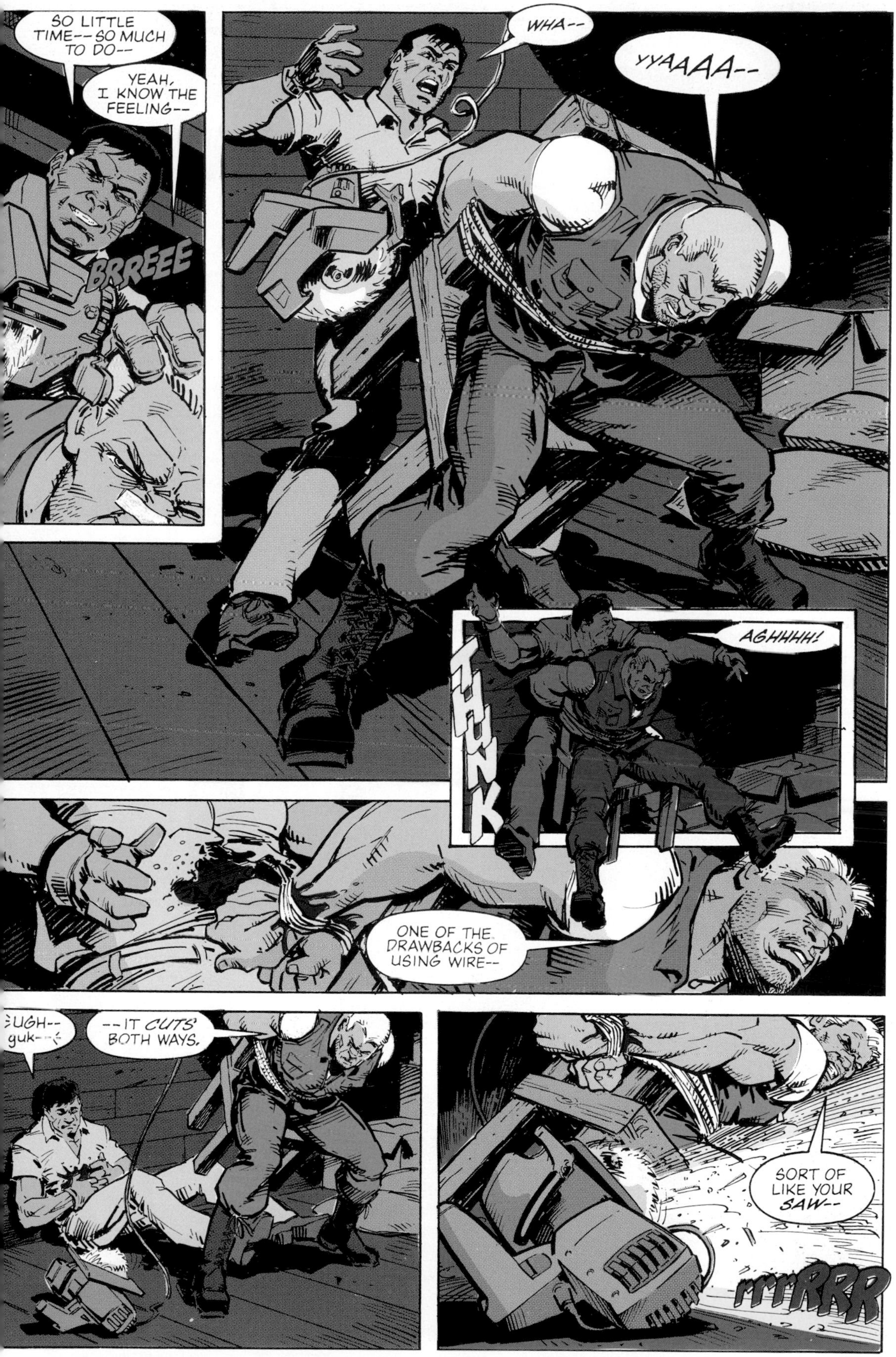
SO LITTLE TIME-- SO MUCH TO DO--
YEAH, I KNOW THE FEELING--
BRREEE
WHA--
YYAAAA--
AGHHHH!
THUNK
ONE OF THE DRAWBACKS OF USING WIRE--
UGH-- guk--
--IT CUTS BOTH WAYS.
SORT OF LIKE YOUR SAW--
rrrRRR

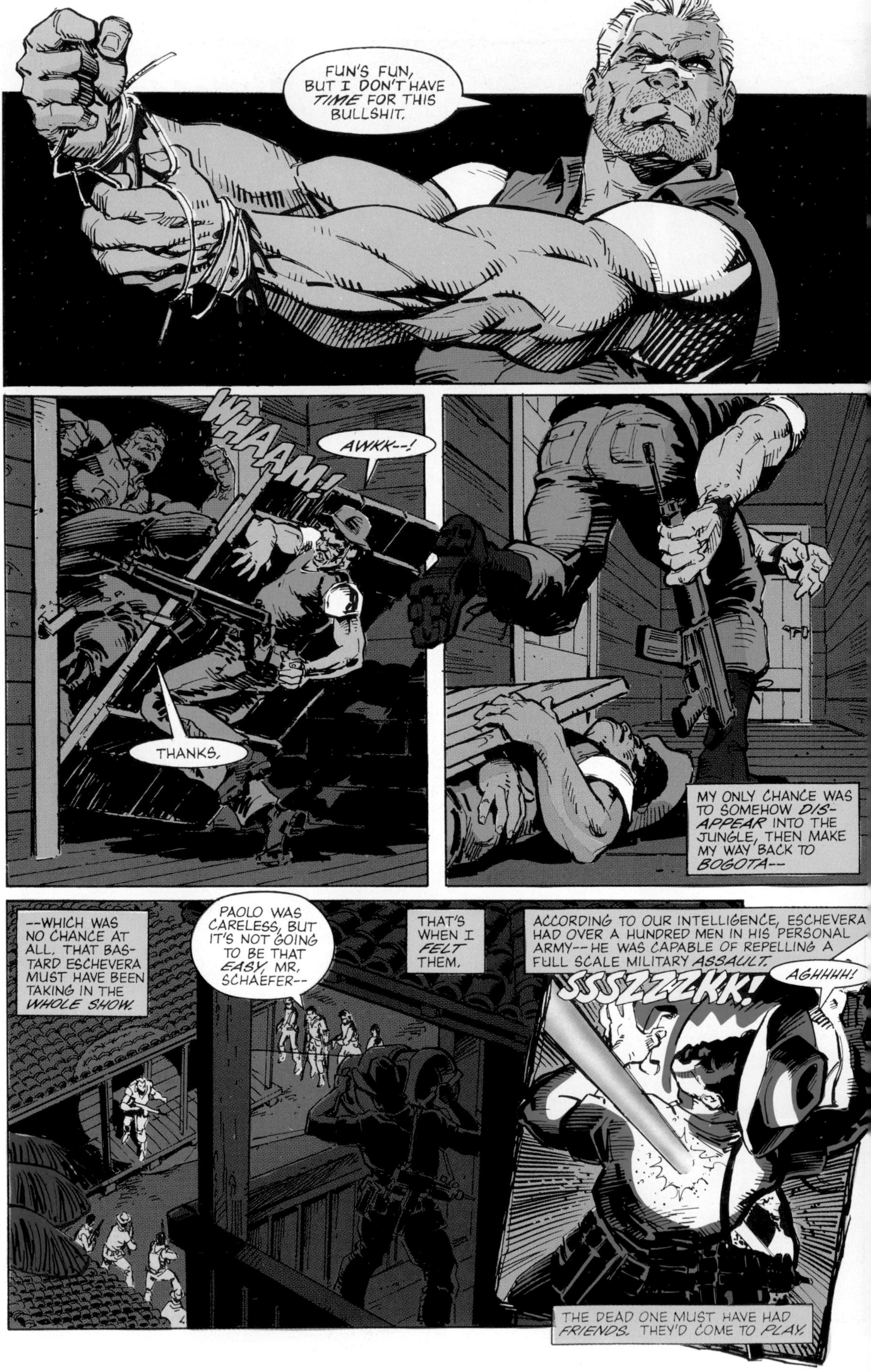
FUN'S FUN, BUT I DON'T HAVE TIME FOR THIS BULLSHIT.
WHAAAM!
AWKK--!
THANKS.
MY ONLY CHANCE WAS TO SOMEHOW DIS-APPEAR INTO THE JUNGLE, THEN MAKE MY WAY BACK TO BOGOTA--
--WHICH WAS NO CHANCE AT ALL. THAT BAS-TARD ESCHEVERA MUST HAVE BEEN TAKING IN THE WHOLE SHOW.
PAOLO WAS CARELESS, BUT IT'S NOT GOING TO BE THAT EASY, MR. SCHAEFER--
THAT'S WHEN I FELT THEM.
ACCORDING TO OUR INTELLIGENCE, ESCHEVERA HAD OVER A HUNDRED MEN IN HIS PERSONAL ARMY--HE WAS CAPABLE OF REPELLING A FULL SCALE MILITARY ASSAULT.
SSSZZZKK!
AGHHHH!
THE DEAD ONE MUST HAVE HAD FRIENDS. THEY'D COME TO PLAY.

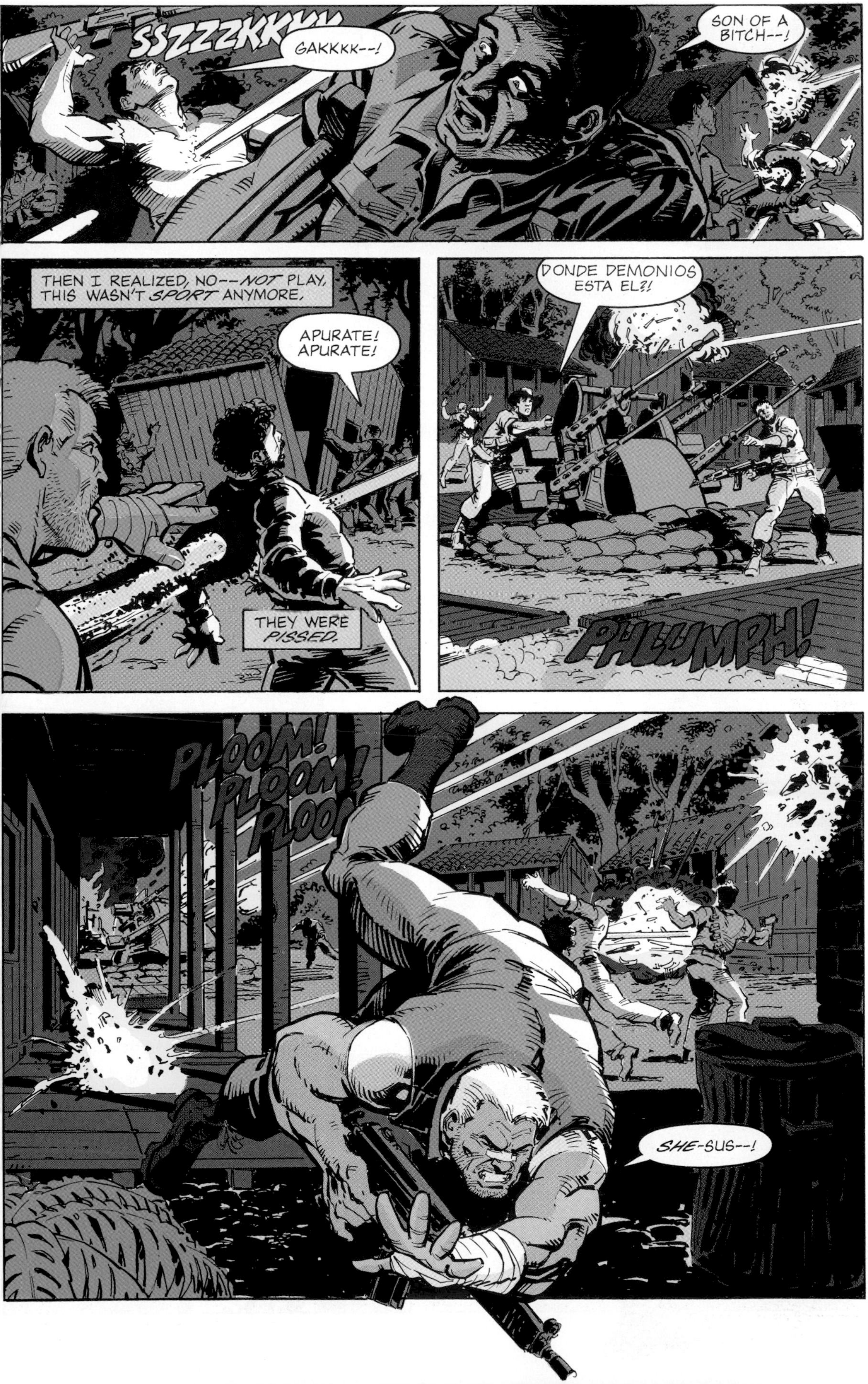
SSZZZKKKK
GAKKKK--!
SON OF A BITCH--!
THEN I REALIZED, NO--*NOT* PLAY, THIS WASN'T *SPORT* ANYMORE,
APURATE! APURATE!
THEY WERE *PISSED*.
DONDE DEMONIOS ESTA EL?!
PHLUMPH!
PLOOM! PLOOM! PLOO
SHE-SUS--!

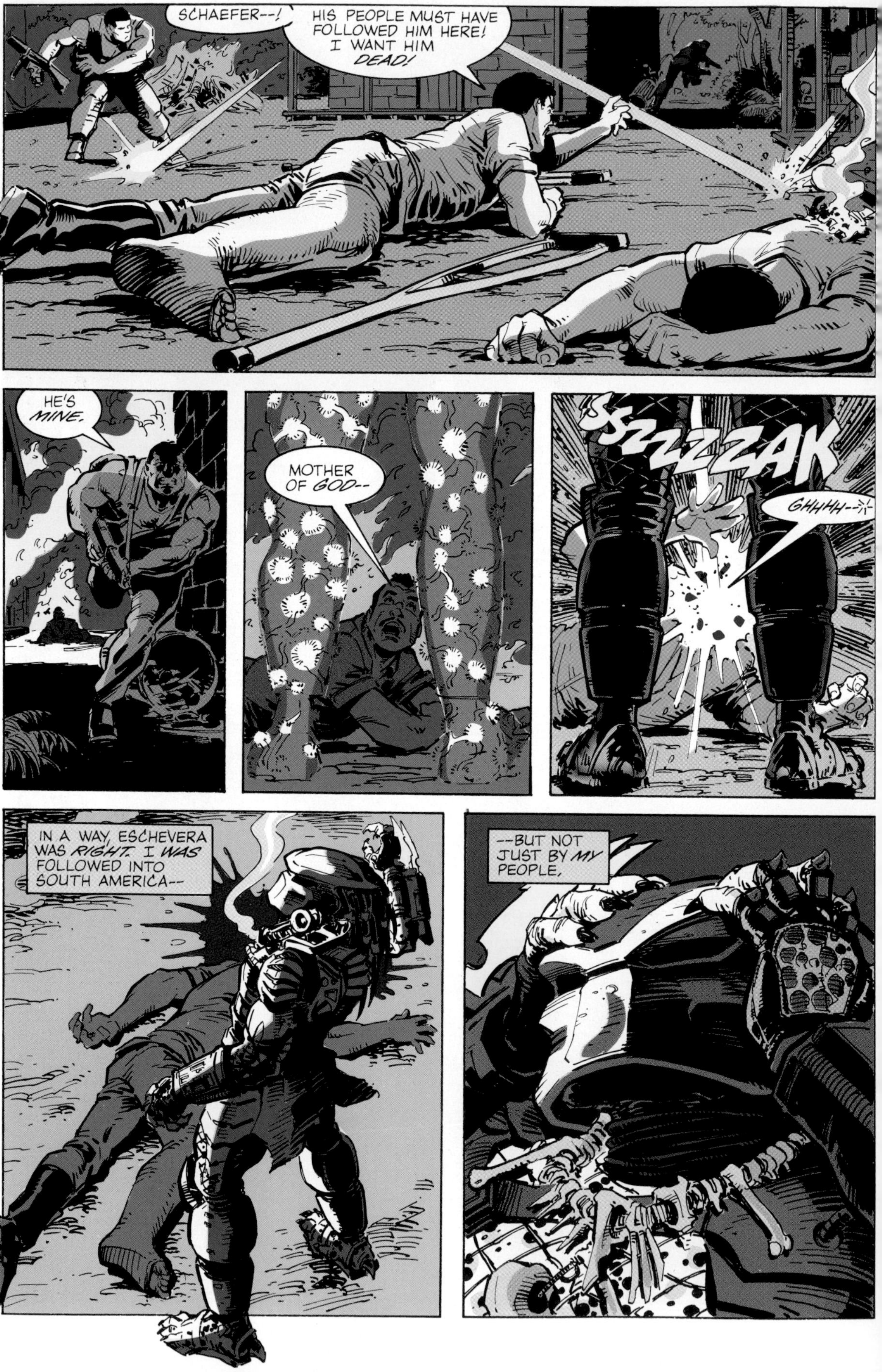
SCHAEFER--!
HIS PEOPLE MUST HAVE FOLLOWED HIM HERE! I WANT HIM DEAD!
HE'S MINE.
MOTHER OF GOD--
SSZZZZAK
GHHHH--
IN A WAY, ESCHEVERA WAS RIGHT. I WAS FOLLOWED INTO SOUTH AMERICA--
--BUT NOT JUST BY MY PEOPLE.

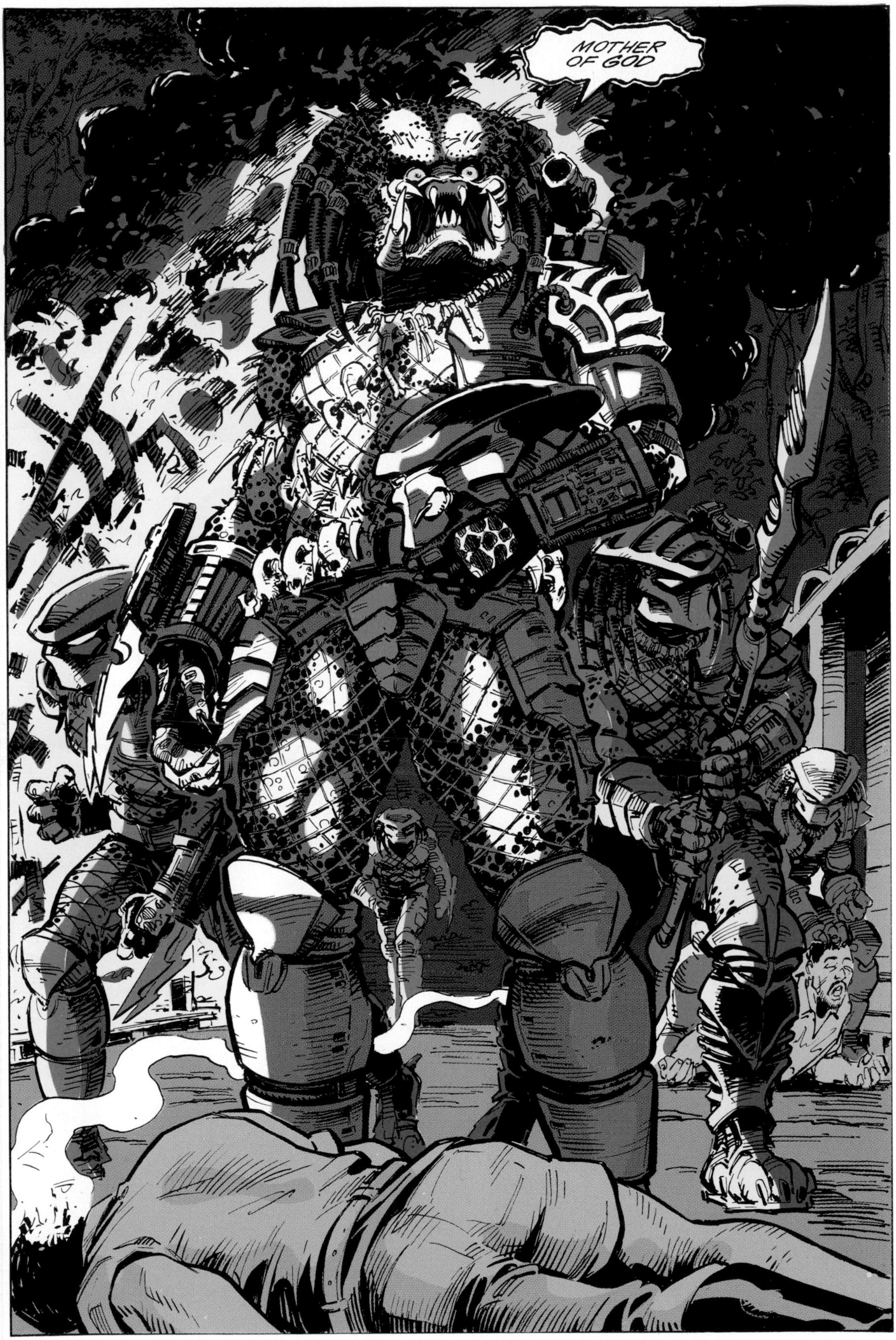
MOTHER OF GOD

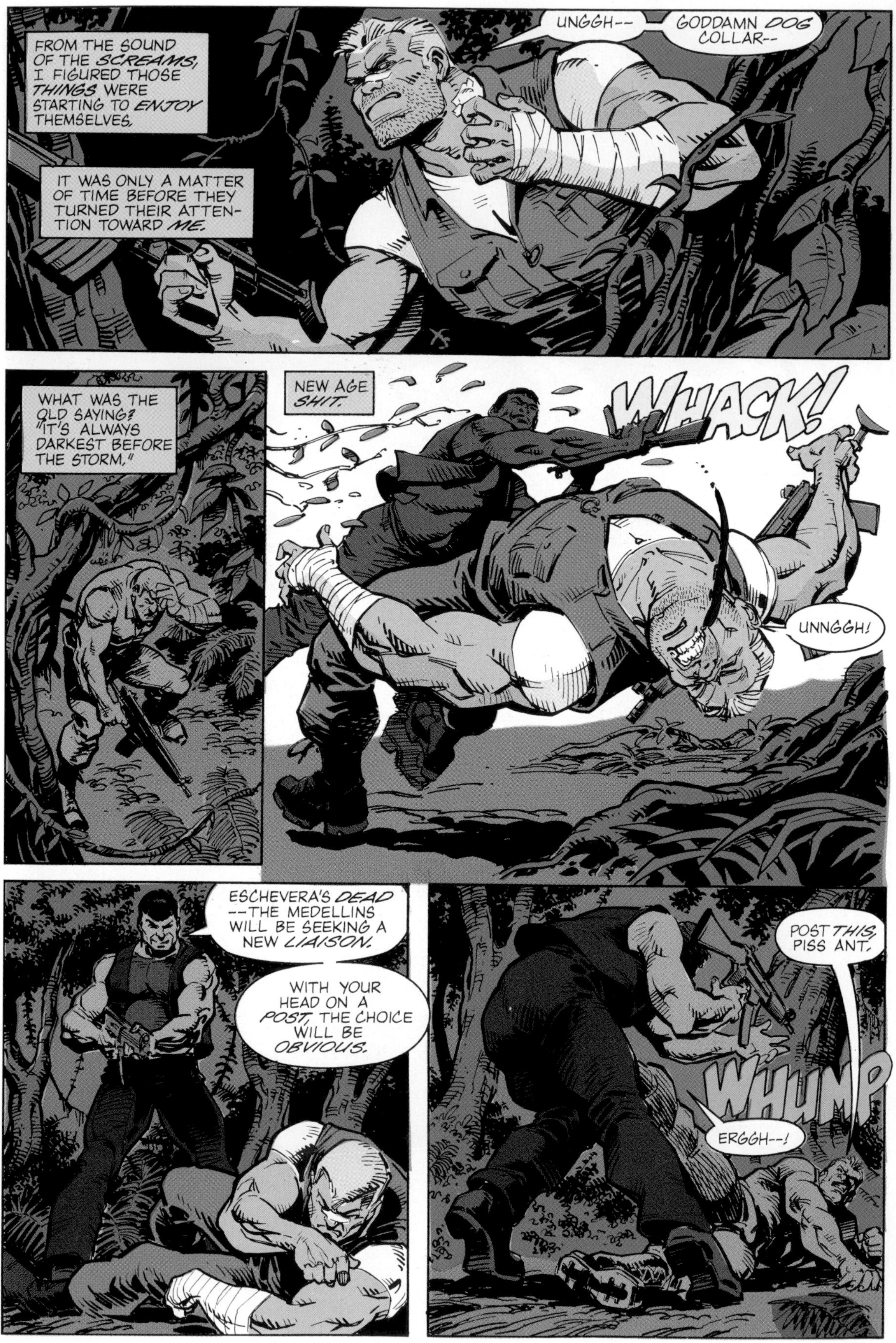
FROM THE SOUND OF THE SCREAMS, I FIGURED THOSE THINGS WERE STARTING TO ENJOY THEMSELVES.
IT WAS ONLY A MATTER OF TIME BEFORE THEY TURNED THEIR ATTENTION TOWARD ME.
UNGGH--
GODDAMN DOG COLLAR--
WHAT WAS THE OLD SAYING? "IT'S ALWAYS DARKEST BEFORE THE STORM."
NEW AGE SHIT.
WHACK!
UNNGGH!
ESCHEVERA'S DEAD --THE MEDELLINS WILL BE SEEKING A NEW LIAISON.
WITH YOUR HEAD ON A POST, THE CHOICE WILL BE OBVIOUS.
POST THIS, PISS ANT.
WHUMP
ERGGH--!

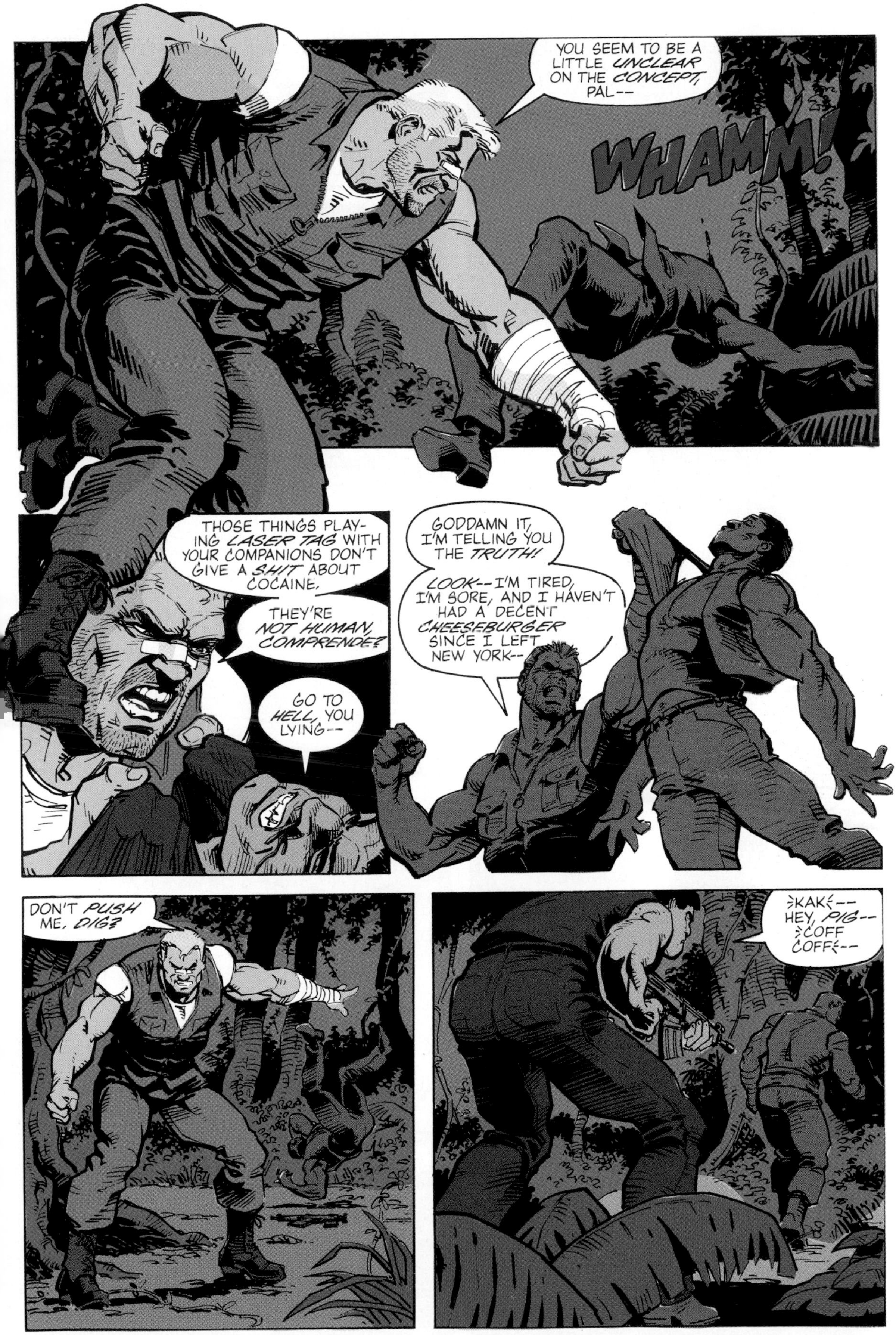
YOU SEEM TO BE A LITTLE UNCLEAR ON THE CONCEPT, PAL--
WHAMM!
THOSE THINGS PLAYING LASER TAG WITH YOUR COMPANIONS DON'T GIVE A SHIT ABOUT COCAINE.
THEY'RE NOT HUMAN, COMPRENDE?
GO TO HELL, YOU LYING--
GODDAMN IT, I'M TELLING YOU THE TRUTH!
LOOK--I'M TIRED, I'M SORE, AND I HAVEN'T HAD A DECENT CHEESEBURGER SINCE I LEFT NEW YORK--
DON'T PUSH ME, DIG?
KAK--
HEY, PIG--
COFF COFF--

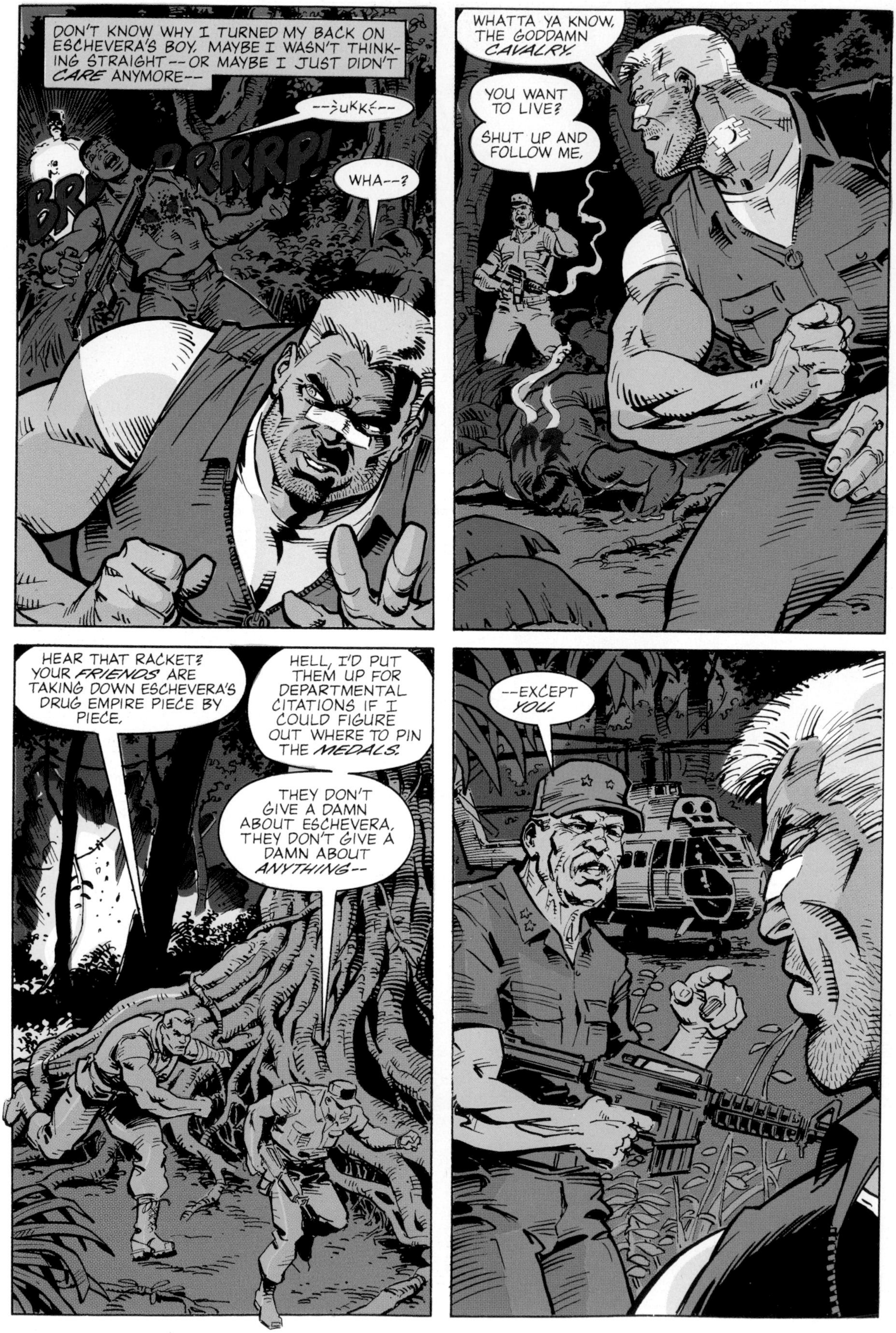

DON'T KNOW WHY I TURNED MY BACK ON ESCHEVERA'S BOY. MAYBE I WASN'T THINKING STRAIGHT--OR MAYBE I JUST DIDN'T CARE ANYMORE--
--UKK--
BRRRRRP!
WHA--?
WHATTA YA KNOW, THE GODDAMN CAVALRY.
YOU WANT TO LIVE?
SHUT UP AND FOLLOW ME.
HEAR THAT RACKET? YOUR FRIENDS ARE TAKING DOWN ESCHEVERA'S DRUG EMPIRE PIECE BY PIECE.
HELL, I'D PUT THEM UP FOR DEPARTMENTAL CITATIONS IF I COULD FIGURE OUT WHERE TO PIN THE MEDALS.
THEY DON'T GIVE A DAMN ABOUT ESCHEVERA. THEY DON'T GIVE A DAMN ABOUT ANYTHING--
--EXCEPT YOU.

THIS *SUCKS!* HOW LONG DO YOU THINK YOU CAN *KEEP* ME HERE?

AS LONG AS WE *HAVE* TO.

HEY, SMITH-- YOUR *SHOES'S* UNTIED--

GET SERIOUS, RASCHE, WE'RE TRAINED PROFESSIONAL-ALS-- THAT RUSE ONLY WORKS ON *CUB SCOUTS.*

AND WHAT THE HELL IS *THIS?* HOMEWORK?

DELINQUENT TAX RETURNS. WE'RE TALKING SOME *TASTY* AUDITS HERE--LATE PENALTIES, INTEREST, MAYBE EVEN SOME *PRISON TIME--*

BRRNNGG..!

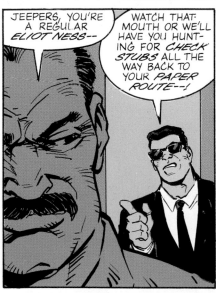

JEEPERS, YOU'RE A REGULAR *ELIOT NESS--*

WATCH THAT MOUTH OR WE'LL HAVE YOU HUNTING FOR *CHECK STUBS* ALL THE WAY BACK TO YOUR *PAPER ROUTE--!*

THAT WAS PETERSON, SCHAEFER'S DUE IN SIX HOURS, THEY'LL CHOPPER HIM STRAIGHT TO THE PAN AM BUILDING AND MAKE DELIVERY THERE--

WAIT A MINUTE-- WHAT DO YOU MEAN, "DELIVERY"?

JESUS, YOU'RE GOING TO *GIVE* HIM TO THEM, AREN'T YOU?

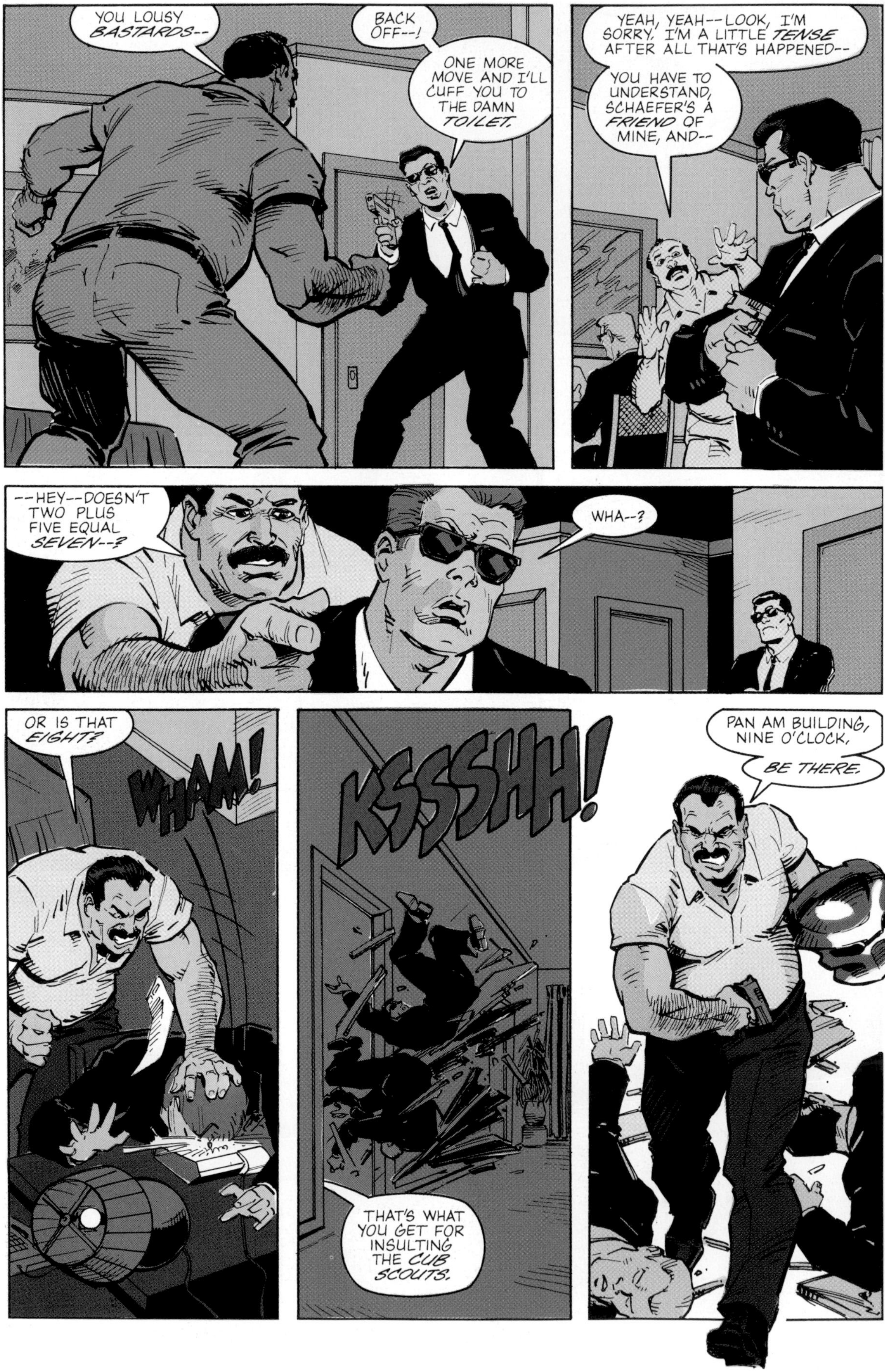
YOU LOUSY BASTARDS--
BACK OFF--!
ONE MORE MOVE AND I'LL CUFF YOU TO THE DAMN TOILET.
YEAH, YEAH--LOOK, I'M SORRY, I'M A LITTLE TENSE AFTER ALL THAT'S HAPPENED--
YOU HAVE TO UNDERSTAND, SCHAEFER'S A FRIEND OF MINE, AND--
--HEY--DOESN'T TWO PLUS FIVE EQUAL SEVEN--?
WHA--?
OR IS THAT EIGHT?
WHAM!
KSSSHH!
THAT'S WHAT YOU GET FOR INSULTING THE CUB SCOUTS.
PAN AM BUILDING, NINE O'CLOCK,
BE THERE.

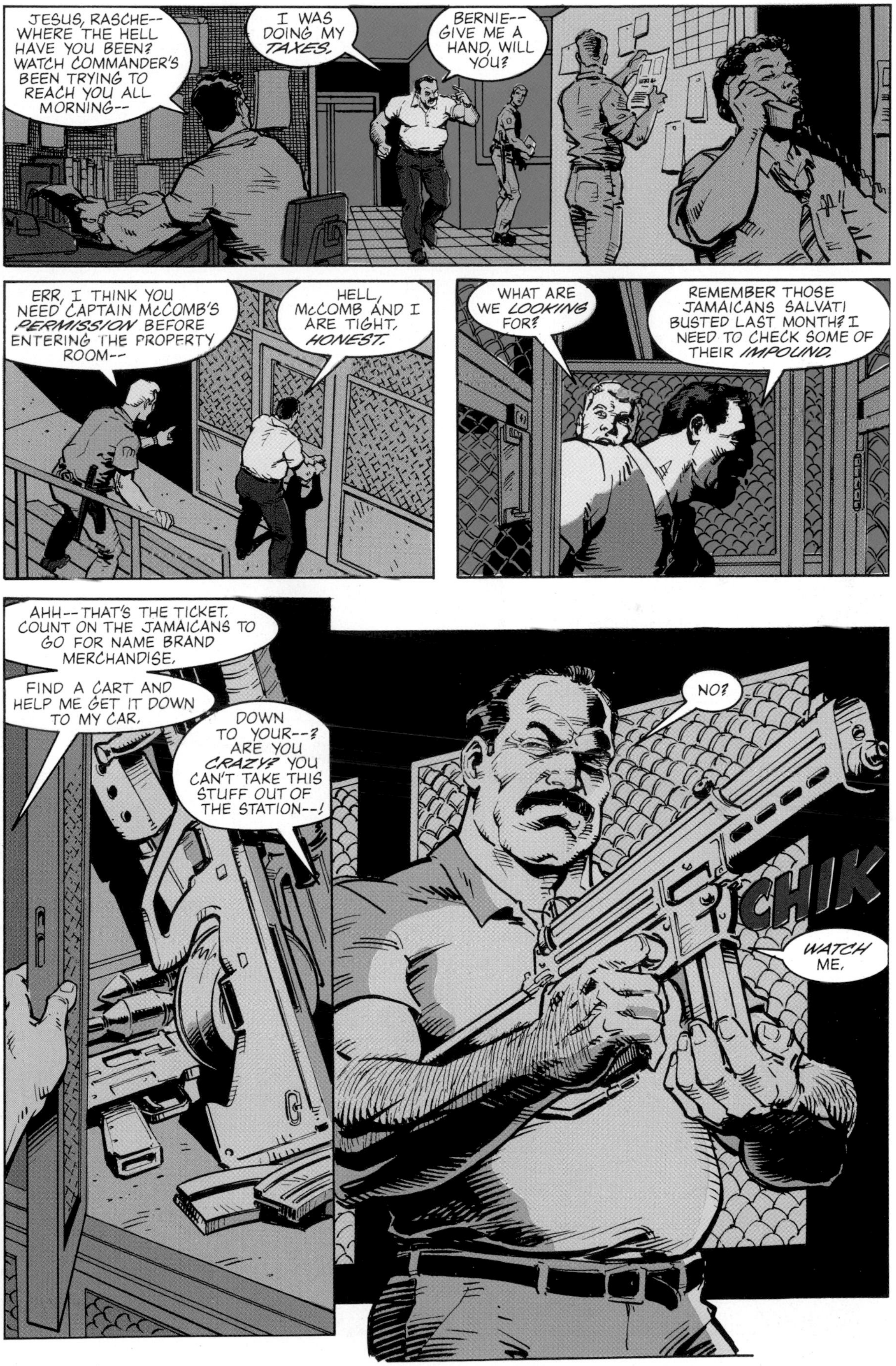
JESUS, RASCHE-- WHERE THE HELL HAVE YOU BEEN? WATCH COMMANDER'S BEEN TRYING TO REACH YOU ALL MORNING--
I WAS DOING MY TAXES.
BERNIE-- GIVE ME A HAND, WILL YOU?
ERR, I THINK YOU NEED CAPTAIN McCOMB'S PERMISSION BEFORE ENTERING THE PROPERTY ROOM--
HELL, McCOMB AND I ARE TIGHT. HONEST.
WHAT ARE WE LOOKING FOR?
REMEMBER THOSE JAMAICANS SALVATI BUSTED LAST MONTH? I NEED TO CHECK SOME OF THEIR IMPOUND.
AHH--THAT'S THE TICKET. COUNT ON THE JAMAICANS TO GO FOR NAME BRAND MERCHANDISE.
FIND A CART AND HELP ME GET IT DOWN TO MY CAR.
DOWN TO YOUR--? ARE YOU CRAZY? YOU CAN'T TAKE THIS STUFF OUT OF THE STATION--!
NO?
CHIK
WATCH ME.

CHOPPERED OUT OF COLOMBIA, PRIVATE JET BACK TO NEW YORK--SUDDENLY I SEEMED TO BE A VERY IMPORTANT PERSON, IT MADE ME *NERVOUS!*

ALL RIGHT, WE'RE *BACK,* NOW I WANT SOME ANSWERS.

WHAT THE HELL ARE WE *DEALING* WITH?

YOU WANT A *NAME?* WE HAVEN'T GOT ONE, YOU WANT A *PLACE?*

NOT *EARTH.*

THEY'VE BEEN COMING HERE FOR *CENTURIES--* ALWAYS IN THE *HEAT,* ALL THAT "ENQUIRER" CRAP ABOUT ALIENS AND ANCIENT ASTRONAUTS-- IT'S ALL *TRUE.*

THEY LIKE THE *CHASE.* THEY HUNTED THE DINOSAURS TO EXTINCTION, SO THEY WENT AFTER *DIFFERENT* PREY.

NEVER THOUGHT WE'D HAVE TO *DEAL* WITH THEM THIS FAR NORTH, MOST OF THE HUNTS WERE CONFINED TO HOT *EQUATORIAL* COUNTRIES-- SOUTH AMERICA, AFRICA--

GODDAMN *GREEN-HOUSE* EFFECT--

OR MAYBE THEY JUST GOT *BORED.*

HELL, IF EARTH'S DISNEY-LAND, THEN NEW YORK'S AN *"E" TICKET.*

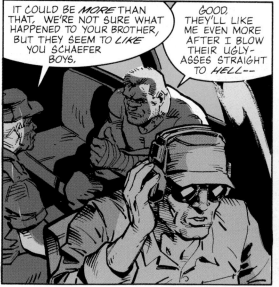

IT COULD BE *MORE* THAN THAT, WE'RE NOT SURE WHAT HAPPENED TO YOUR BROTHER, BUT THEY SEEM TO *LIKE* YOU SCHAEFER BOYS.

GOOD, THEY'LL LIKE ME EVEN MORE AFTER I BLOW THEIR UGLY-ASSES STRAIGHT TO *HELL--*

I'M SORRY, SON, WE'VE GOT SOME-THING *ELSE* IN MIND.

SHOULD HAVE GUESSED.

YOU'RE *GIVING* ME TO THEM.

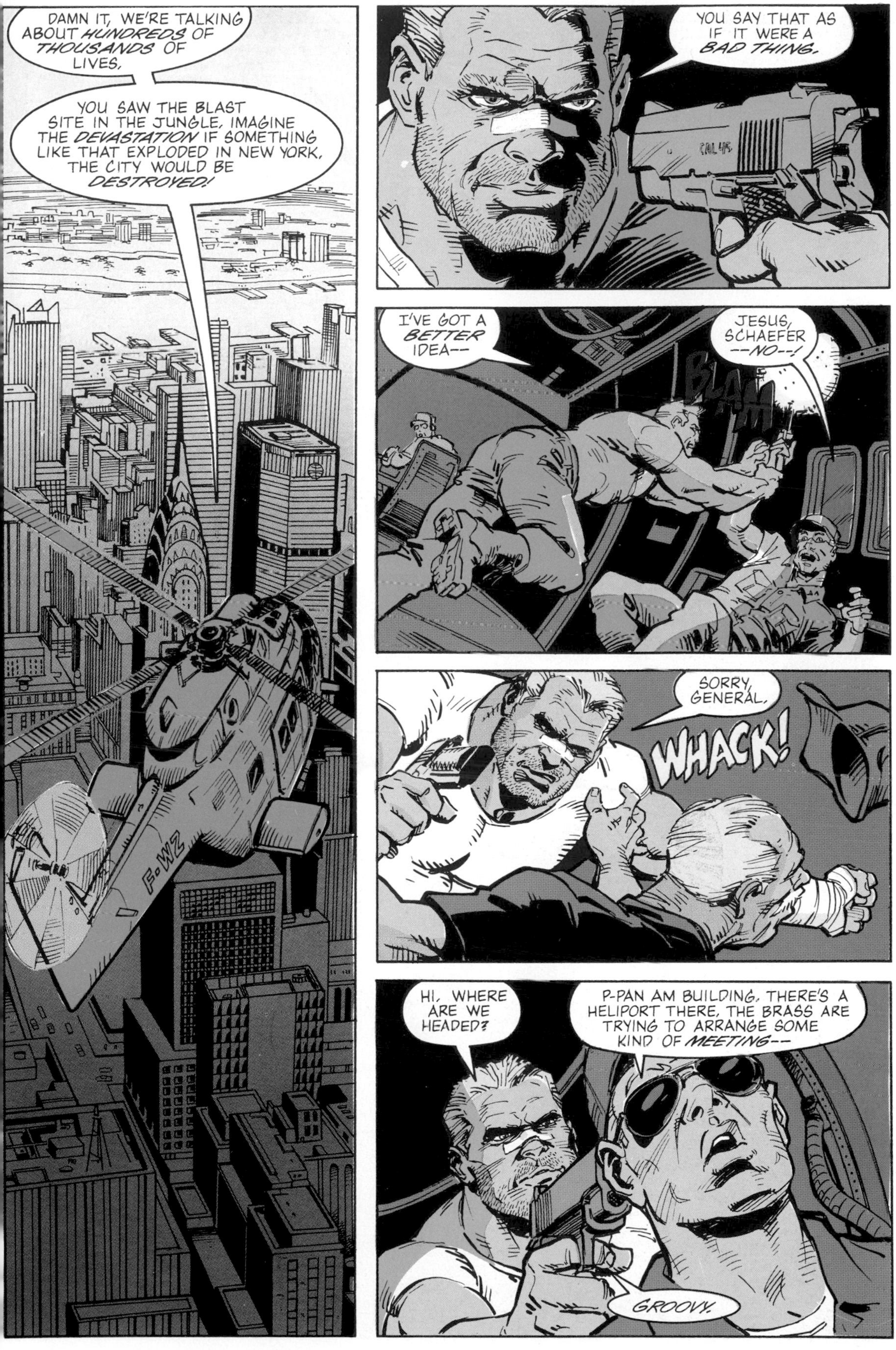
DAMN IT, WE'RE TALKING ABOUT HUNDREDS OF THOUSANDS OF LIVES.
YOU SAW THE BLAST SITE IN THE JUNGLE. IMAGINE THE DEVASTATION IF SOMETHING LIKE THAT EXPLODED IN NEW YORK. THE CITY WOULD BE DESTROYED!
YOU SAY THAT AS IF IT WERE A BAD THING.
I'VE GOT A BETTER IDEA--
JESUS, SCHAEFER --NO--!
BLAM
SORRY, GENERAL.
WHACK!
HI. WHERE ARE WE HEADED?
P-PAN AM BUILDING. THERE'S A HELIPORT THERE. THE BRASS ARE TRYING TO ARRANGE SOME KIND OF MEETING--
GROOVY.

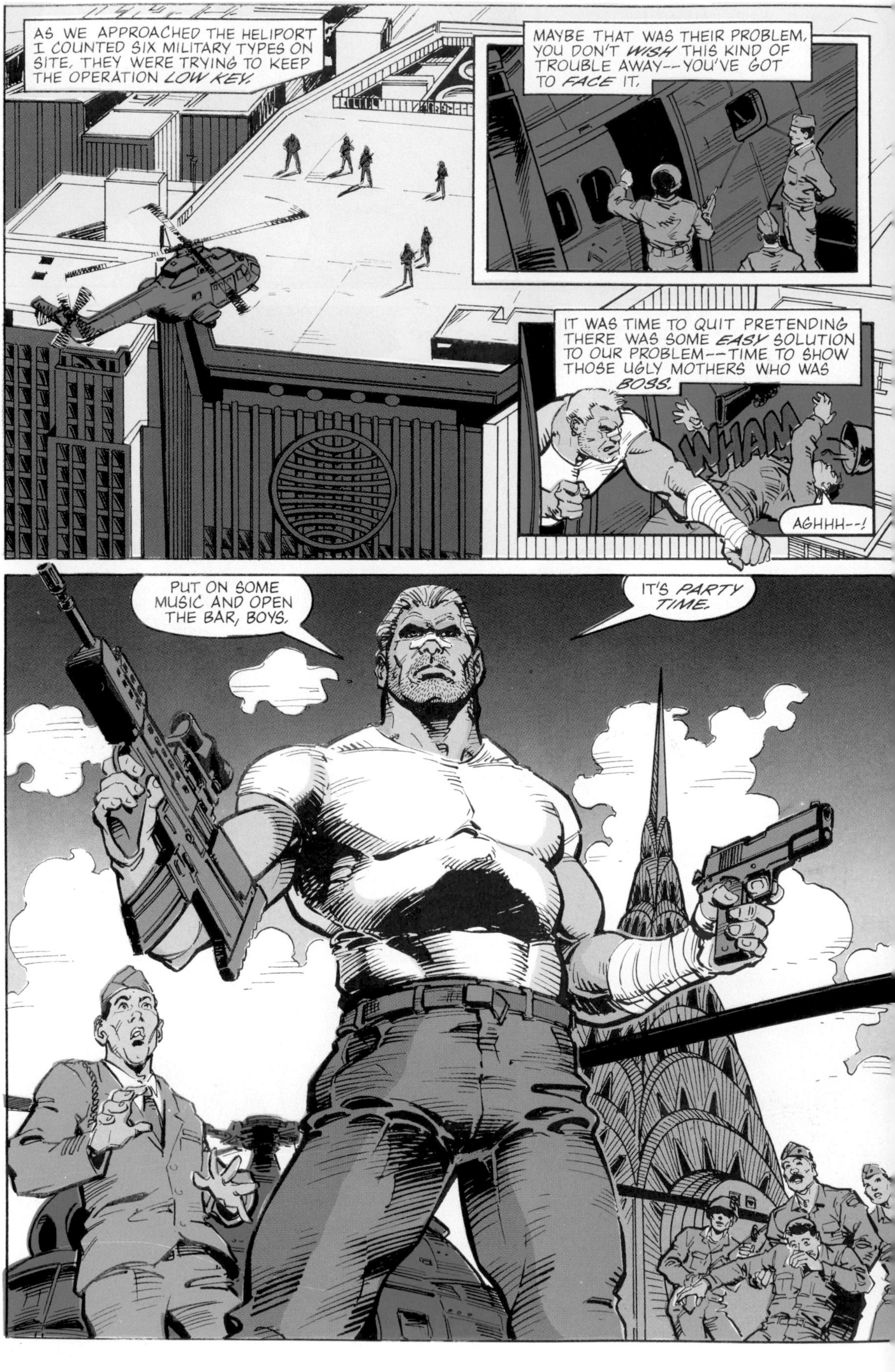
AS WE APPROACHED THE HELIPORT I COUNTED SIX MILITARY TYPES ON SITE, THEY WERE TRYING TO KEEP THE OPERATION LOW KEY.
MAYBE THAT WAS THEIR PROBLEM, YOU DON'T WISH THIS KIND OF TROUBLE AWAY--YOU'VE GOT TO FACE IT.
IT WAS TIME TO QUIT PRETENDING THERE WAS SOME EASY SOLUTION TO OUR PROBLEM--TIME TO SHOW THOSE UGLY MOTHERS WHO WAS BOSS.
WHAM
AGHHH--!
PUT ON SOME MUSIC AND OPEN THE BAR, BOYS.
IT'S PARTY TIME.

1

2

3

CHAPTER 4

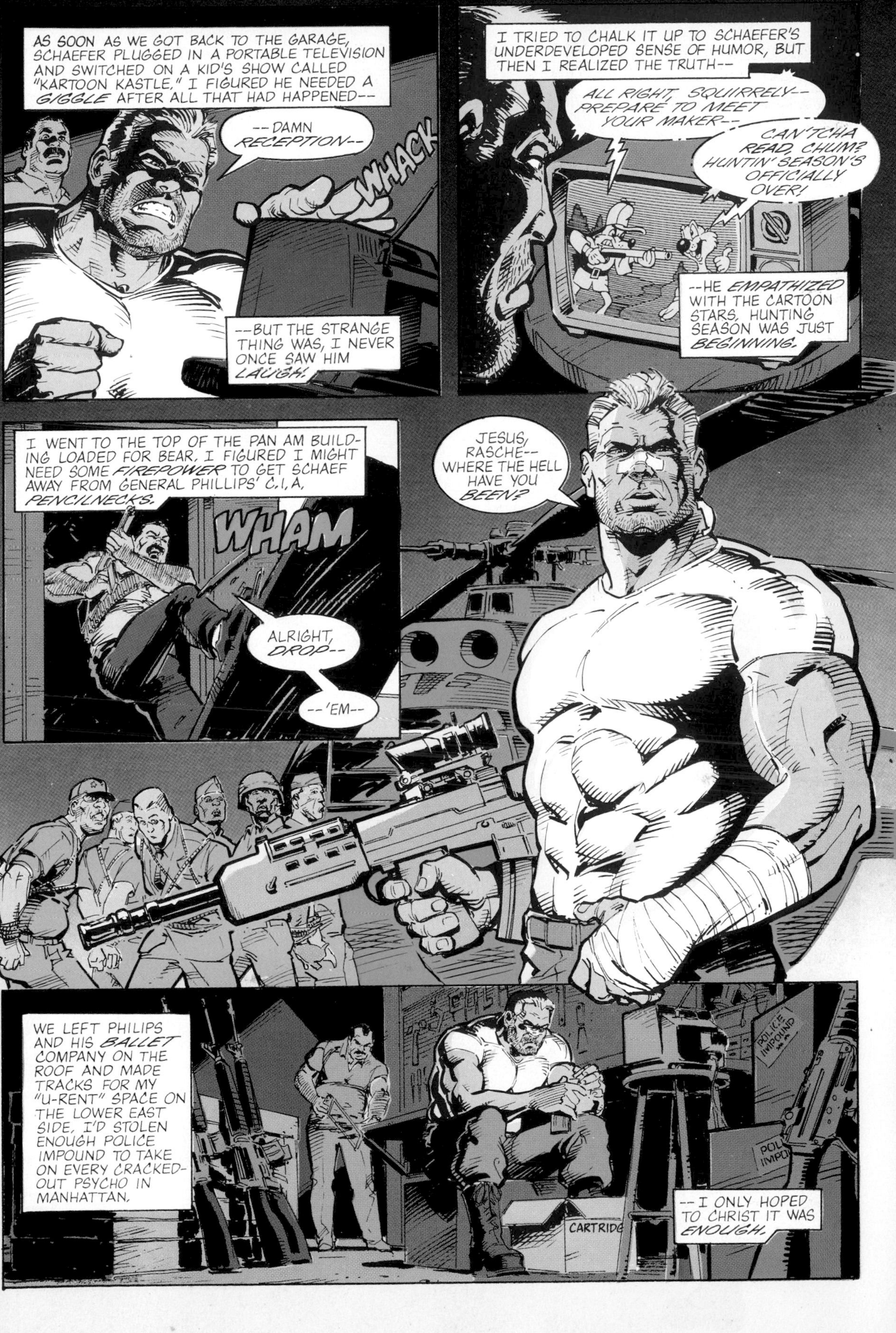

AS SOON AS WE GOT BACK TO THE GARAGE, SCHAEFER PLUGGED IN A PORTABLE TELEVISION AND SWITCHED ON A KID'S SHOW CALLED "KARTOON KASTLE," I FIGURED HE NEEDED A GIGGLE AFTER ALL THAT HAD HAPPENED--
--DAMN RECEPTION--
WHACK
--BUT THE STRANGE THING WAS, I NEVER ONCE SAW HIM LAUGH!
I TRIED TO CHALK IT UP TO SCHAEFER'S UNDERDEVELOPED SENSE OF HUMOR, BUT THEN I REALIZED THE TRUTH--
ALL RIGHT, SQUIRRELY-- PREPARE TO MEET YOUR MAKER--
CAN'TCHA READ, CHUM? HUNTIN' SEASON'S OFFICIALLY OVER!
--HE EMPATHIZED WITH THE CARTOON STARS, HUNTING SEASON WAS JUST BEGINNING.
I WENT TO THE TOP OF THE PAN AM BUILDING LOADED FOR BEAR, I FIGURED I MIGHT NEED SOME FIREPOWER TO GET SCHAEF AWAY FROM GENERAL PHILLIPS' C.I.A. PENCILNECKS.
WHAM
ALRIGHT, DROP--
--'EM--
JESUS, RASCHE-- WHERE THE HELL HAVE YOU BEEN?
WE LEFT PHILIPS AND HIS BALLET COMPANY ON THE ROOF AND MADE TRACKS FOR MY "U-RENT" SPACE ON THE LOWER EAST SIDE, I'D STOLEN ENOUGH POLICE IMPOUND TO TAKE ON EVERY CRACKED-OUT PSYCHO IN MANHATTAN.
POLICE IMPOUND
CARTRIDG
--I ONLY HOPED TO CHRIST IT WAS ENOUGH.

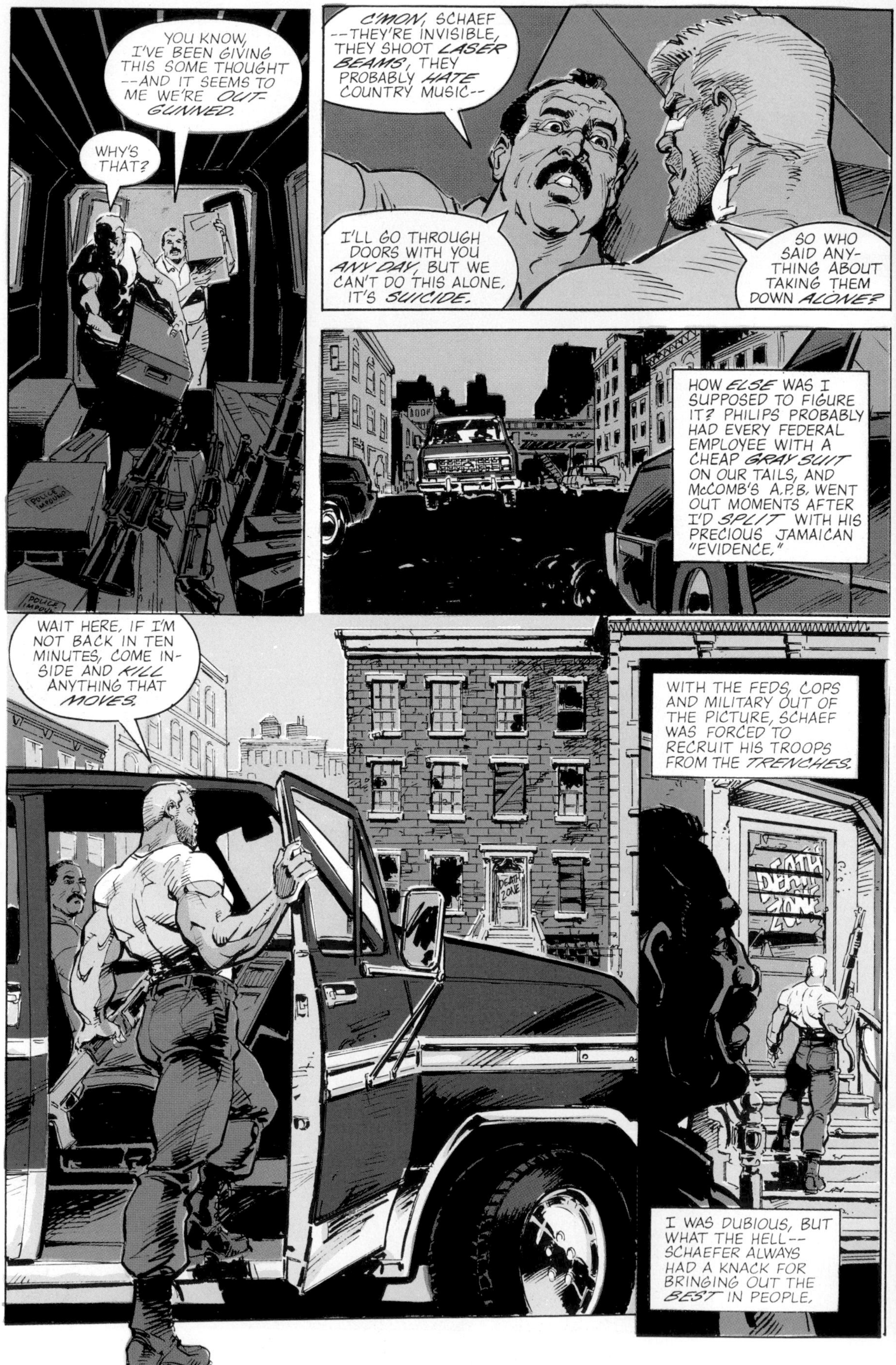
YOU KNOW, I'VE BEEN GIVING THIS SOME THOUGHT --AND IT SEEMS TO ME WE'RE OUT-GUNNED.
WHY'S THAT?
POLICE IMPOUND
C'MON, SCHAEF --THEY'RE INVISIBLE, THEY SHOOT LASER BEAMS, THEY PROBABLY HATE COUNTRY MUSIC--
I'LL GO THROUGH DOORS WITH YOU ANY DAY, BUT WE CAN'T DO THIS ALONE, IT'S SUICIDE.
SO WHO SAID ANY-THING ABOUT TAKING THEM DOWN ALONE?
HOW ELSE WAS I SUPPOSED TO FIGURE IT? PHILIPS PROBABLY HAD EVERY FEDERAL EMPLOYEE WITH A CHEAP GRAY SUIT ON OUR TAILS, AND McCOMB'S A.P.B. WENT OUT MOMENTS AFTER I'D SPLIT WITH HIS PRECIOUS JAMAICAN "EVIDENCE."
WAIT HERE, IF I'M NOT BACK IN TEN MINUTES, COME IN-SIDE AND KILL ANYTHING THAT MOVES.
DEATH ZONE
WITH THE FEDS, COPS AND MILITARY OUT OF THE PICTURE, SCHAEF WAS FORCED TO RECRUIT HIS TROOPS FROM THE TRENCHES.
I WAS DUBIOUS, BUT WHAT THE HELL-- SCHAEFER ALWAYS HAD A KNACK FOR BRINGING OUT THE BEST IN PEOPLE.

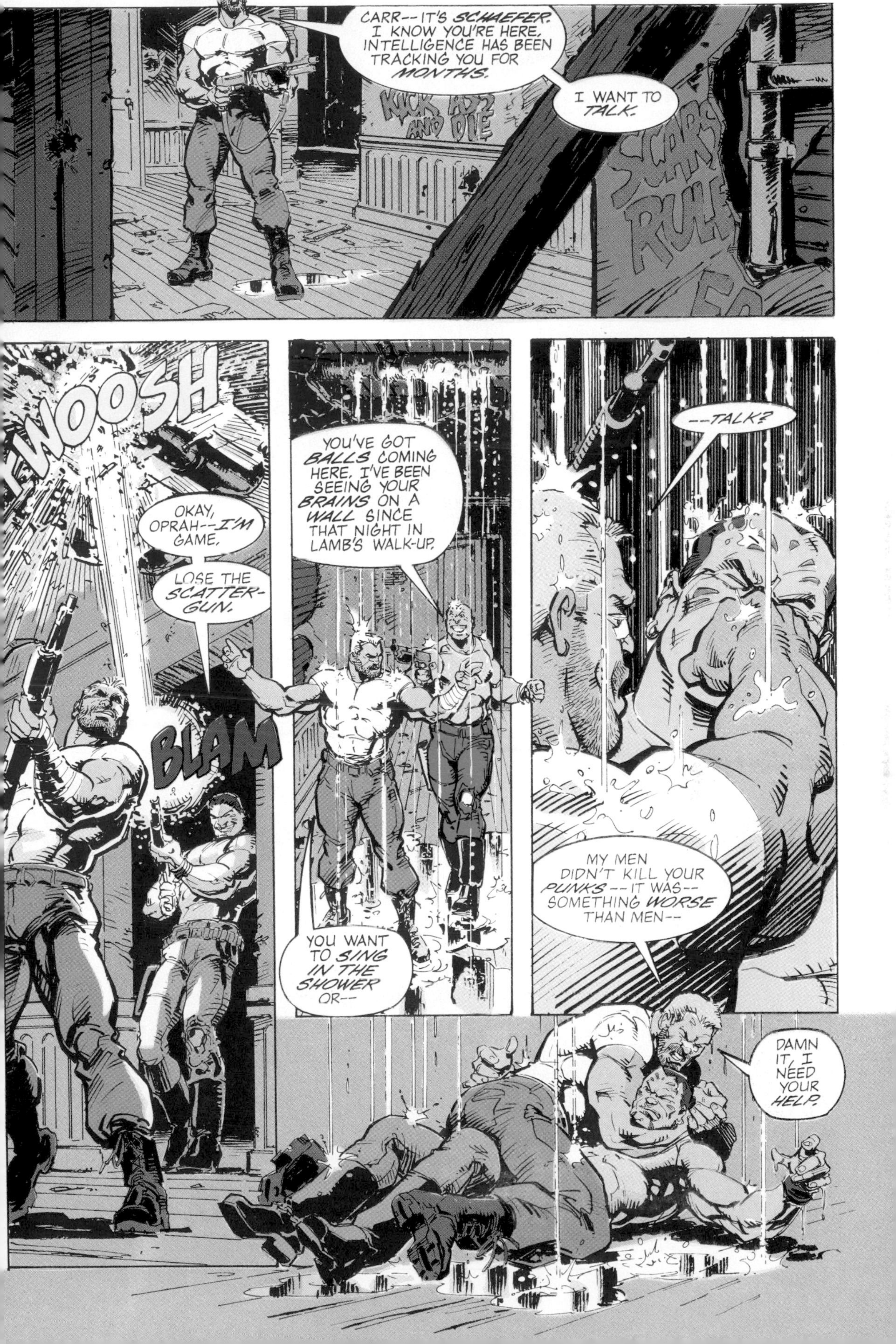
CARR-- IT'S SCHAEFER. I KNOW YOU'RE HERE. INTELLIGENCE HAS BEEN TRACKING YOU FOR MONTHS.
I WANT TO TALK.
KICK ASS AND DIE
SCARS RULE
WOOSH
OKAY, OPRAH-- I'M GAME.
LOSE THE SCATTER-GUN.
BLAM
YOU'VE GOT BALLS COMING HERE. I'VE BEEN SEEING YOUR BRAINS ON A WALL SINCE THAT NIGHT IN LAMB'S WALK-UP.
YOU WANT TO SING IN THE SHOWER OR--
--TALK?
MY MEN DIDN'T KILL YOUR PUNKS -- IT WAS-- SOMETHING WORSE THAN MEN--
DAMN IT, I NEED YOUR HELP.

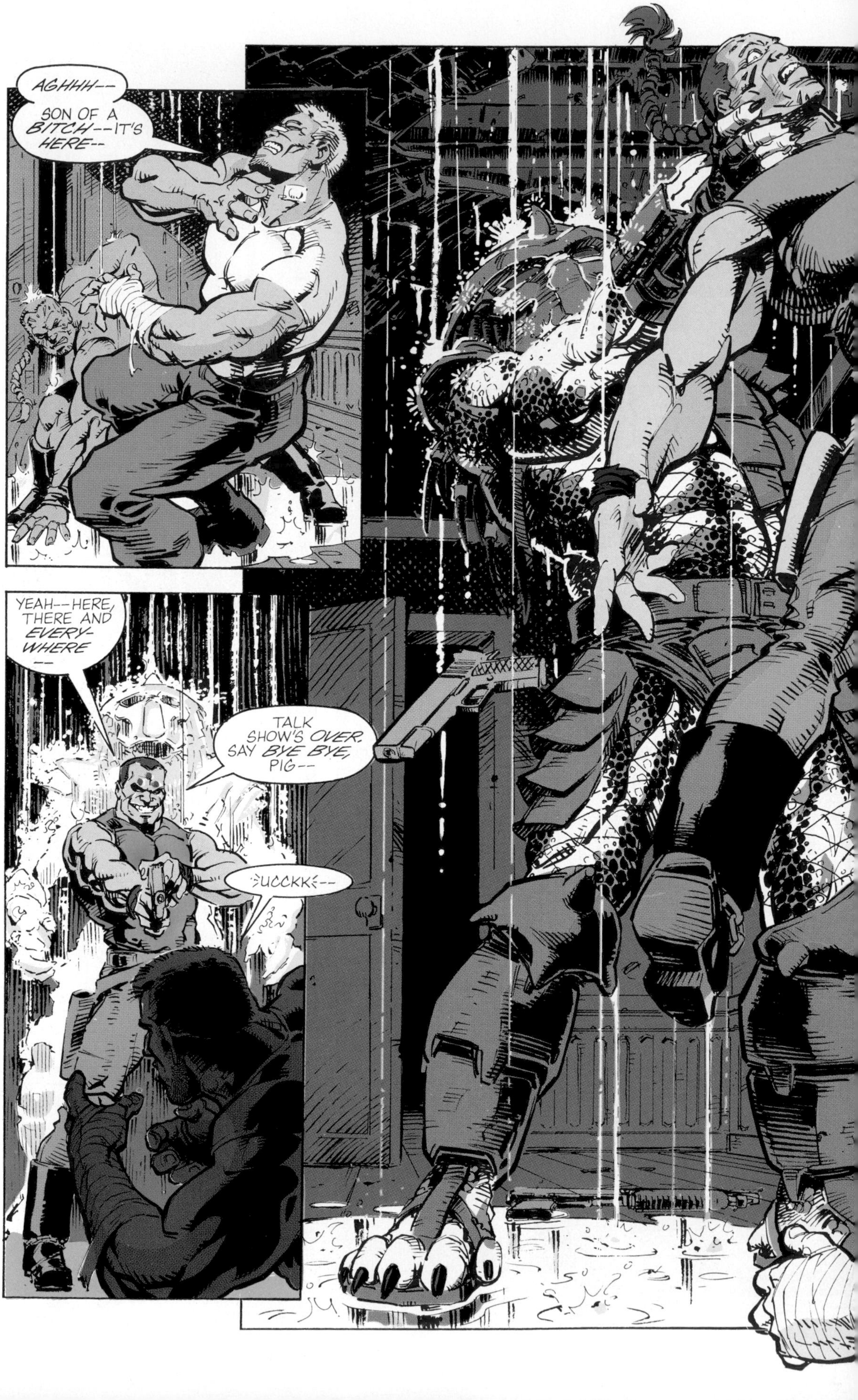
AGHHH--
SON OF A BITCH--IT'S HERE--
YEAH--HERE, THERE AND EVERY-WHERE--
TALK SHOW'S OVER. SAY BYE BYE, PIG--
UCCKK--

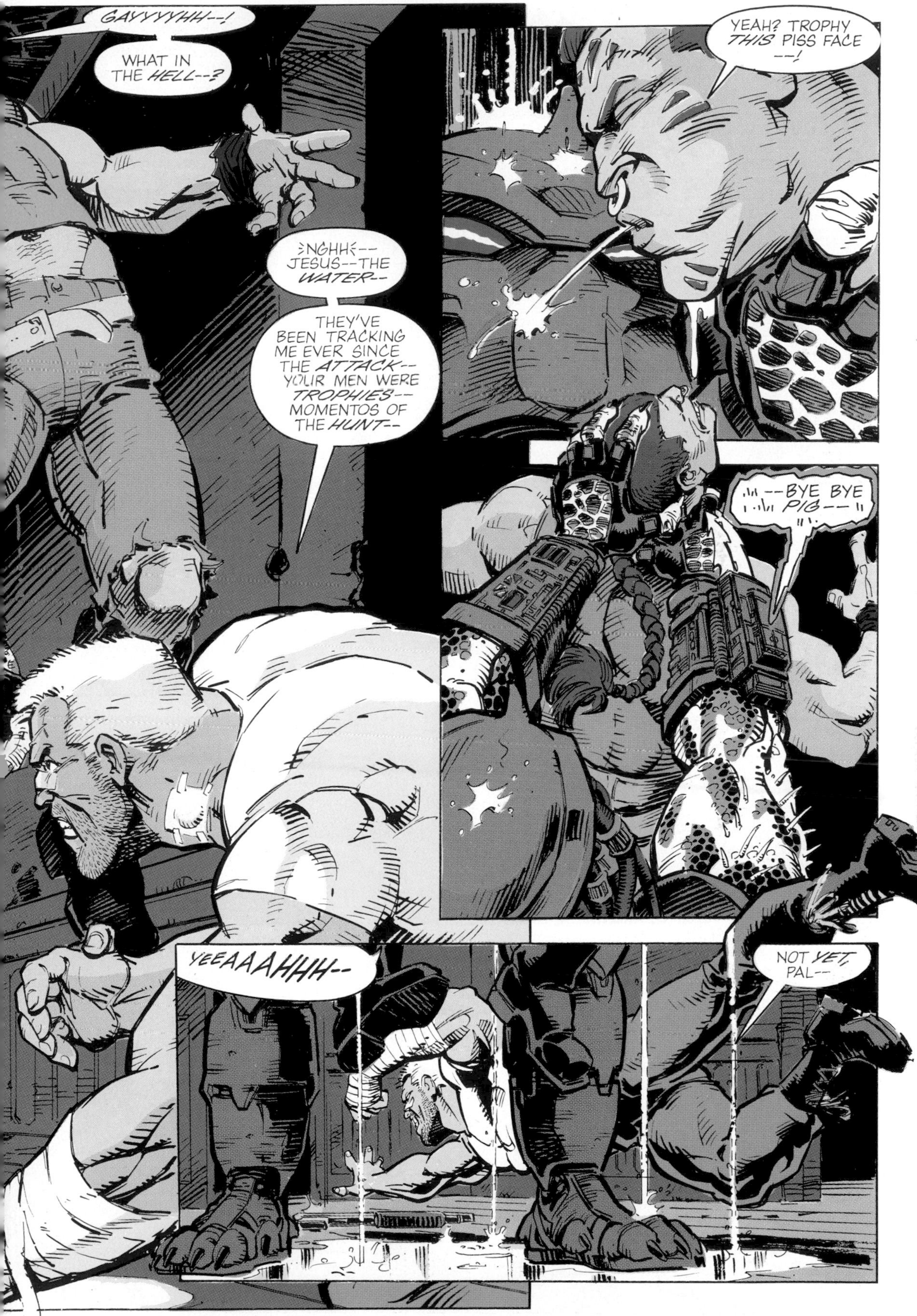
GAYYYYHH--!
WHAT IN THE HELL--?
YEAH? TROPHY THIS PISS FACE --!
NGHH-- JESUS--THE WATER--
THEY'VE BEEN TRACKING ME EVER SINCE THE ATTACK-- YOUR MEN WERE TROPHIES-- MOMENTOS OF THE HUNT--
--BYE BYE PIG--
YEEAAAAHHH--
NOT YET, PAL--

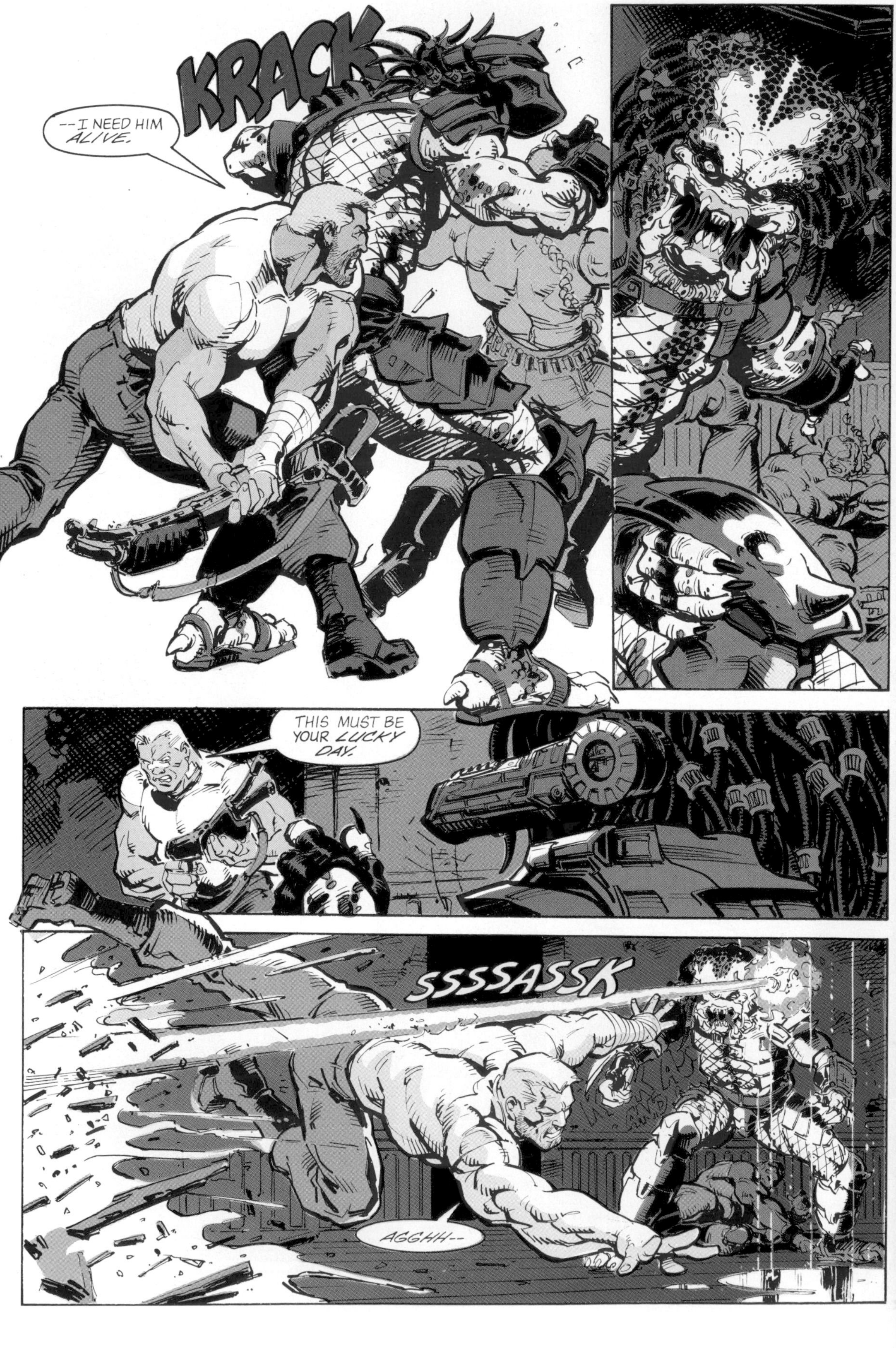

KRACK
--I NEED HIM ALIVE.
THIS MUST BE YOUR LUCKY DAY.
SSSSASSK
AGGHH--

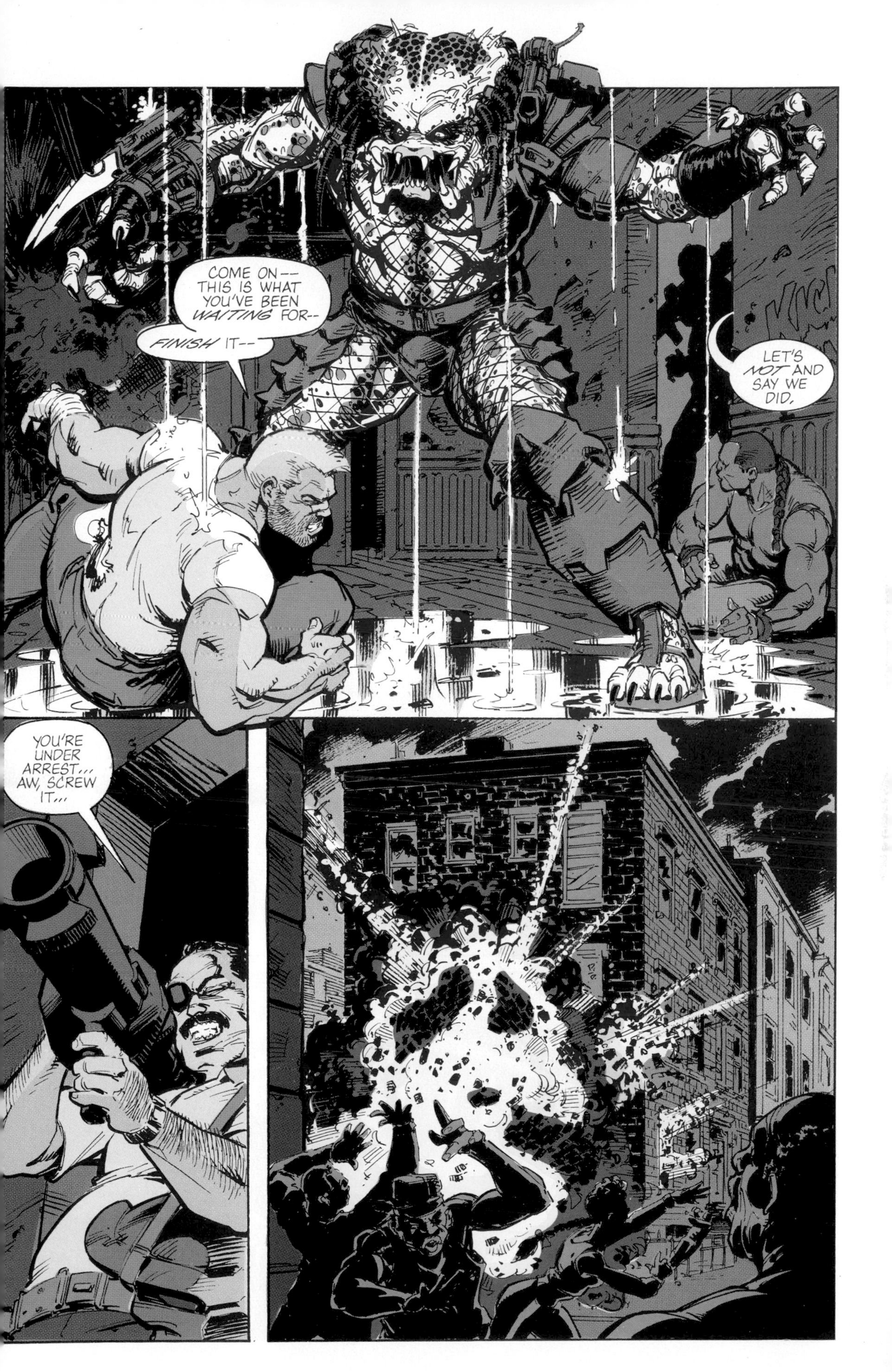
COME ON-- THIS IS WHAT YOU'VE BEEN WAITING FOR--
FINISH IT--
LET'S NOT AND SAY WE DID.
YOU'RE UNDER ARREST... AW, SCREW IT...

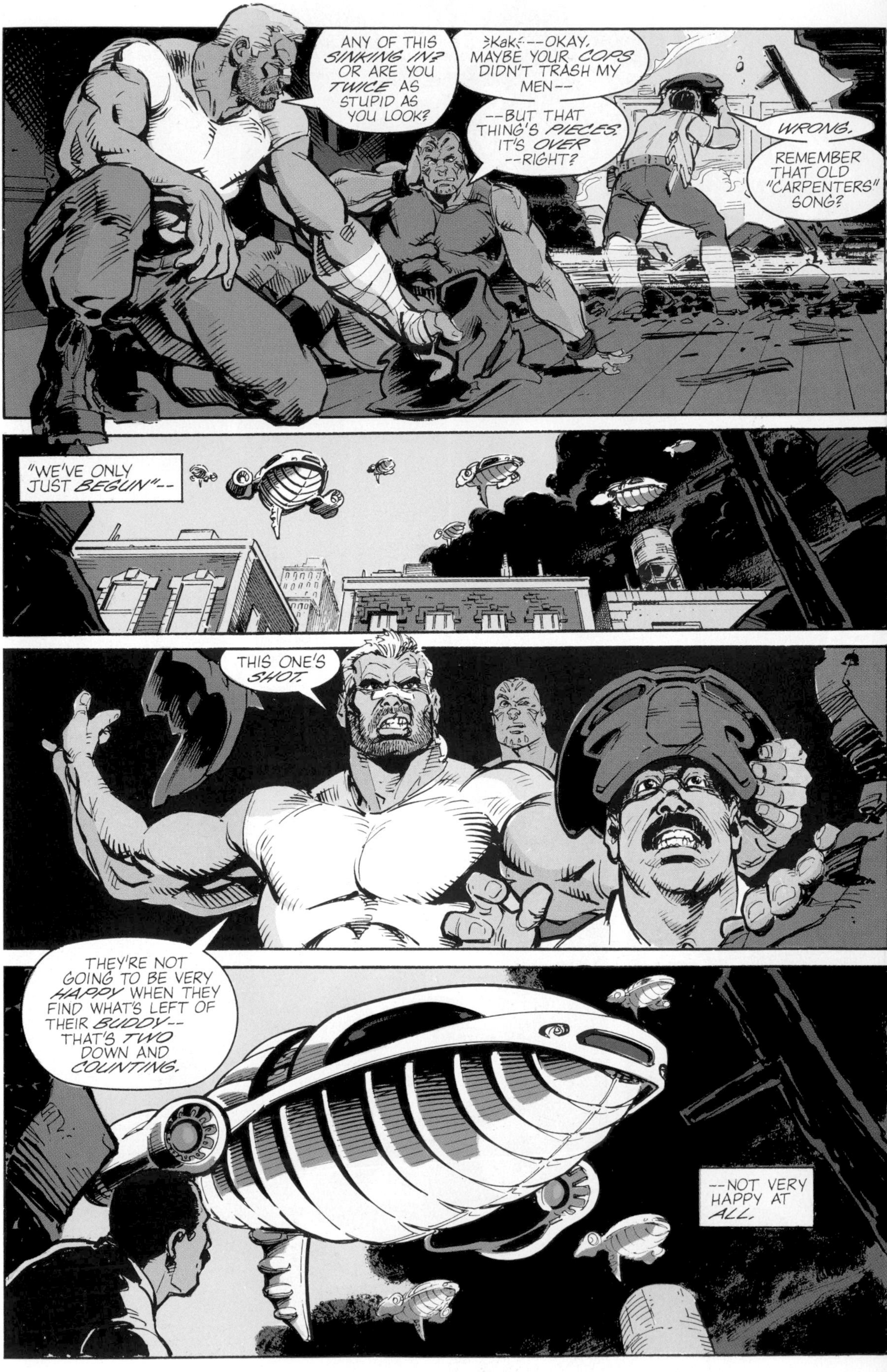

ANY OF THIS SINKING IN? OR ARE YOU TWICE AS STUPID AS YOU LOOK?
Kak--OKAY, MAYBE YOUR COPS DIDN'T TRASH MY MEN--
--BUT THAT THING'S PIECES. IT'S OVER --RIGHT?
WRONG.
REMEMBER THAT OLD "CARPENTERS" SONG?
"WE'VE ONLY JUST BEGUN"--
THIS ONE'S SHOT.
THEY'RE NOT GOING TO BE VERY HAPPY WHEN THEY FIND WHAT'S LEFT OF THEIR BUDDY-- THAT'S TWO DOWN AND COUNTING.
--NOT VERY HAPPY AT ALL.

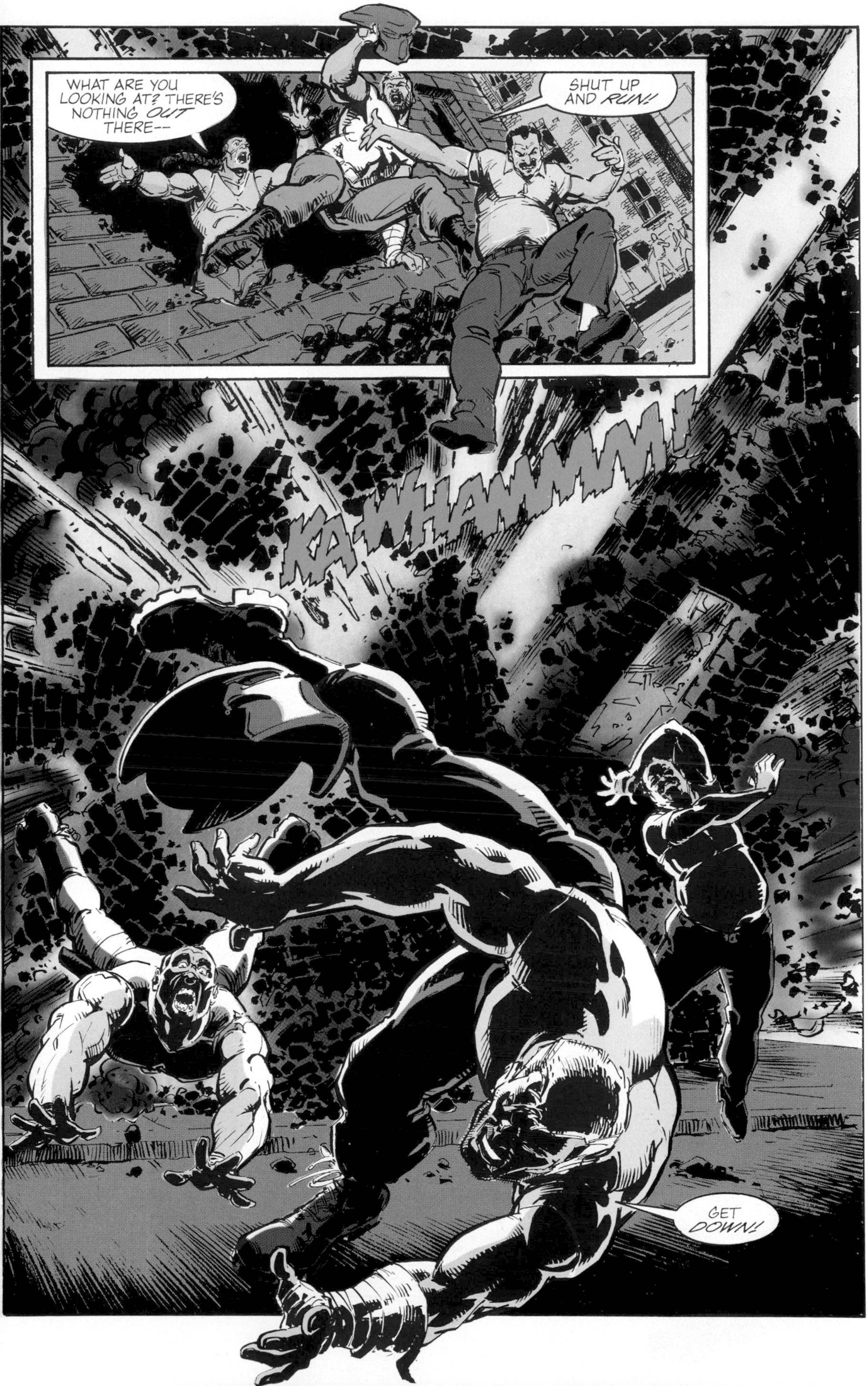
WHAT ARE YOU LOOKING AT? THERE'S NOTHING OUT THERE--
SHUT UP AND RUN!
KA-WHAMMMM!
GET DOWN!

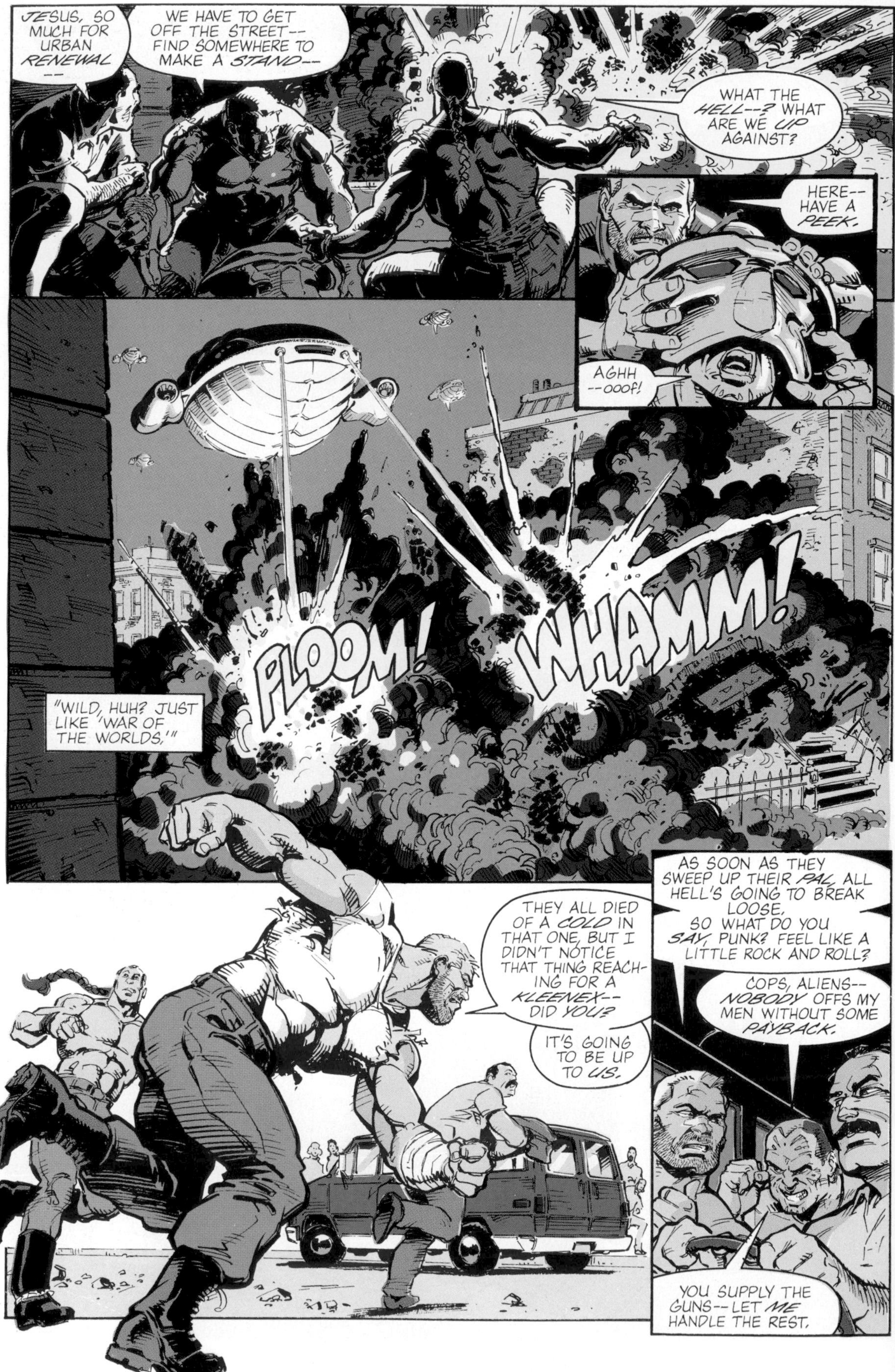

JESUS, SO MUCH FOR URBAN RENEWAL --
WE HAVE TO GET OFF THE STREET-- FIND SOMEWHERE TO MAKE A STAND--
WHAT THE HELL--? WHAT ARE WE UP AGAINST?
HERE-- HAVE A PEEK.
AGHH --ooof!
PLOOM!
WHAMM!
"WILD, HUH? JUST LIKE 'WAR OF THE WORLDS,'"
THEY ALL DIED OF A COLD IN THAT ONE, BUT I DIDN'T NOTICE THAT THING REACHING FOR A KLEENEX-- DID YOU?
IT'S GOING TO BE UP TO US.
AS SOON AS THEY SWEEP UP THEIR PAL, ALL HELL'S GOING TO BREAK LOOSE. SO WHAT DO YOU SAY, PUNK? FEEL LIKE A LITTLE ROCK AND ROLL?
COPS, ALIENS-- NOBODY OFFS MY MEN WITHOUT SOME PAYBACK.
YOU SUPPLY THE GUNS-- LET ME HANDLE THE REST.

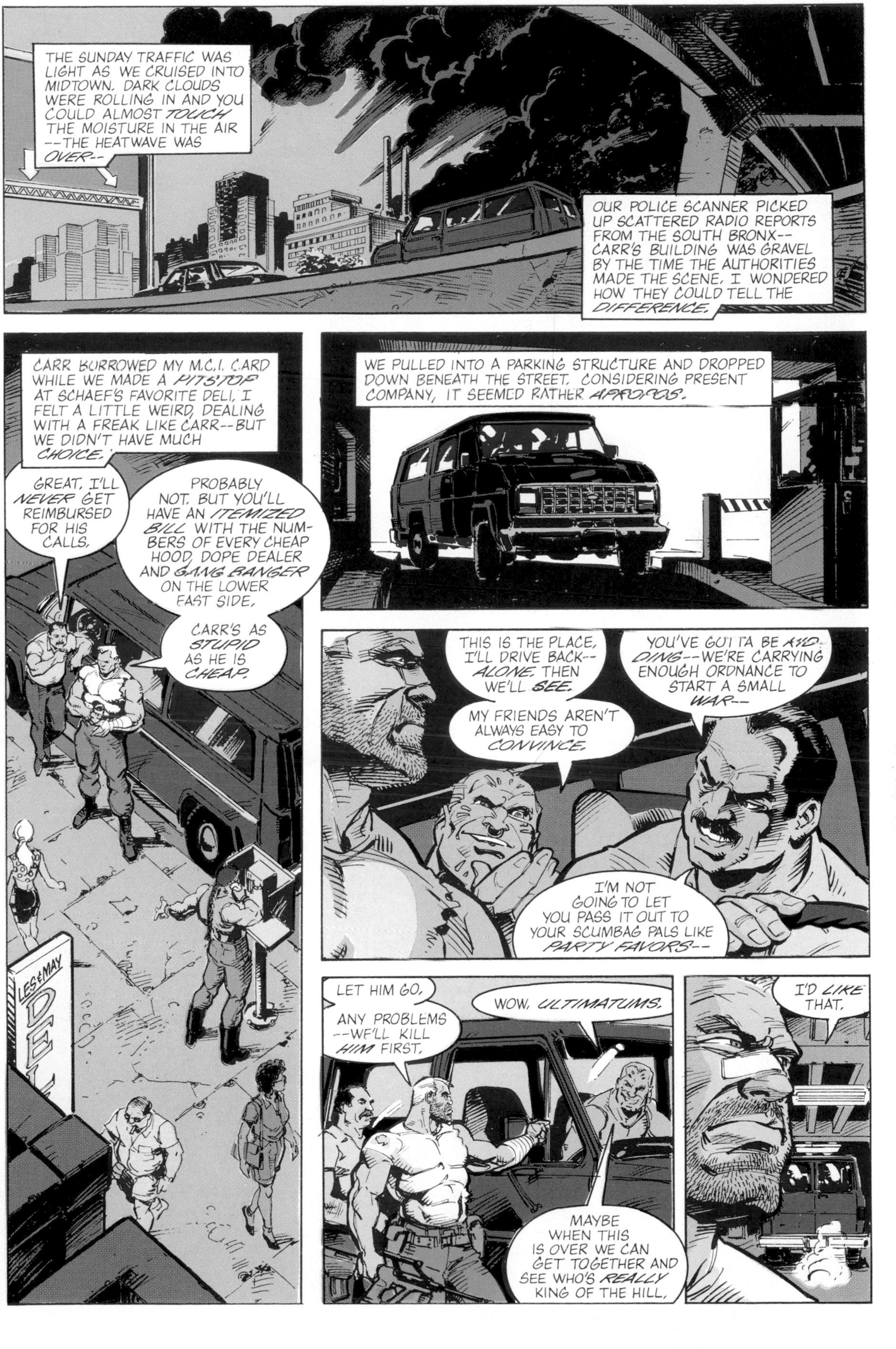
THE SUNDAY TRAFFIC WAS LIGHT AS WE CRUISED INTO MIDTOWN. DARK CLOUDS WERE ROLLING IN AND YOU COULD ALMOST TOUCH THE MOISTURE IN THE AIR --THE HEATWAVE WAS OVER--
OUR POLICE SCANNER PICKED UP SCATTERED RADIO REPORTS FROM THE SOUTH BRONX-- CARR'S BUILDING WAS GRAVEL BY THE TIME THE AUTHORITIES MADE THE SCENE. I WONDERED HOW THEY COULD TELL THE DIFFERENCE.
CARR BORROWED MY M.C.I. CARD WHILE WE MADE A PITSTOP AT SCHAEF'S FAVORITE DELI. I FELT A LITTLE WEIRD, DEALING WITH A FREAK LIKE CARR--BUT WE DIDN'T HAVE MUCH CHOICE.
GREAT. I'LL NEVER GET REIMBURSED FOR HIS CALLS.
PROBABLY NOT. BUT YOU'LL HAVE AN ITEMIZED BILL WITH THE NUMBERS OF EVERY CHEAP HOOD, DOPE DEALER AND GANG BANGER ON THE LOWER EAST SIDE.
CARR'S AS STUPID AS HE IS CHEAP.
LES & MAY
DELI
WE PULLED INTO A PARKING STRUCTURE AND DROPPED DOWN BENEATH THE STREET. CONSIDERING PRESENT COMPANY, IT SEEMED RATHER APROPOS.
THIS IS THE PLACE. I'LL DRIVE BACK-- ALONE. THEN WE'LL SEE.
MY FRIENDS AREN'T ALWAYS EASY TO CONVINCE.
YOU'VE GOTTA BE KID-DING--WE'RE CARRYING ENOUGH ORDNANCE TO START A SMALL WAR--
I'M NOT GOING TO LET YOU PASS IT OUT TO YOUR SCUMBAG PALS LIKE PARTY FAVORS--
LET HIM GO.
ANY PROBLEMS --WE'LL KILL HIM FIRST.
WOW, ULTIMATUMS.
MAYBE WHEN THIS IS OVER WE CAN GET TOGETHER AND SEE WHO'S REALLY KING OF THE HILL.
I'D LIKE THAT.

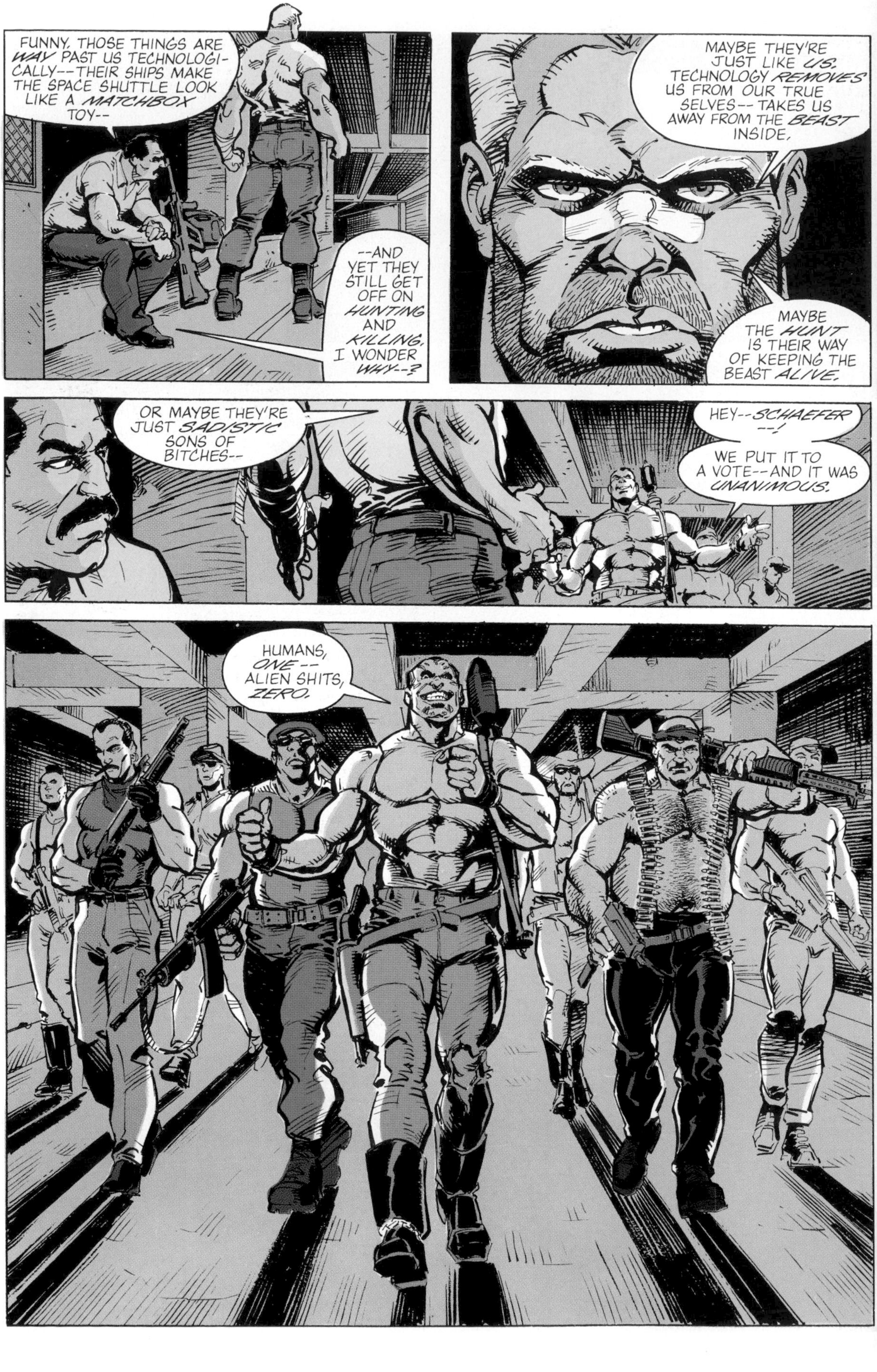
FUNNY, THOSE THINGS ARE WAY PAST US TECHNOLOGICALLY--THEIR SHIPS MAKE THE SPACE SHUTTLE LOOK LIKE A MATCHBOX TOY--
--AND YET THEY STILL GET OFF ON HUNTING AND KILLING. I WONDER WHY--?
MAYBE THEY'RE JUST LIKE US. TECHNOLOGY REMOVES US FROM OUR TRUE SELVES-- TAKES US AWAY FROM THE BEAST INSIDE.
MAYBE THE HUNT IS THEIR WAY OF KEEPING THE BEAST ALIVE.
OR MAYBE THEY'RE JUST SADISTIC SONS OF BITCHES--
HEY--SCHAEFER--!
WE PUT IT TO A VOTE--AND IT WAS UNANIMOUS.
HUMANS, ONE-- ALIEN SHITS, ZERO.

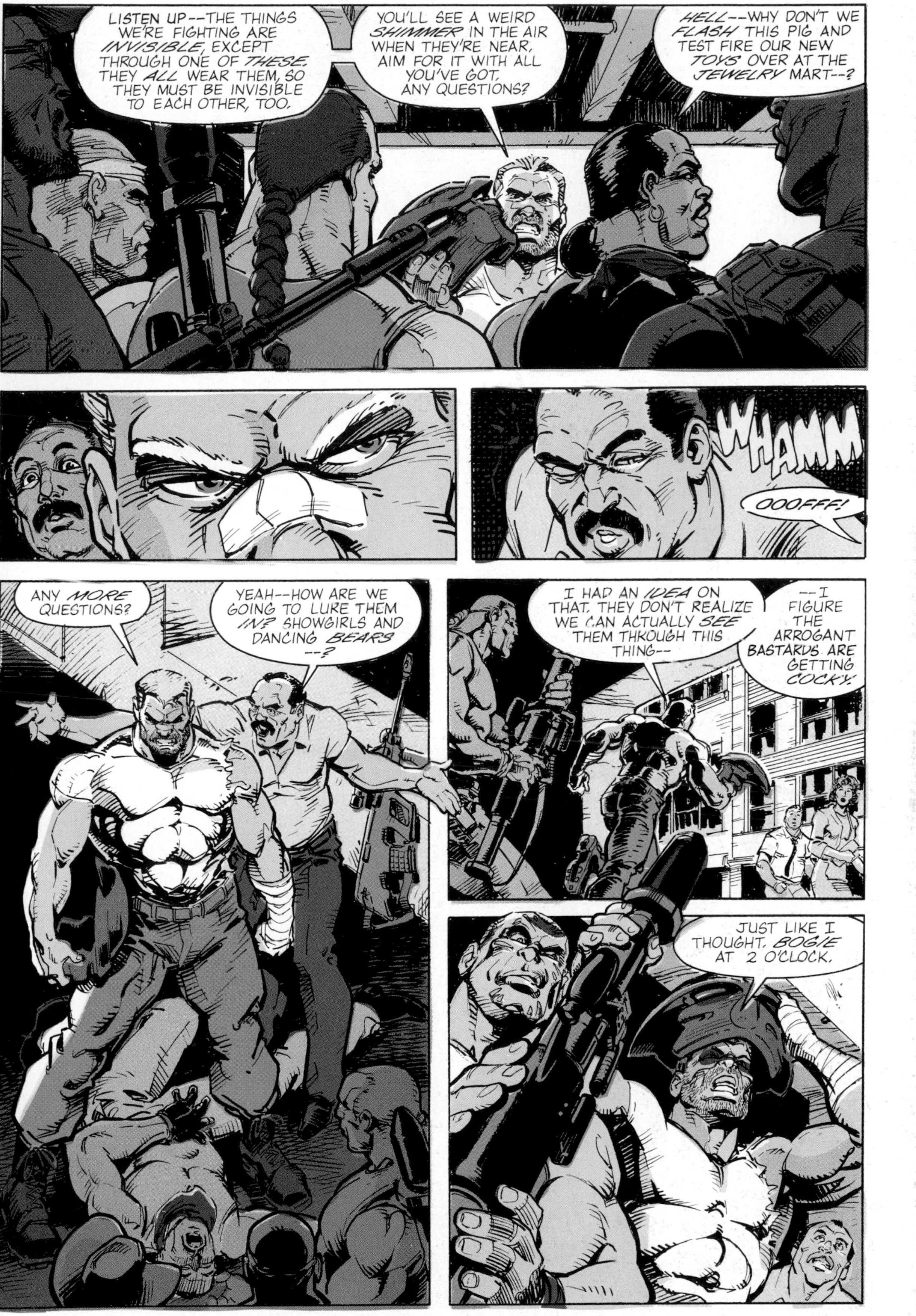
LISTEN UP--THE THINGS WE'RE FIGHTING ARE INVISIBLE, EXCEPT THROUGH ONE OF THESE. THEY ALL WEAR THEM, SO THEY MUST BE INVISIBLE TO EACH OTHER, TOO.
YOU'LL SEE A WEIRD SHIMMER IN THE AIR WHEN THEY'RE NEAR. AIM FOR IT WITH ALL YOU'VE GOT. ANY QUESTIONS?
HELL--WHY DON'T WE FLASH THIS PIG AND TEST FIRE OUR NEW TOYS OVER AT THE JEWELRY MART--?
WHAMM
OOOFFF!
ANY MORE QUESTIONS?
YEAH--HOW ARE WE GOING TO LURE THEM IN? SHOWGIRLS AND DANCING BEARS--?
I HAD AN IDEA ON THAT. THEY DON'T REALIZE WE CAN ACTUALLY SEE THEM THROUGH THIS THING--
--I FIGURE THE ARROGANT BASTARDS ARE GETTING COCKY.
JUST LIKE I THOUGHT. BOGIE AT 2 O'CLOCK.

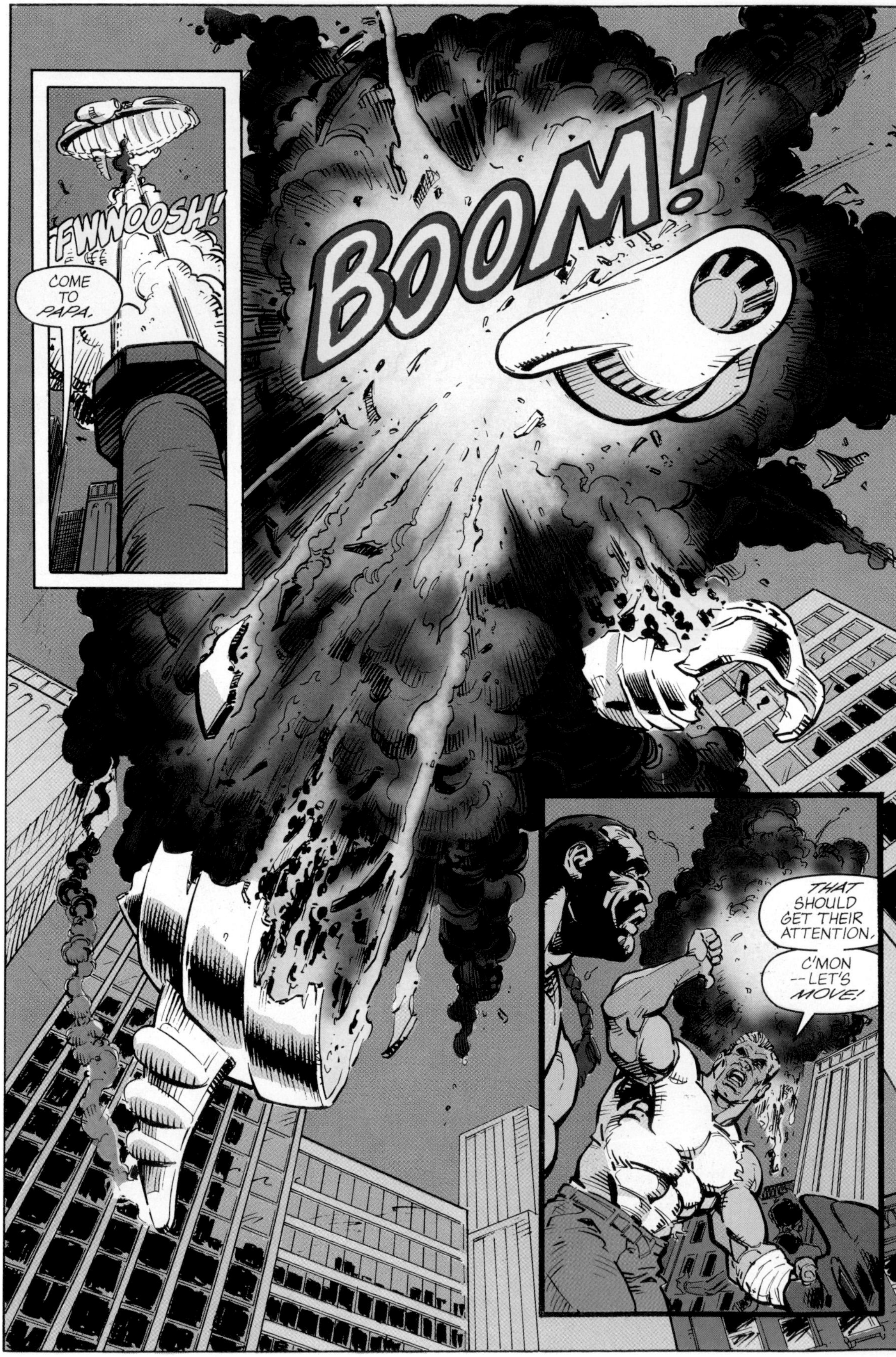
FWWOOSH!
COME TO PAPA.
BOOM!
THAT SHOULD GET THEIR ATTENTION.
C'MON --LET'S MOVE!

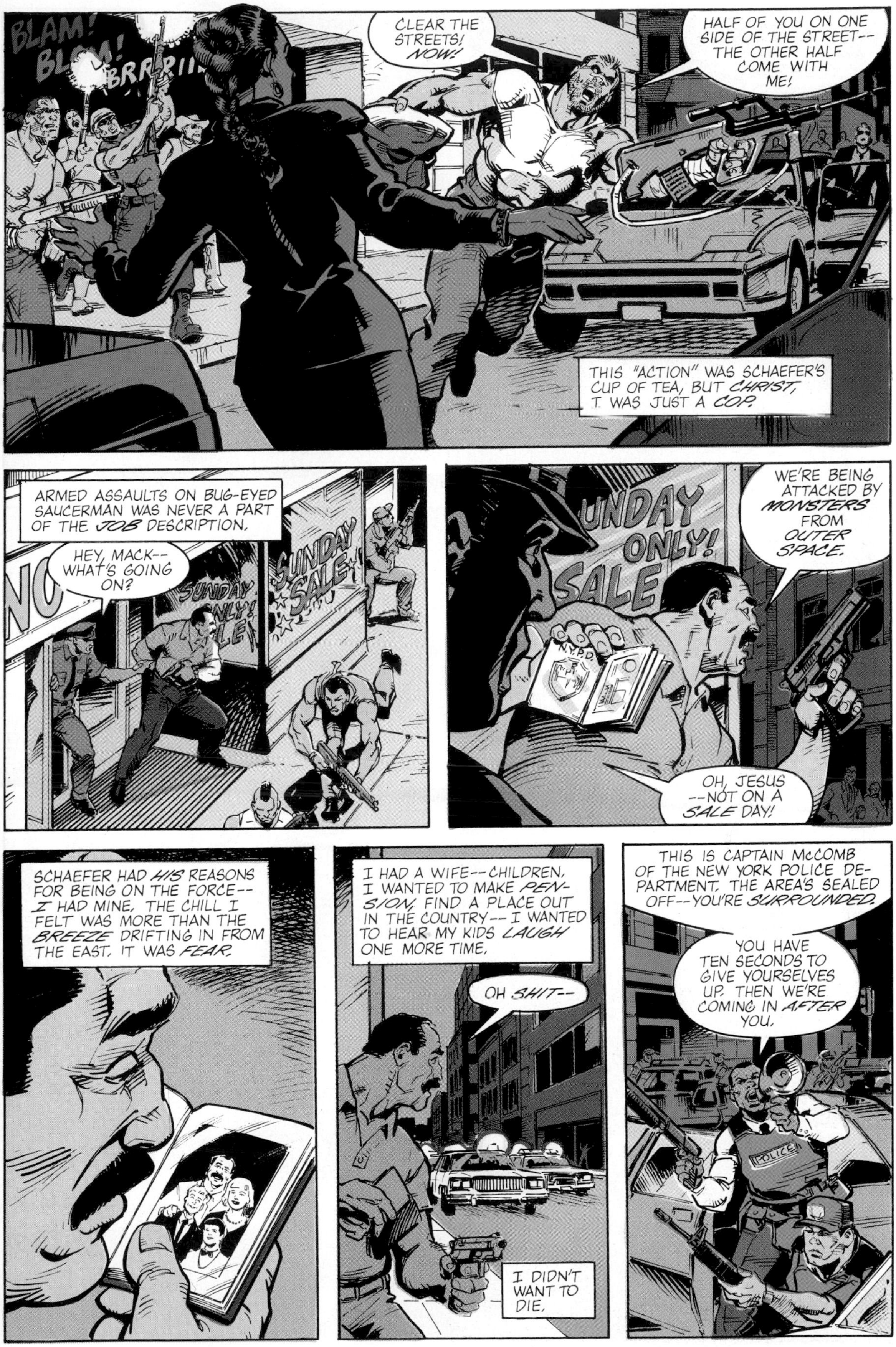
BLAM! BLAM! BRRRIIII
CLEAR THE STREETS! NOW!
HALF OF YOU ON ONE SIDE OF THE STREET-- THE OTHER HALF COME WITH ME!
THIS "ACTION" WAS SCHAEFER'S CUP OF TEA, BUT CHRIST, T. WAS JUST A COP.
ARMED ASSAULTS ON BUG-EYED SAUCERMAN WAS NEVER A PART OF THE JOB DESCRIPTION.
HEY, MACK-- WHAT'S GOING ON?
SUNDAY SALE
WE'RE BEING ATTACKED BY MONSTERS FROM OUTER SPACE.
OH, JESUS --NOT ON A SALE DAY!
SUNDAY ONLY! SALE
N.Y.P.D.
SCHAEFER HAD HIS REASONS FOR BEING ON THE FORCE-- I HAD MINE. THE CHILL I FELT WAS MORE THAN THE BREEZE DRIFTING IN FROM THE EAST. IT WAS FEAR.
I HAD A WIFE--CHILDREN. I WANTED TO MAKE PENSION, FIND A PLACE OUT IN THE COUNTRY--I WANTED TO HEAR MY KIDS LAUGH ONE MORE TIME.
OH SHIT--
I DIDN'T WANT TO DIE.
THIS IS CAPTAIN McCOMB OF THE NEW YORK POLICE DEPARTMENT. THE AREA'S SEALED OFF--YOU'RE SURROUNDED.
YOU HAVE TEN SECONDS TO GIVE YOURSELVES UP. THEN WE'RE COMING IN AFTER YOU.
POLICE

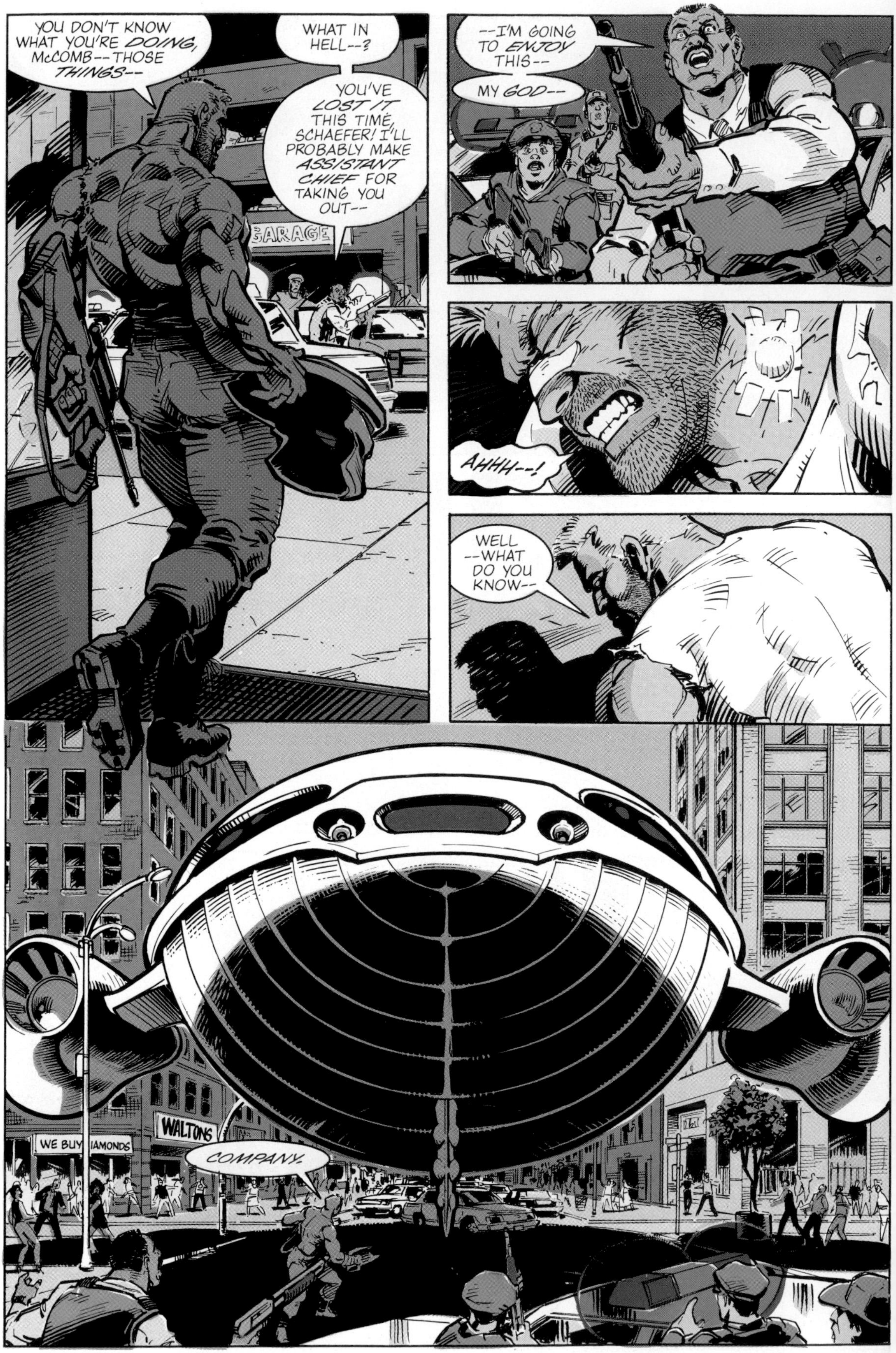
YOU DON'T KNOW WHAT YOU'RE DOING, McCOMB--THOSE THINGS--
WHAT IN HELL--?
YOU'VE LOST IT THIS TIME, SCHAEFER! I'LL PROBABLY MAKE ASSISTANT CHIEF FOR TAKING YOU OUT--
GARAGE
--I'M GOING TO ENJOY THIS--
MY GOD--
AHHH--!
WELL --WHAT DO YOU KNOW--
WALTONS
WE BUY DIAMONDS
COMPANY.

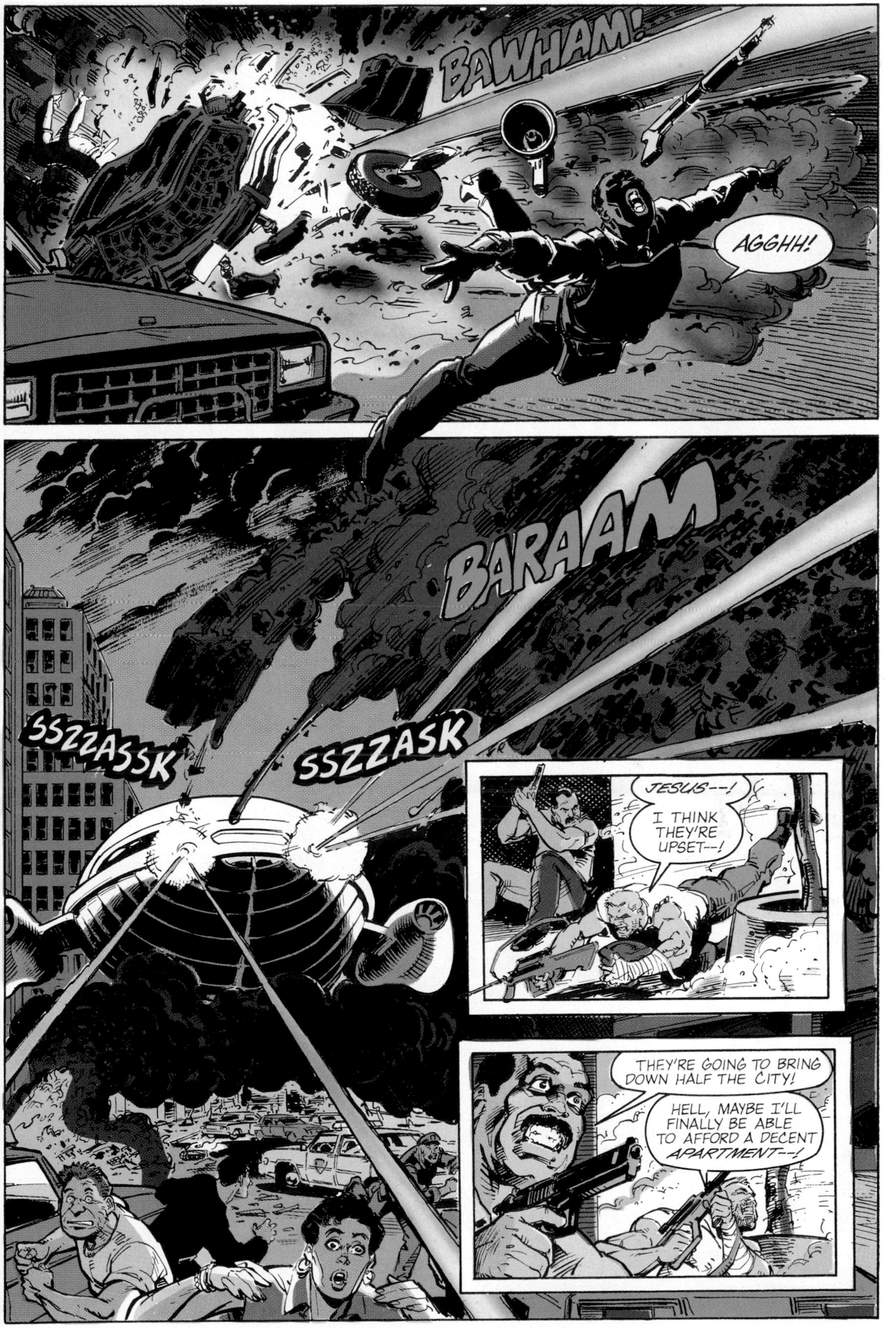
BAWHAM!
AGGHH!
BARAAM
SSZZASSK
SSZZASK
JESUS--!
I THINK THEY'RE UPSET--!
THEY'RE GOING TO BRING DOWN HALF THE CITY!
HELL, MAYBE I'LL FINALLY BE ABLE TO AFFORD A DECENT *APARTMENT*--!

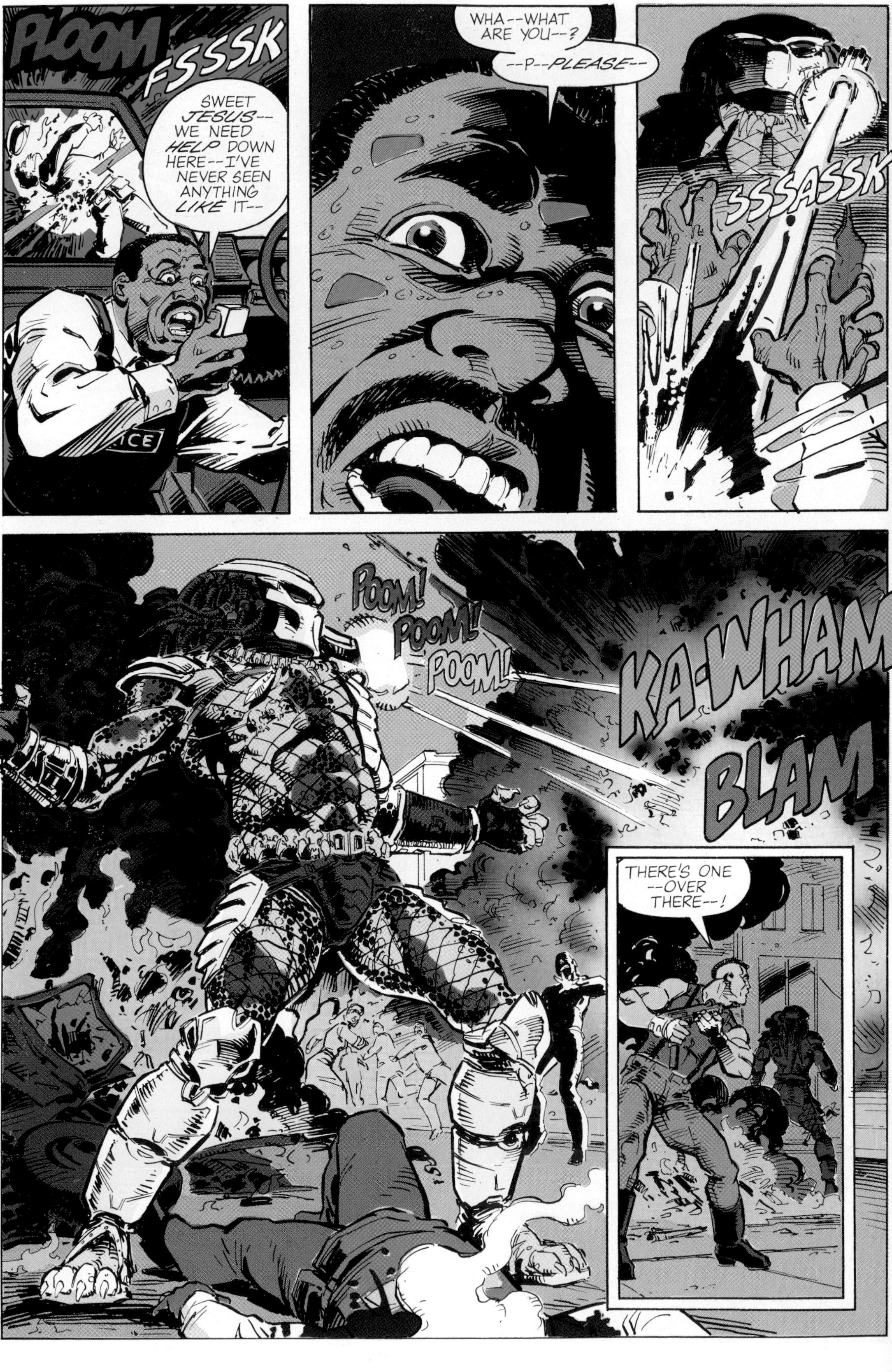
PLOOM
FSSSSK
SWEET JESUS-- WE NEED HELP DOWN HERE--I'VE NEVER SEEN ANYTHING LIKE IT--
WHA--WHAT ARE YOU--?
--P--PLEASE--
SSSASSK
POOM!
POOM!
POOM!
KA-WHAM
BLAM
THERE'S ONE --OVER THERE--!

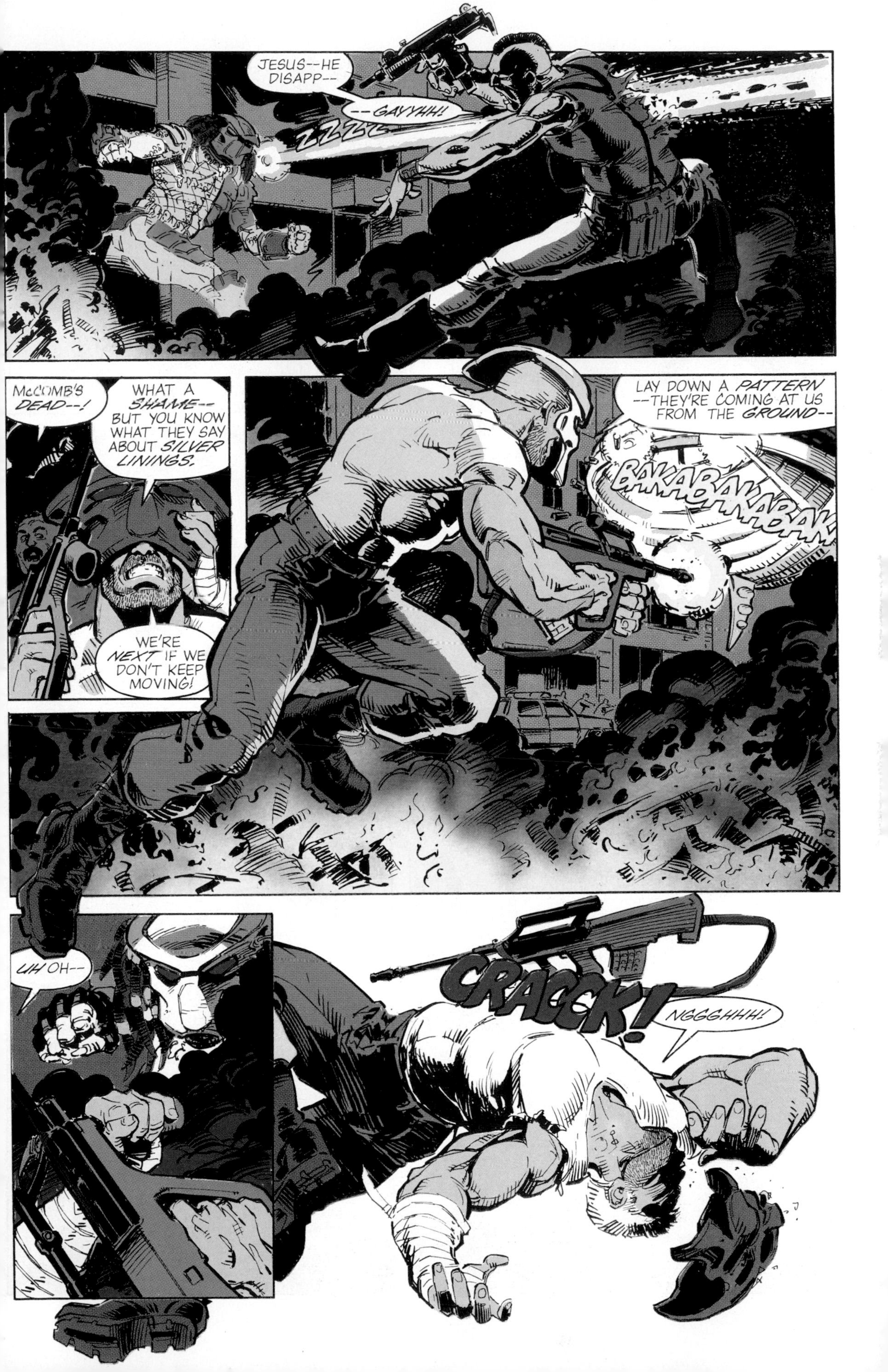
JESUS--HE DISAPP--
--GAYYHH!
ZZZZ
McCOMB'S DEAD--!
WHAT A SHAME-- BUT YOU KNOW WHAT THEY SAY ABOUT SILVER LININGS.
WE'RE NEXT IF WE DON'T KEEP MOVING!
LAY DOWN A PATTERN --THEY'RE COMING AT US FROM THE GROUND--
BAKABAKABAKABAK
UH OH--
CRACCK!
NGGGHHH!

SSSASSKKK!

THEY'RE ALL *OVER* US!

HELMET'S *GONE*--WE'RE *BLIND* AND THEY *KNOW* IT!

HELL--THEY'RE *ENJOYING* THIS--

BLAM

AGHHH--!

KSSSH

RASCHE--!

THE SHIT'S IN THE FAN *NOW,* BOY.

YOU HAD TO DO THIS THE *HARD* WAY.

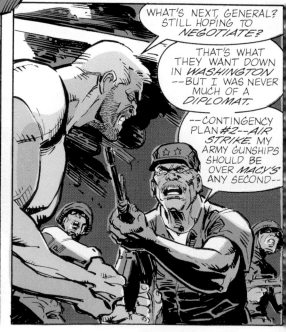

WHAT'S NEXT, GENERAL? STILL HOPING TO *NEGOTIATE?*

THAT'S WHAT THEY WANT DOWN IN *WASHINGTON*--BUT I WAS NEVER MUCH OF A *DIPLOMAT.*

--CONTINGENCY PLAN *#2--AIR STRIKE.* MY ARMY GUNSHIPS SHOULD BE OVER *MACY'S* ANY SECOND--

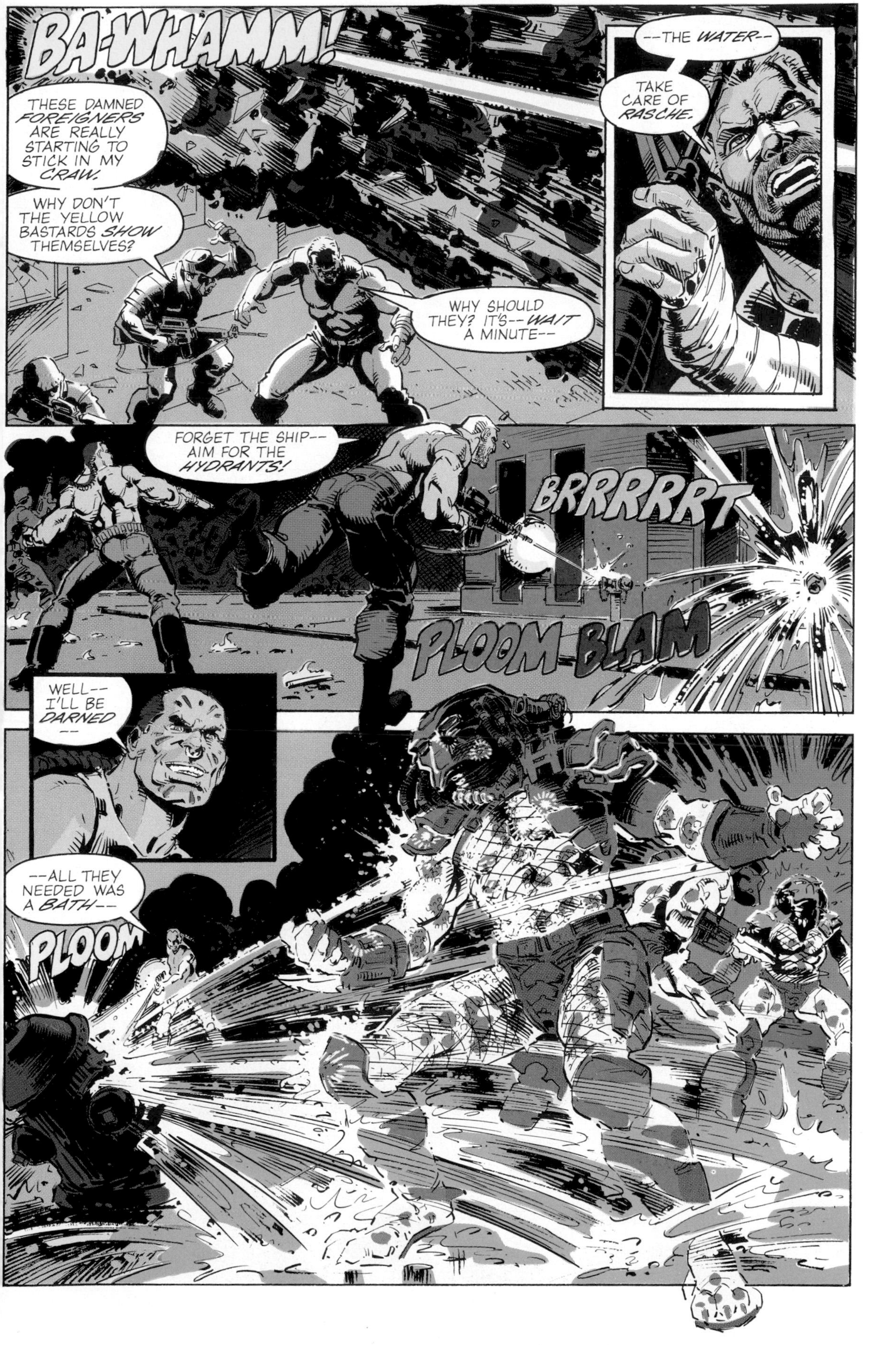
BA-WHAMM!
THESE DAMNED FOREIGNERS ARE REALLY STARTING TO STICK IN MY CRAW.
WHY DON'T THE YELLOW BASTARDS SHOW THEMSELVES?
WHY SHOULD THEY? IT'S--WAIT A MINUTE--
--THE WATER--
TAKE CARE OF RASCHE.
FORGET THE SHIP--AIM FOR THE HYDRANTS!
BRRRRRT
PLOOM BLAM
WELL--I'LL BE DARNED--
--ALL THEY NEEDED WAS A BATH--
PLOOM

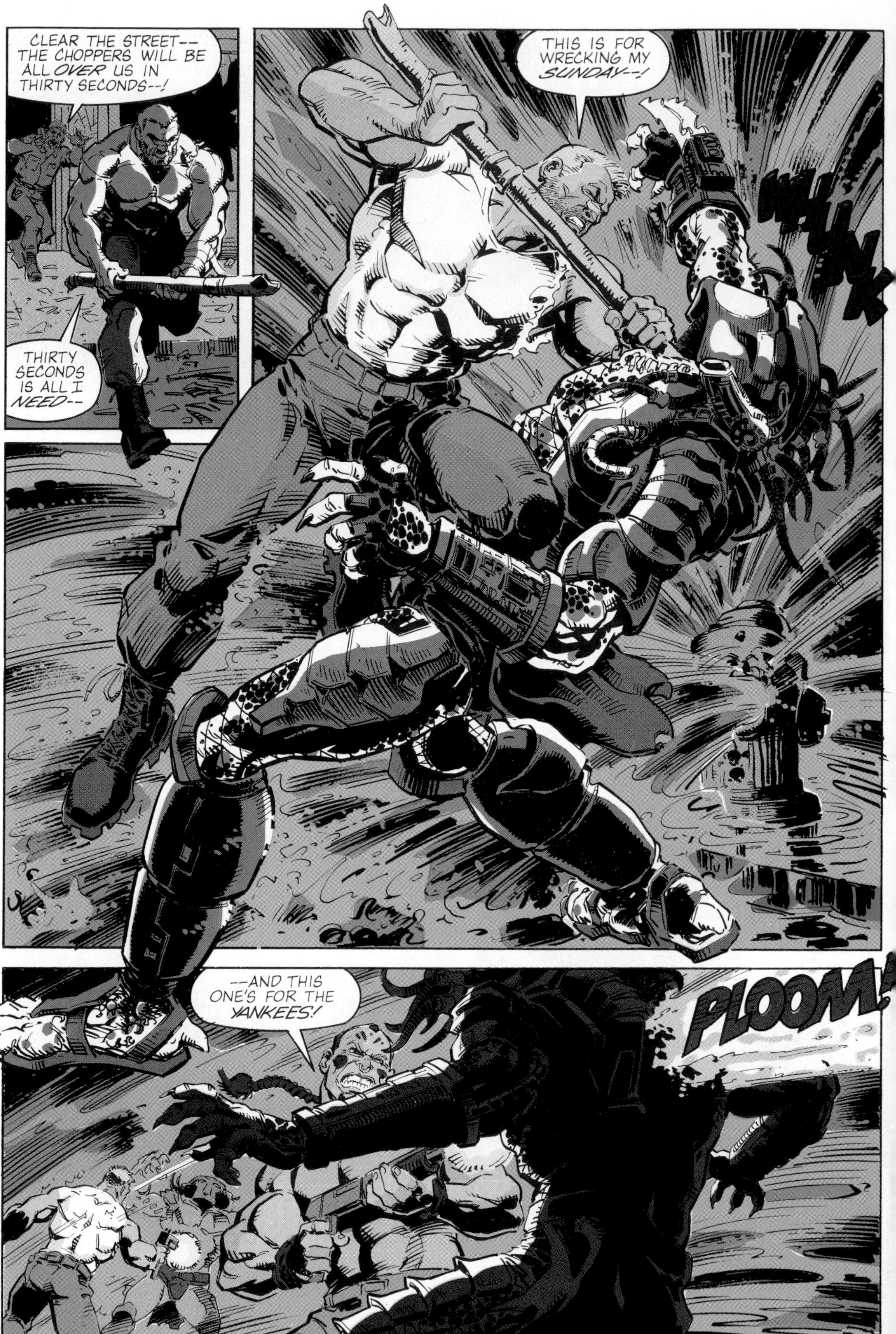

CLEAR THE STREET-- THE CHOPPERS WILL BE ALL OVER US IN THIRTY SECONDS--!
THIRTY SECONDS IS ALL I NEED--
THIS IS FOR WRECKING MY SUNDAY--!
--AND THIS ONE'S FOR THE YANKEES!
PLOOM!

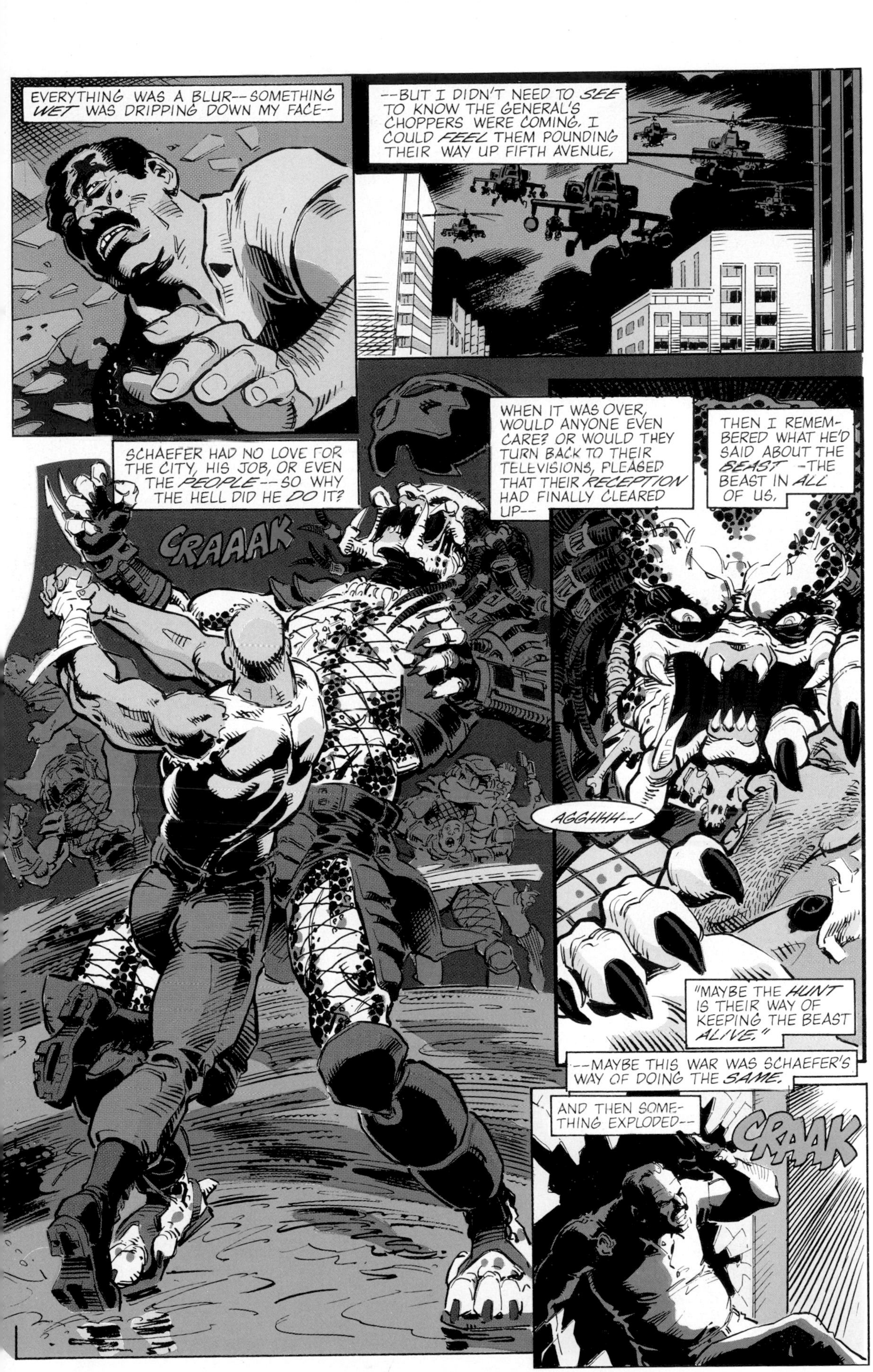
EVERYTHING WAS A BLUR--SOMETHING WET WAS DRIPPING DOWN MY FACE--
--BUT I DIDN'T NEED TO SEE TO KNOW THE GENERAL'S CHOPPERS WERE COMING. I COULD FEEL THEM POUNDING THEIR WAY UP FIFTH AVENUE.
SCHAEFER HAD NO LOVE FOR THE CITY, HIS JOB, OR EVEN THE PEOPLE--SO WHY THE HELL DID HE DO IT?
CRAAAK
WHEN IT WAS OVER, WOULD ANYONE EVEN CARE? OR WOULD THEY TURN BACK TO THEIR TELEVISIONS, PLEASED THAT THEIR RECEPTION HAD FINALLY CLEARED UP--
THEN I REMEMBERED WHAT HE'D SAID ABOUT THE BEAST -THE BEAST IN ALL OF US.
AGGHHH--!
"MAYBE THE HUNT IS THEIR WAY OF KEEPING THE BEAST ALIVE."
--MAYBE THIS WAR WAS SCHAEFER'S WAY OF DOING THE SAME.
AND THEN SOMETHING EXPLODED--
CRAAK

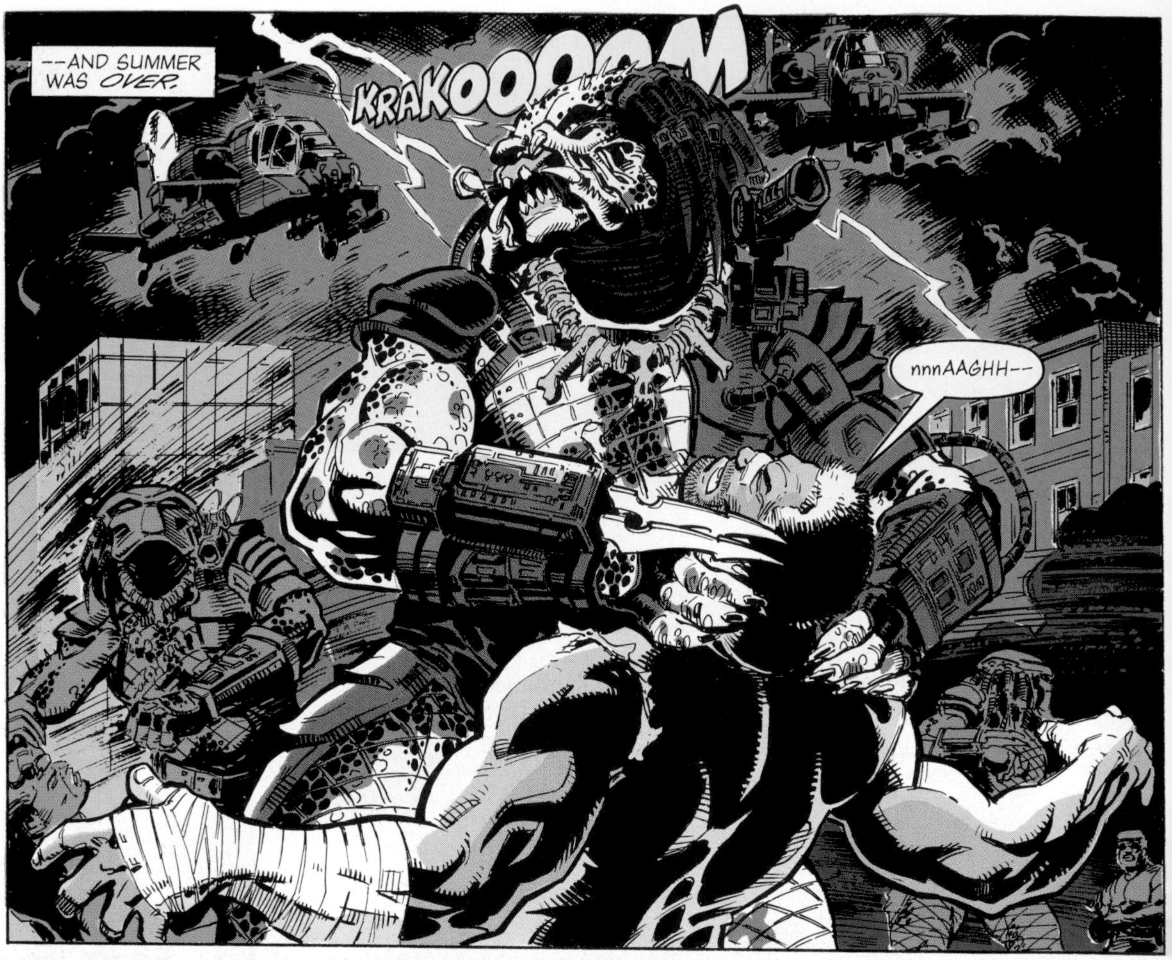
--AND SUMMER WAS OVER.
KRAKOOOOOM
nnnAAGHH--

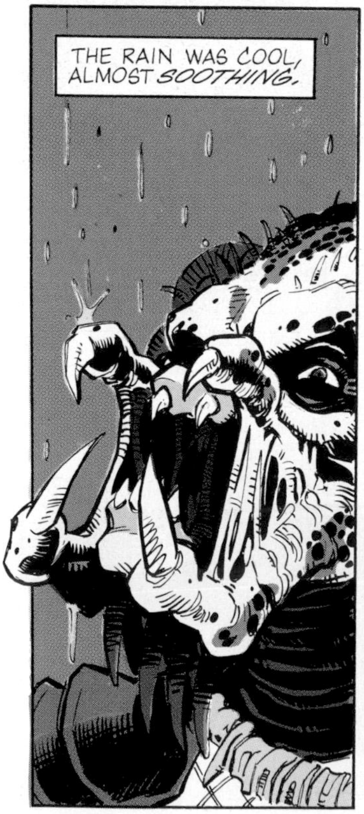
THE RAIN WAS COOL, ALMOST SOOTHING.

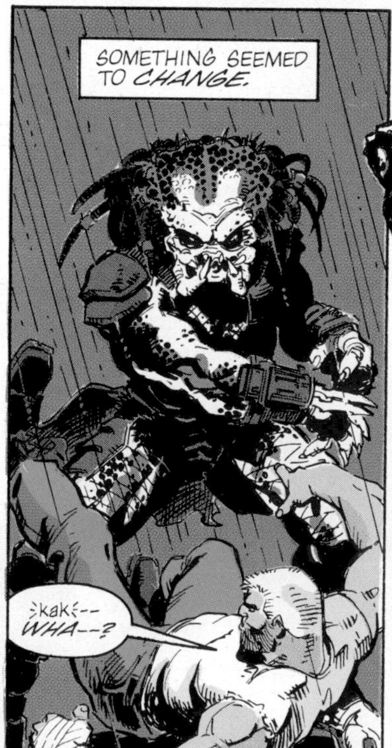
SOMETHING SEEMED TO CHANGE.
kak--
WHA--?

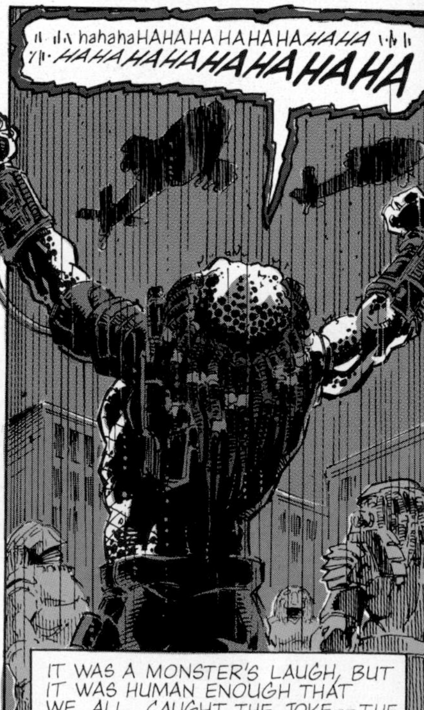
hahahaHAHAHA HAHAHAHAHA HAHAHAHAHAHAHAHAHA
IT WAS A MONSTER'S LAUGH, BUT IT WAS HUMAN ENOUGH THAT WE ALL CAUGHT THE JOKE--THE SHOWDOWN HAD TURNED INTO A FREE-FOR-ALL.

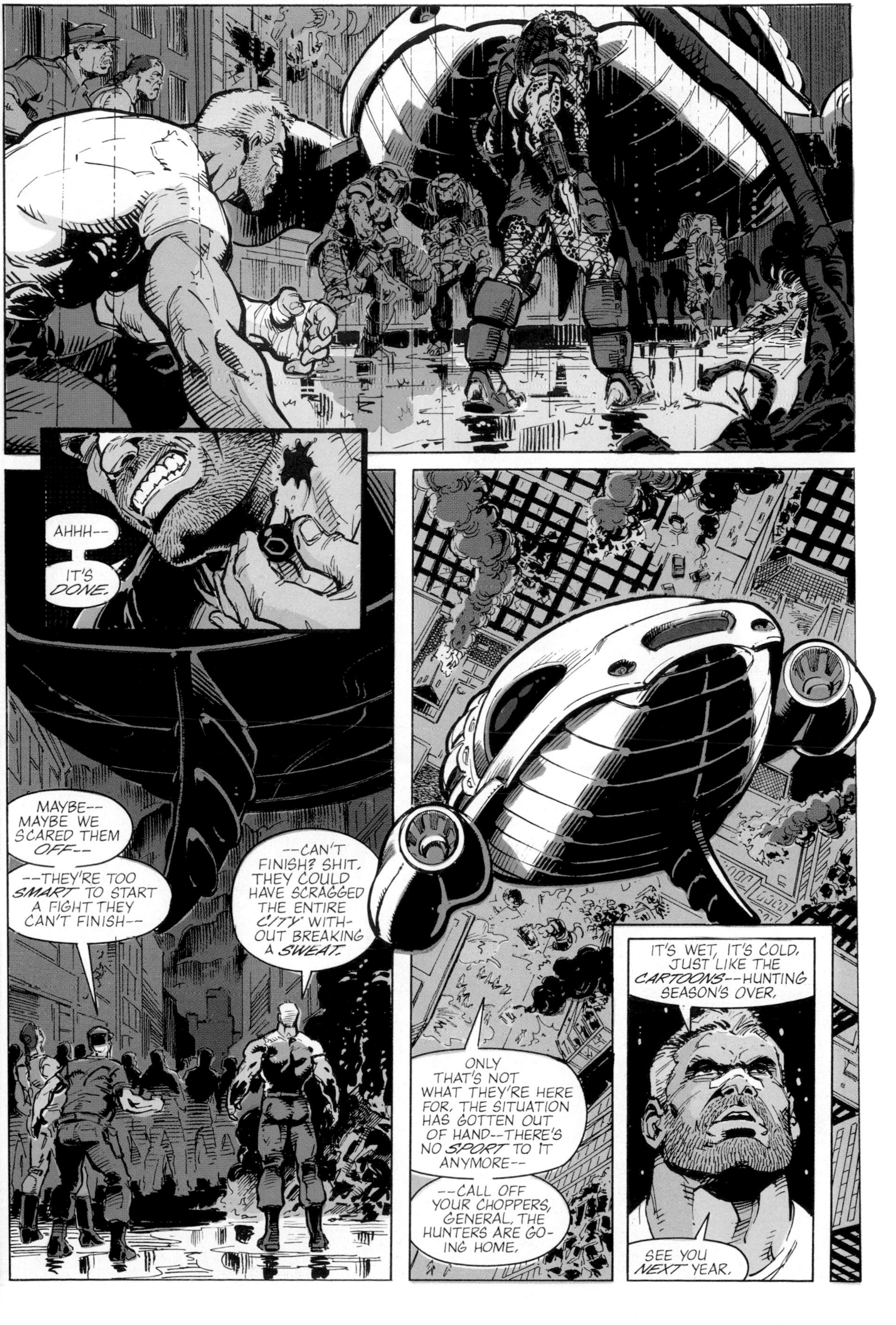
AHHH--
IT'S DONE.
MAYBE--MAYBE WE SCARED THEM OFF--
--THEY'RE TOO SMART TO START A FIGHT THEY CAN'T FINISH--
--CAN'T FINISH? SHIT. THEY COULD HAVE SCRAGGED THE ENTIRE CITY WITHOUT BREAKING A SWEAT.
ONLY THAT'S NOT WHAT THEY'RE HERE FOR. THE SITUATION HAS GOTTEN OUT OF HAND--THERE'S NO SPORT TO IT ANYMORE--
--CALL OFF YOUR CHOPPERS, GENERAL. THE HUNTERS ARE GOING HOME.
IT'S WET, IT'S COLD, JUST LIKE THE CARTOONS--HUNTING SEASON'S OVER.
SEE YOU NEXT YEAR.

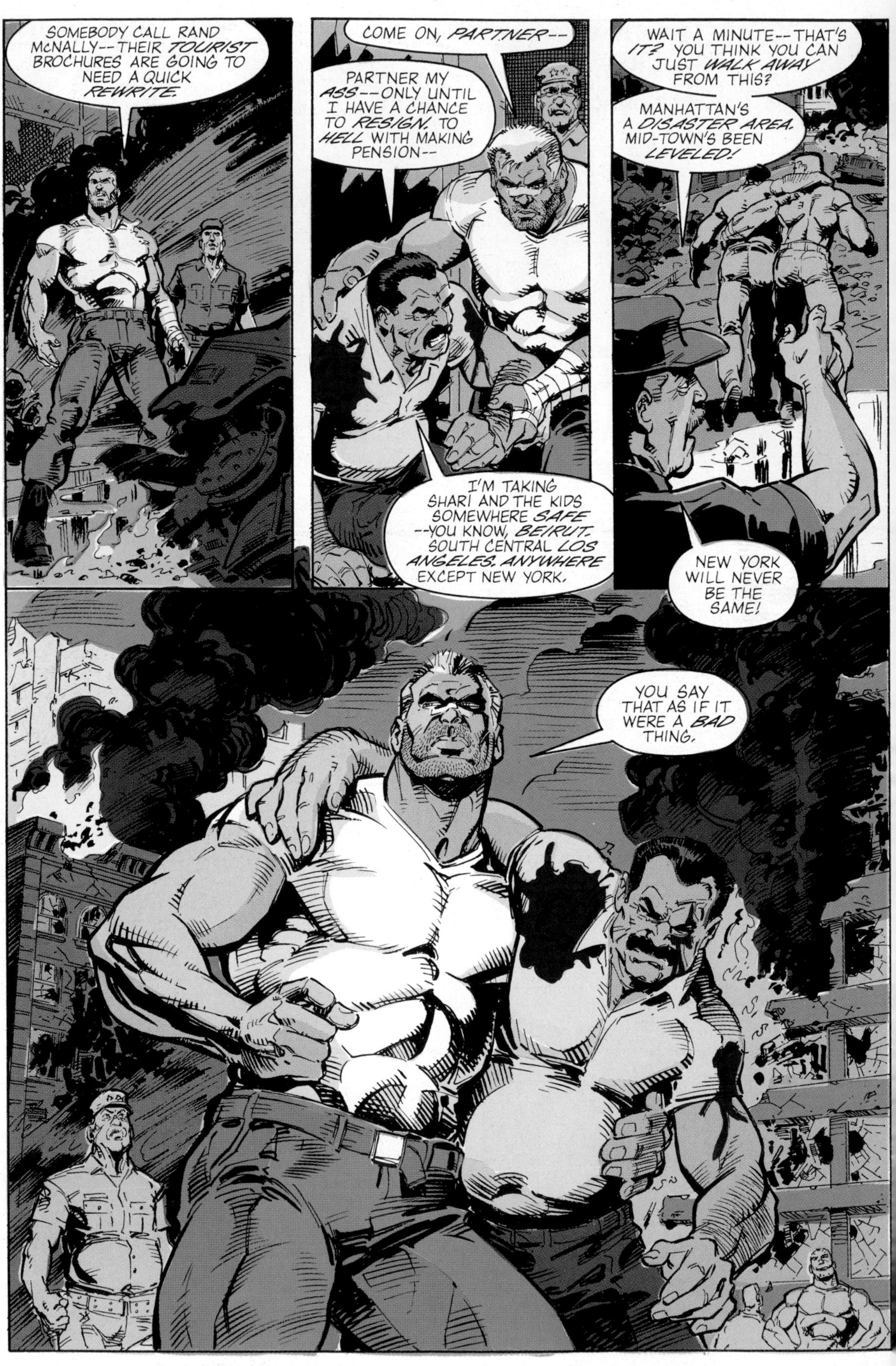
SOMEBODY CALL RAND McNALLY--THEIR TOURIST BROCHURES ARE GOING TO NEED A QUICK REWRITE.
COME ON, PARTNER--
PARTNER MY ASS--ONLY UNTIL I HAVE A CHANCE TO RESIGN. TO HELL WITH MAKING PENSION--
I'M TAKING SHARI AND THE KIDS SOMEWHERE SAFE --YOU KNOW, BEIRUT. SOUTH CENTRAL LOS ANGELES. ANYWHERE EXCEPT NEW YORK.
WAIT A MINUTE--THAT'S IT? YOU THINK YOU CAN JUST WALK AWAY FROM THIS?
MANHATTAN'S A DISASTER AREA. MID-TOWN'S BEEN LEVELED!
NEW YORK WILL NEVER BE THE SAME!
YOU SAY THAT AS IF IT WERE A BAD THING.